Silas Marcus Macvane

The Working Principles of Political Economy in a New and Practical Form

A Book for Beginners

Silas Marcus Macvane

The Working Principles of Political Economy in a New and Practical Form
A Book for Beginners

ISBN/EAN: 9783744645041

Printed in Europe, USA, Canada, Australia, Japan

Cover: Foto ©Suzi / pixelio.de

More available books at **www.hansebooks.com**

THE

WORKING PRINCIPLES

OF

POLITICAL ECONOMY

IN A NEW AND PRACTICAL FORM

A BOOK FOR BEGINNERS

BY

S. M. MACVANE

McLean Professor of History in Harvard College

NEW YORK
EFFINGHAM MAYNARD & CO.
771 Broadway and 67 and 69 Ninth Street
1893

COPYRIGHT,
1890,
BY S. M. MACVANE

To my Teacher and Friend,

PROFESSOR HENRY WARREN TORREY,

IN GRATEFUL ACKNOWLEDGMENT OF THE DEBT I OWE TO HIS

LEARNING AND KINDNESS,

THIS BOOK IS

AFFECTIONATELY INSCRIBED.

PREFACE.

THE aim of this book is to give, in small compass, a sufficient view of economic doctrine for the ordinary needs of intelligent citizens. I have had two principal motives in writing it. In the first place, I wished to show that the principles of Political Economy may be developed in such a form as to bring out, more clearly than is done in the standard books, their close and vital connection with every-day industry. In the second place, I wished to suggest some modifications, chiefly in points of detail, of the conclusions commonly accepted hitherto by the leading economists.

Political Economy is among the most practical of sciences, yet it has been made to look very much like an abstract philosophy. The great writers seem to have been more concerned about the logical validity of their reasoning, than they were to keep their work, at all points, plainly and closely in touch with the mechanism of practical business. The result is, that their readers, after mastering the doctrine as a matter of abstract theory, are too often quite in the dark as to the precise mode of its application in practice. Economic truth can hardly obtain general acceptance, as the basis of industrial hygiene, until it is so presented as to apply, directly and without laborious interpretation, to the visible facts of industrial life.

In the little book here offered, the attempt is made to work out the leading principles of economics with a constant eye on actual affairs. The facts discussed are taken in their ordinary, observable form; the student is asked and helped to analyze them, with a view of perceiving their relations to each other, and the underlying principles by which they are controlled. The plan has difficulties which the more abstract treatment avoids; but I hope the character of the result may be found a sufficient compensation.

The modifications of theory which I have ventured to suggest grow naturally out of the method I have followed. In all fundamental points, my results are in substantial harmony with the teachings of the older economists. But in the analysis of cost of production, and in the consequent distinction between savings and working capital, I have ventured on an innovation which seems to be called for in the interest of clearness, both in the discussion of wages and in the law of value. In the treatment of money and prices, I have departed considerably, in secondary points, from the beaten track. In developing the theory of prices, I found it necessary to have the use of a term which should recognize bank deposits as an integral part of the circulation. The term "bank currency," though not free from objection, seemed on the whole to be the one most suitable for the case. I accordingly adopted it, with the understanding that it includes, on the side of Notes, those issued by Governments as well as those issued by ordinary banks.

In the great question of Protection and Free Trade, I have simply tried to indicate the grounds of controversy. So long as the Tariff is a political issue, it seems only fair that a book intended, in part, for use in High Schools should contain nothing offensive to either of the parties into which our citizens are divided.

This book makes no pretence of being easy reading. The subject-matter is, I think, too complex, and at some points too elusive, to admit of a treatment that shall be at once easy and adequate. The best a writer can hope for is that his work shall be found clear and instructive by those who give time to the study of it. Not that Political Economy is, on the whole, a very difficult study. It merely calls for some patient reflection, especially at those critical points where sound reason is opposed to superficial appearances. There is nothing in the science that young persons of ordinary ability may not master, if only they apply themselves. It would be a happy reform in our national education, if a portion of the time that is now spent by our youth over barren puzzles in percentage, and the arid subtleties of formal grammar (English and other), were devoted to intelligent study of elementary economics. I cherish a hope that this little book may do something towards promoting such a reform.

CAMBRIDGE, MASS.,
    Dec. 1889.

CONTENTS.

CHAPTER		PAGE
I.	THE STUDY OF POLITICAL ECONOMY	11
II.	DIVISION OF LABOR: EXCHANGE OF PRODUCTS: WRONG VIEW OF MONEY	17
III.	THE USES OF MONEY: BUYING AND SELLING	25
	Questions and Exercises	35
IV.	OF WEALTH AND THE DISTINCTION BETWEEN NATURAL WEALTH AND WEALTH PRODUCED BY LABOR	36
V.	WHY NATURAL WEALTH, ORIGINALLY A GIFT TO MEN, CANNOT ALWAYS BE OBTAINED FOR NOTHING	43
VI.	OF LABOR, AND ITS PRODUCTIVENESS	52
VII.	NATURE AND NECESSITY OF CAPITAL	58
VIII.	CAPITAL REPRESENTS INDUSTRIAL IMPROVEMENTS	65
IX.	TWO CLASSES OF PRODUCERS, LABORERS AND EMPLOYERS	72
	Questions and Exercises	83
X.	OF VALUE IN EXCHANGE	86
XI.	COST OF PRODUCTION AS THE ULTIMATE REGULATOR OF VALUE	92
XII.	EXCEPTIONS TO THE GENERAL LAW OF VALUE	109
	Questions and Exercises	120

		PAGE
XIII.	Of Prices, or the Value of Money	122
XIV.	Production of the Precious Metals	141
XV.	Bank Currency	150
XVI.	Questions between Gold and Silver	165
XVII.	Inconvertible Legal Tender Notes	182
	Questions and Exercises	192
XVIII.	Wages and Profits as Portions of the Product of Industry	194
XIX.	Wages of Individual Laborers	212
XX.	Further Considerations Regarding Wages	231
XXI.	Profits of Individual Employers	251
XXII.	Interest on Borrowed Savings	270
XXIII.	Productiveness of Natural Agents: Economic Rent	286
XXIV.	Consequences of Diminishing Returns	310
	Questions and Exercises	321
XXV.	Exchange of Products between Separate Communities, or International Trade	323
XXVI.	Free Trade and Protection	349
XXVII.	Concluding Suggestions	364
	Questions and Exercises	377
Appendix:	The Tariff on Imports	381
	Summary of Duties	386
	Internal Revenue	387
	Note on Analysis of Cost of Production	387
Index		389

POLITICAL ECONOMY.

CHAPTER I.

THE STUDY OF POLITICAL ECONOMY.

1. Political Economy and Daily Life. — The general subject of political economy is wealth, which is simply a short name for the numberless things we all like to have and to own. Everybody needs some wealth in order to live; most persons are eager to get a great deal of it, — more, perhaps, than would be good for them, if they got it. How to get the wealth we need in the world is, for most of us, a very serious question. Few therefore, even among young people, can be entirely ignorant of some at least of the ways by which wealth may be obtained. There are few who have not seen some kinds of wealth actually produced.

Those who live in the country, or have even spent their holidays there, must have seen something of the ways by which a very important part of wealth, namely, our food, is produced. Those who live in the city witness the activity of mills and factories and the busy operations of commerce. We have all seen men at work, and know in a general way what labor accomplishes. There are but few of us who have not seen machinery in operation, or are ignorant of the powerful aid it gives to human labor. Everybody knows what it is to buy and to sell. We are all familiar with the use of money, and checks, and bank-notes. We all know the difference between saving and spending, and between diligence and sloth. No intelligent person can grow up in a civilized community without often hearing and thinking about these matters, for they are part and parcel of our daily life.

Now these are the chief topics of political economy. The object of the science is to study the conditions under which we carry on the struggle for the means to supply our daily wants, — the struggle for wealth. It aims to discover the principles that govern the production and sharing of wealth; the circumstances that favor and those that obstruct the largest production and the fairest sharing of the product.

2. True and False Political Economy. — It is at once an advantage and a disadvantage for political economy that it deals with subjects that enter so closely into our daily life. The advantage is that the science must always possess great interest for every intelligent lover of his country and his fellow-men; it can never lack earnest and devoted students. The disadvantage is that beginners in political economy are seldom wholly beginners. Their familiarity, in practical ways, with many of the topics and questions of the science, —

things they hear and ideas they pick up in one way or another,—give them a sort of political economy before coming to the set study of it.

Now if this political economy were good and sound so far as it goes, it would save us the necessity of much elementary explanation and definition. But, unfortunately, it is for the most part wrong. It is adopted without sufficient reflection, is not tested at all, and has usually no better basis than half-seen facts or wholly misinterpreted relations of things.

Economic subjects are peculiarly ill adapted for hasty treatment, being full of pitfalls for the unwary. They often have, superficially, an appearance of great simplicity, while they are in fact highly complicated. The motions of the earth and its true relations to the heavenly bodies are not more effectually disguised to the careless observer than are the real facts of economic life. To pierce through the illusions, and gain a clear view of things as they really are, demands an amount of thought and study that busy people are seldom able, and careless people are seldom willing, to bestow.

So it comes to pass that popular political economy is so often erroneous. So also it comes to pass that beginners in the set study of political economy have usually much to unlearn. They have to give up ideas which they previously regarded as familiar and unquestionable truths. Much of the space in every book on political economy has to be devoted to the refutation of false theories. In fact, the prevalence of wrong ideas is one of the chief causes for the existence of political economy. If the laws of production, wages, currency, etc., were so clear and simple that he who runs might read, there would be no occasion to spend time in writing or studying books about them.

But it is not only false theories that beginners have to unlearn. They have to unlearn wrong ways of looking at things and fallacious modes of reasoning about them. This is more difficult. Habits of thought are hard to shake off. Long after the student has perceived the faultiness of his former way of thinking, he is apt to find himself unconsciously falling back into it. Other sciences have no such obstacles to contend against. In chemistry, for example, the student has everything to learn; but then he has nothing to unlearn. He comes to the study with a mind open to the truth, and can advance from point to point unembarrassed by any relics of past errors.

3. Political Economy and Politics. — The fact that political economy has to appeal to reason in opposition to appearances, and has to reject as false so many views held by the unthinking, makes the spread of economic truth slow and difficult. The close connection of economic questions with the daily life and welfare of the people tends rather to aggravate than to diminish this difficulty. There must be laws about trade, and the currency, and banking, and taxes. Now men are almost certain to disagree as to the kind of laws it would be wise to pass in relation to such matters. Thus in every free country economic questions often become political questions. This view or that principle becomes the rallying-cry of a party. In the debates that ensue men are prone to seek arguments rather than the truth, and political success rather than the public welfare. In such contests it is unfortunately true that sound and just principles are often difficult to explain and uphold in opposition to false and glittering theories, that seem to be more in harmony with daily observation.

Fallacies exist only because false doctrine often looks truer than the truth. As political economy has many such strongly entrenched fallacies to expose and refute, and has to run counter to the cherished opinions of large classes of men in relation to subjects that interest them deeply, it is inevitable that it should be regarded by many as a tissue of idle dreams, or even something worse.

The science has also suffered from the denunciations of benevolent enthusiasts whose schemes for the improvement of the world it has had to oppose. Well-intending visionaries take it amiss to be reminded of the hard realities of life. The offence of political economy is that it insists on getting at the true causes of the poverty and misery that are so sadly prevalent in the world. It rejects all remedies that do not address themselves to the seat and source of the disease. For this, eloquent enthusiasts have denounced it as "the gloomy science," and an enemy of human progress. They have no doubt turned many against it.

Yet political economy is but reason and common sense applied to practical affairs. It has made great progress in the last hundred years, and is steadily, if slowly, winning its way to general acceptance. Even in quarters where it is rejected as a system, many of its most important principles are followed in practice.

CHAPTER II.

DIVISION OF LABOR.—EXCHANGE OF PRODUCTS.—WRONG VIEW OF MONEY.

1. The Struggle for Money.—The source of many wrong theories about economic subjects is found in the use of money in business transactions. Money is exceedingly important to us in practical ways, and at the same time hard to get. To a superficial observer the struggle of life may well seem to be a struggle for money. All our gains, and the worth of all our possessions, are expressed in money. The man who has plenty of money is regarded as rich; the man who has none is regarded as poor.

Industrial labors of all kinds are apt to be thought of merely as ways of getting money. The laborer who works in the factory or in the field; the employer who plans and directs the work; the merchant who buys the product and sells it again; the builders of houses and ships and railways; the inventors of machinery and the owners of land,—all seem to exert themselves only for the sake of the money they hope to get in return.

2. Money not Useful in Itself.—Now this view of industrial activity, though natural and convenient for practical purposes, is totally false and misleading when used as the basis of economic theories. The first step in the study of political economy is to gain a larger and truer view of industrial operations. One who reflects a little will perceive that money, in and of itself, has no qualities that should make it an object of universal quest. It is, in truth, the one form of wealth that has no independent use for us. Every other thing is useful in itself; money is useful only as a means of getting other things.

If some unseen power were suddenly to deprive everybody of all things that are good to eat or to drink or to wear or to enjoy in other ways, leaving even a most liberal price in money for everything so taken away, it is easy to see that the money would not save us from cold, hunger, and misery. Money is useful only where we can get other things in exchange for it, — useful only when we part with it.

3. Division of Labor.—Why, then, are men so much concerned about money? Why care for it or use it at all? In order to answer these questions we must consider a point of the very highest importance in actual life as well as in political economy. Civilized life demands the use of many different commodities. One has only to think of the various things a person in ordinary circumstances makes use of in the course of a single day, in order to perceive how great the number and variety of commodities necessary for comfortable living.

Now, no one person could possibly succeed in making so many things. Life is too short to learn the way of making even a small part of them. If each person were limited to the things he could produce for himself, we could never rise above the condition of rude barbarians. Civilization is possible only by dividing up the work of production, — by arranging that each producer shall make enough of one commodity for a considerable number besides himself. This is called *Division of Labor*. The following great advantages are gained by the use of it.

4. **Advantages of Division of Labor.** — (*a*) A great saving of time in learning how to make things. There are but few things that can be made properly without some degree of skill and special knowledge. Skill can be acquired only by practice. All fine and complicated products require much skill and knowledge: years of practice are necessary for learning the art of making them. If every man had to learn the art of making shoes, for example, merely in order to supply his own need of them, one can readily see how great a waste of time there would be. By arranging that one man shall learn the art, and shall make shoes for many others, a great saving is effected in the work of learning.

(*b*) A man who devotes himself to the production of one thing learns the art of making that one thing thoroughly. He learns all about the materials and tools. He seldom wastes time and materials by bungling. He learns to turn everything to the best account.

Thus he is able to make a better article, and to make it more quickly than would be possible for one who had to divide his time among many different kinds of production.

(c) Division of labor enables each person to do the work for which he or she is best fitted. Those who have great muscular strength and endurance can do the kinds of work in which strength and endurance are necessary. Those who have deft fingers and delicate taste can devote themselves to occupations in which there is need of taste and dainty workmanship. Thus division of labor enables all the talents of the community to be turned to the best account. The result is to increase production and improve its quality, besides promoting in other ways the comfort and happiness of the producers.

By an extension of the principle, people living in different parts of the country are enabled to make full use of the natural advantages which their neighborhood possesses. Thus local peculiarities of soil climate, water-power, mineral resources, etc., become available for supplying the needs of the people living in other places.

(d) Division of labor makes the use of machinery possible. No man would build a cotton-mill in order to make cotton cloth for his own family. There would be no saving of labor in doing so. When the mill can be used to supply a whole city or a whole country the case is different. It then becomes the means of saving a great deal of labor; or, better, of adding greatly to the productiveness of labor. By division of employments, and the machinery it makes possible, men are enabled to use the forces of nature with great effect, as aids in production.

(*e*) Division of labor is applied with great advantages to the different parts or stages of the production of things that are made up of several different materials, or go through a number of different processes. For example, take the production of penknives. For making the blades, iron ore must be dug from the earth; then it must be smelted and turned into steel; then it must be cut up and beaten into the required shapes; then each piece must be ground and polished. Each of these operations is distinct from the rest, requiring different tools, a different kind of skill, and a different sort of place for carrying it on.

Again, the production of the handles is an entirely different sort of work from that of making the blades, and is itself broken up into several distinct operations. There is, therefore, the same reason for subdividing the work of making penknives that there is for division of labor in producing different commodities. The only difference is that here the different sets of laborers co-operate towards the production of a single commodity. This difference has led some to distinguish this sort of division of labor by a separate name: viz., *Combination of Labor.*

Whatever we call it, the important thing to be clear

about is that the production of all complicated articles is greatly cheapened, and the quality greatly improved, by dividing the work of making them among a number of different sets of laborers.

5. Necessity of Exchange. — Enough has been said, it may be hoped, to suggest the great power of division of labor to increase the productiveness of industry. But obviously production of things by division of labor has the awkward result of leaving them in the wrong hands when they are finished. Nobody has the things he needs; everybody has, instead, a great stock of a single article. In order that all persons shall get the things they need for their own use, a most complicated set of exchanges must take place. This is the one serious drawback in division of labor: it is the price we pay for all the advantages.

6. Exchange by Barter: its Difficulties. — Now it is at least conceivable that the producers should meet each other at appointed times and places, and exchange products one with another. In a very small community this might perhaps be done. But one readily sees that exchange of products conducted on that plan would be very laborious, if not quite impracticable, in a large community.

Two very great difficulties would be encountered. In the first place, the man who has produced, we will suppose, a carriage, and wishes to get in exchange for it a watch, a coat, and a barrel of flour, must find a man who not only wishes to get a carriage, but also has a watch, a suit of clothes, and a barrel of flour,—all of the kind desired,—to give in exchange for it. Since, under division of labor the man who wishes the carriage has presumably but one commodity to offer in exchange, and that one commodity would rarely happen to be one of the things needed by the carriage-maker, we readily see how awkward the situation would be.

Exchange by direct barter between producers would involve so much trouble and so great risks of failure, that the whole advantage arising from division of labor might be lost thereby.

7. A Central Exchange.—The only plan by which barter could be made possible in practice would be to have some very wealthy man or company undertake the business of making the exchanges. The undertaking would be a vast one. A stock would have to be kept on hand of all the various commodities that people want, including many different sorts and qualities of each commodity; and not merely a single specimen of each thing, but so large a supply of it that all persons in the community could get access to it and obtain the desired quantity.

The universal exchange, we may assume, would have to be about as large as all the present shops and warehouses put together. Probably the management of so vast a business would exceed human capacity. To say nothing of the knowledge of all articles of trade that the business would call for, the mere size of the establishment and the extent of its operations would render the supervision of it exceedingly difficult if not impossible.

8. Difficulty of Exchange without a Standard of Value. — But supposing these difficulties to be overcome, there would remain, in the second place, the problem of finding some ready way of expressing the proportions in which things should exchange for each other. The persons concerned could not say, as we do, that a thing is worth so many dollars, for that would imply the use of money, which they are supposed not to have. In order to express the value of each article, they would need a list stating how much of every other article a given quantity of it would exchange for. In fact, the company would need two such lists for each article, one for use in buying and the other for use in selling it; for they could not afford to buy and sell at the same value.

The number of commodities of all kinds entering into the trade of a civilized community being so great, each list would be extremely long, and the number of lists would be extremely great. There would, further, be endless labor in correcting them from day to day, owing to the continual changes that occur in the market value of things. A single change in any article would involve a correction of every list.

Altogether, then, it is clear that exchange of products by means of direct barter would be very costly and laborious. The institutions for making exchanges would necessarily be few in number, so that most producers would have to travel considerable distances in order to get their products exchanged. There would also be a danger that the community might have to pay very dearly for the services of the exchangers.

CHAPTER III.

THE USE OF MONEY AS A MEDIUM OF EXCHANGE.—NATURE OF BUYING AND SELLING.

1. Money facilitates Exchange.—It is only by considering the difficulties attending the use of barter that one can get clear views as to the true nature and use of money. The great and true service rendered by money is, that it makes the exchange of commodities easy.

This it accomplishes in two ways. First, by breaking up the exchange into two parts or stages. It substitutes two comparatively easy exchanges for one exceedingly difficult one. The man who wishes to exchange a carriage for a coat, a watch, and a barrel of flour, first sells the carriage for money, and then with the money buys the things he wants wherever he can buy them most favorably. This enables the work of exchanging things to go on without the help of a great central exchange.

Secondly, money makes exchange easy by making it possible to have a *price* for everything. Instead of cumbersome lists, showing how much of every other article a thing is worth, we need only to say how much money it is worth. Money serves as a standard of value.

2. Exchange is obscured by the Use of Money. — In these two ways the use of money renders the work of exchanging commodities comparatively easy and expeditious. But it greatly increases the difficulty of studying political economy. The use of money gives rise to most of the wrong ideas against which political economy has to contend. Exchange of commodities is very much disguised by it, — so much so, in fact, that many men who do a great deal of exchanging never once think of it as exchanging at all. They think of selling as a thing by itself, and of buying as a thing by itself, — not waiting to consider that these are in reality the separated halves of an exchange.

Two circumstances tend to conceal the real nature of the case. In the first place, the two halves of the exchange are transacted with different persons. The man to whom, in our example, the carriage is sold, is not the man from whom the watch or the coat or the barrel of flour is bought; so that the transaction lacks the appearance of an exchange. Secondly, the two parts of the exchange may be separated by a considerable interval of time. It may suit the convenience of the carriage-builder not to buy the watch or the coat or the barrel of flour at once. With the money in his pocket, he can safely wait. He may in the meantime make and sell another carriage, and the money derived from the new sale may get mixed up with the other money, so that when he buys a thing he could not easily tell for which of the carriages he receives it in exchange.

How Money Obscures Exchanges. 27

Thus the use of money, while making exchange easy, has made it complicated. When men sell things, they do not usually think of the particular things they are to buy with the money they get. They may not have decided yet. Their immediate object is to get money. They know that to him who has this, the whole market is open.

Money has been very fitly called "general purchasing power," because it can be so readily exchanged for any desired commodity. Until the actual moment of purchase the owner of money is free to choose what he will have. Yet when he does buy, it is clear that he is simply completing the exchange that was begun when he obtained the money. The money served as a pledge that he should receive an equivalent for the thing sold leaving him free to choose the time and the form in which he should receive it.

Thus the use of money enables each producer to exchange on free terms with the general body of other producers, instead of being limited to the particular individual who buys his product and to the particular moment at which he buys it. These facts disguise the exchange, but they do not affect its real character. In the end each producer has parted with certain things, and has received certain other things in return.

3. Buying easier than Selling. — There are some other circumstances that tend to obscure this fundamental relation between buying and selling. In the first place the use of money affects the two halves of exchange very unequally. As there are always stocks of goods for sale, the possession of money makes it comparatively easy to get what we want. But the difficulty of finding the persons who want our product remains precisely as great as it would be under a system of barter. Thus the chief remaining difficulty in making the exchanges is thrown on the side of selling.

There is usually no small difficulty in getting things sold at satisfactory prices. The attention of business men, producers as well as traders, is thus ordinarily fixed on their sales. Every other part of their business they can control, but for their sales they must await the pleasure of other men. This is, therefore, the part that causes anxiety. A natural result of this is a tendency to forget the other part of the exchanges they are carrying on, and to view all sorts of industrial activity merely as so many different ways of getting money. From this state of mind manifold errors spring.

The student of political economy has made his first real step in the science, when he has perceived clearly that buying and selling are merely the easiest way of exchanging products, and that, though buying is so much easier than selling, it is not a whit less important. In fact, what is selling for one man is buying for another.

4. Function of Traders. — It may occur to the reader that there are some facts of daily life which seem to conflict with this view of buying and selling. To begin with, there is the fact that merchants and traders constantly buy and sell the same thing. When the cloth merchant has sold his cloth he does not buy a stock of other commodities: he buys more cloth. In this sort of buying and selling there would seem to be no exchange of commodities. But we must note the fact that merchants and traders buy of one set of men and sell to quite a different set. As a class, they buy of those who produce and sell to those who consume. The truth, then, is that they are the men who manage the exchange of products for us.

Money allows division of labor to be used in exchange as well as in production. Instead of one great central place of general exchange, money enables us to have many small establishments, in each of which some part of the work is done. Each dealer devotes himself to trading in some one commodity, or in a limited number of commodities. His buying and selling are part of the process by which commodities find their way from the farms, mines, factories, and mills where they are produced, to the hands of those who are to consume them.

Things are usually bought and sold at least three times in passing from the producer to the consumer. The manufacturer sells to the wholesale dealer, the wholesale dealer to the shopkeeper, and the shopkeeper to the consumer. In some trades there are several other intermediate changes of ownership.

These transfers from dealer to dealer are for convenience and economy. They simplify the operations of each dealer, and are commercially of great importance. But for political economy they have little significance beyond their effect in lessening the labor of carrying on exchange. In all respects except that of economy and convenience the man who buys of the producer might be the same who sells to the consumer. These are the essential transactions in economic exchange; all the intermediate transfers are merely helps towards making these easy.

5. Buying and Selling do not create Wealth.— The gains made by buying and selling are often very large,— so large that many think of buying and selling as the true source of wealth. But one who reflects at all readily sees that mere buying and selling can produce nothing. Individuals may grow rich by fortunate operations of that kind; but the whole community cannot do so. The general wealth can be increased only by producing more or by saving more.

If all the commodities in the world were bought and sold fifty times in a day, with a rise of price at each new sale. the world would be no richer at the end of the day than it was at the beginning. Some individuals might no doubt be richer; but others would be poorer by the same amount.

6. Speculative Buying and Selling.— Every change in the price of an article usually brings gain or loss to those who happen to have stocks of it on hand. Such changes are an unavoidable evil. They disturb the course of trade and production. The opportunities they present for making large and sudden gains give rise, in every community, to a class of men called speculators.

Speculators perform no necessary part of the work of exchange. They carry things no step forward from the producer to the consumer. They merely aim to profit by the fluctuations of the market. By buying things that are about to rise in price, and selling again after the rise, they are able to gain the difference. If prices were steady, they would have no basis for their operations.

So far as speculators merely anticipate the natural course of the market, their operations are entirely legitimate, and even at times beneficial to the community. By buying in seasons of plenty and carrying over a stock that might otherwise be partly wasted, they sometimes help out the deficiency in seasons of dearth. But when, for purposes of gain, they impose on the ignorance or timidity of their neighbors, when they resort to knavery and deception, — when, by combinations and "corners," they create artificial fluctuations of the market, — they become enemies of honest industry and a burden to the community.

7. Some appear only as Buyers. — There is another circumstance which seems to conflict with the view that buying and selling are at bottom exchange of commodities. Many persons appear only as buyers. They have nothing to sell, for they produce nothing. The large class who live in idleness are in this position. Also the more numerous class who, though doing useful service in other ways, take no part in the production of commodities. Even the hired laborers, who do the chief work of production, appear in the market as buyers only. How, then, shall we maintain the doctrine that buying and selling are mainly exchanging of things?

As it is of the highest importance that the beginner should be quite clear on this point, let us consider these cases. First the case of the idlers. It is obvious that these, in order to be able to buy anything, must have an income from some source. Some of them own estates of land and receive rents from their tenants; others own buildings or building-lots in the cities; still others hold bonds, mortgages, railway stocks, etc. Their income from these sources is now commonly paid in money. But this is merely for the convenience of all concerned. If there were no money in the world, there would still be farms and city lots and the various other forms of property named. The rents, however, would have to be paid in commodities: so many bushels of wheat, so many tons of coal, so many yards of cloth.

In some countries rent of land is actually paid in products of the land itself. If all rents, dividends, and interest were paid in commodities, the objection we are considering would not be thought of. The persons receiving income from such sources would receive it either in the precise commodities they happened to need for their own use, or in other things. If they received the things needed for their own use, they would not appear in the market at all: they would be neither buyers nor sellers. If, on the other hand, they received things unsuitable for their own use, they would appear in the market both as sellers and as buyers. It would then be clear that their purchases are in fact part and parcel of the general exchange of commodities.

At present the troublesome half of their exchange is done for these persons by those who pay them rents, interest, or dividends. Others are compelled to sell more than they buy by the full amount of the money paid to the receivers of rent, interest, and dividends. If those others were allowed to spend the money for themselves, their buying would simply be equal to their selling, and there would be no difficulty in perceiving the reality of the exchange. That they hand over a part of their buying power to their landlords and creditors does not change the essential features of the case. Their landlords and creditors simply complete exchanges whereof the difficult half has been done already.

The same remarks apply to all payments of money in the form of fees, salaries, and wages. Men nominally work for money, but in reality they work for commodities. By getting paid in money, they really get the commodities, without any danger of disputes about quality or kind, and without the trouble and risks attending the difficult half of exchange.

If each laborer were paid in the product of his own labor, he would run great risks of loss and suffering in the effort to sell it. The arrangement whereby laborers receive money for their labor frees them from all that trouble and risk. The employer does the selling for them. His purchases of commodities fall short of his sales by the whole amount of the laborers' purchases. Their buying simply completes the exchange that his selling begins.

8. Money and Prices. — Since the final object of all our industrial exertions is to obtain enjoyable commodities or services, it follows that the amount of money we receive does not, of itself, determine our reward. In order to know how much we are receiving for our labors, we must also know the prices of the things we wish to buy with the money. If the prices be fixed, any increase of our money income means a corresponding increase of our real rewards. Similarly if our money incomes be fixed, a fall in the prices of the things we buy means a corresponding increase of our real rewards. But an increase of our money income, accompanied by an equal rise in the prices of the things we buy, would leave us no better off than before.

These are important principles and need to be steadily borne in mind. Many speak and act as if mere increase of money were, in and of itself, a general blessing. But to one who reflects at all, it must be clear that what we need in order to have an increase of the general wealth is not more money, but more commodities. If every person's money income were doubled, without any increased production of commodities, nobody would be better off than before.

QUESTIONS AND EXERCISES.

1. Describe the advantages arising from division of labor.
2. Show that the trouble of exchanging products is a disadvantage attending division of labor.
3. Could exchange be carried on by barter?
4. Show how the use of money facilitates exchange.
5. How does the use of money disguise the exchange of products?
6. Why is it usually so much harder to sell than to buy?
7. Trace carefully the exchanges of products in the following cases:

(a) A farmer receives $25 for wheat, uses $20 of the amount to pay his debt to the coal-dealer, and with the balance buys a dozen of spoons.

(b) The coal-dealer pays the $20 to his bookkeeper, who buys with it a suit of clothes from the tailor.

(c) The tailor uses the money to pay his house rent, and the owner of the house buys a watch with it.

8. A teacher receives her salary from the town treasury and spends half of it in buying books and deposits the balance in a savings bank. [Consider the tax-payers as well as the teacher and the book-sellers.]

CHAPTER IV.

OF WEALTH AND THE DISTINCTION BETWEEN NATURAL WEALTH AND WEALTH PRODUCED BY LABOR.

1. **Wealth consists of Material Objects.**—It has been stated that the word "wealth" is simply a short name for the numberless things we all like to have and to own. It is now necessary to define wealth somewhat more fully, in order that there may be no misunderstanding as to the nature and extent of our subject.

The first point to be noted is that the wealth of which political economy treats is material wealth. The things comprised in it are material objects. Our invisible possessions, our powers of body and mind, even those of them that come into play in getting material wealth, are not themselves included in the definition of our wealth, since they are rather part of ourselves than of our worldly goods. The wealth we speak of in political economy is such as one may part with at will. Therefore we exclude our personal gifts and attainments, such as knowledge, intelligence, skill, good health, physical strength, social position, a good name, the love of friends, and the like. This implies no contempt for these unseen possessions, which are, in fact, far more important and precious than mere material wealth. We only mean that political economy does not undertake to deal with them. It wisely confines itself to the humbler task of considering those material things that men need for the support of life, or desire as aids to comfortable living.

2. Useless Things are not Wealth.—Wealth, then, consists of material objects; but not all material objects are wealth. Things that have no known use for us, things that nobody wants, are not wealth. This principle excludes from wealth a large part of the material objects in the world. It applies not only to useless things found in nature, such as desert lands, useless rocks, weeds, noxious animals, etc., but also to products of labor that are worn out or have proved to be useless.

Of course a thing may have useful properties not yet discovered. To men who are ignorant of the good in it, it is not wealth. Thus wealth depends on knowledge. The metallic ores were not wealth till men learned to smelt and forge them. Linen rags were not wealth till men learned the art of making them into paper. We cannot tell how many substances now regarded as useless rubbish may become, through new discoveries, valuable portions of the world's wealth.[1]

[1] The words useful and useless, as here employed, have no necessary reference to any real or intrinsic usefulness. A thing

It may be well to add that wealth implies possession, or the ability on the part of somebody to have the use of it. Therefore things that are beyond our reach are not wealth. Mineral beds that lie too deep to be dug up, treasures at the bottom of the sea, game that is too wary to be caught, are examples. Here again new discoveries and inventions may bring within our reach things that have hitherto been of no use to us because unknown, or regarded as inaccessible.

Our wealth, then, consists of all the useful and agreeable material objects we own, or have the right to use and enjoy without asking the consent of any other person.

3. Rights over Human Beings are not Wealth.—We have seen that a man's powers of body and mind are not included in his wealth. Much less can they, in any case, be regarded as the wealth of another. Men, the owners of wealth, can never themselves be regarded as mere wealth, even when reduced to a state of slavery. To the slave-owner, indeed, the possession of slaves may be a source of income; it may suit him in his pride of mastery over his fellowmen to regard them as his property. But to adopt that view would be to forget the poor slaves, who are members of the community, with as good a claim to be considered as the master has. All that

is useful, in the sense here intended, if it is an object of desire to any portion of the human race. It may be in itself strictly worthless, or even injurious to those who use it: the fact that men desire to have it makes it a part of wealth.

the master gains by the existence of slavery they lose. If he is richer by reason of his power to exact their service, they are poorer to the same extent by the loss of their freedom and the products of their labor. Therefore, in any country where slavery exists, the wealth of the community as a whole would not be lessened by freeing the slaves; nor, in free countries, would it be increased by making one part of the population slaves of the other part.

The same principle applies to all other claims and rights of one man over the person or the property of other men. Debts of all kinds, as well as all mere proofs of debt, such as notes, bonds, mortgages, etc., must be excluded from our idea of wealth. They merely show to whom the wealth belongs, or will belong when the debts are paid. If every debt were forgiven, and every bond, note, and mortgage were cancelled, we should still have precisely as much wealth in the country as we had before. We create no riches by getting into debt or by writing mortgages on our property.

4. **Natural Wealth and Wealth produced by Labor.**— The wealth of the people of the United States is of two general kinds. Partly it consists of what remains of the natural resources that originally fitted our country to be the home of a civilized nation. This part, which we may call our Natural Wealth, our forefathers acquired for themselves and us simply by coming over the sea and taking possession;

it cost no labor beyond the trouble of taking and holding it. The other part of our wealth consists of products of human industry, — things for which, or upon which, labor in some form has been expended. This part we may call Wealth produced by Labor.

Natural wealth includes the land, with its spontaneous growth of forest-trees, etc., its bearing capacity under tillage, and its varied uses as our home; also all such things as deposits of coal, iron, and other useful metals and minerals; water and water-power; electricity; the expansive force of steam, and all other physical forces; harbors and navigable rivers; fisheries, wild game and the like; a pleasant and healthful climate; a favorable position for commerce; — in a word every resource and advantage of a material kind bestowed on men by the beneficence of the Creator. We must also include in natural wealth some things that ordinarily come to us so freely, without care or effort on our part, that we rarely give them even a thought. It may seem strange, at first, to give the name of wealth to air, water, and sunlight; but they are surely among the most important things in the world, as anybody quickly discovers who is cut off from adequate supplies of them. That they come to us so easily would be a poor reason for excluding them from the list of things constituting our natural wealth.

The modes in which natural wealth is useful are highly varied; it would be difficult to mention all of them. Some things are directly useful to us just as we find them and where we find them; *e. g.* air, sunlight, and (merely as a lodging-place) land. Other things are made useful by merely bringing them to the place where we need them; for example, coal and other fuel, mineral oil, game, fish, etc. Other things serve mainly as materials for the production of useful commodities; *e. g.* metallic ores, wool, cotton, silk; skins of animals, woods other than fuel, marble, etc. Still other parts of natural wealth are useful chiefly as necessary agents in the production of commodities or materials, or as aids in producing and transporting commodities and materials from one place to another; *e. g.* the soil, the motive power of wind, water, and steam, and the various physical forces that come into play in the growth of plants and animals.

Wealth produced by labor includes all useful things that have been prepared for use by exertion of any kind on the part of men; for example, houses, furniture, pictures, food, clothing, horses, and other domestic animals, machinery, ships, railways, money, etc.

Land in its wild state, fishes in the sea, coal in the seam, trees in the forest, belong to natural wealth. Cultivated farms, fish that has been caught, coal that has been mined, lumber that has been cut, belong to wealth produced by labor.

5. The Nature of Production.—Obviously natural

wealth is the basis or source of all wealth produced by labor. Men create nothing. They can only make use of the materials, forces, and opportunities they find in the world about them. Strictly, what we call Production consists, so far as men are concerned, in moving things or parts of things from one place or position to another. Consider carefully, for example, what men do in building a house, or in making clothes, or in procuring food, and you will perceive that it is confined to moving things, or placing things in particular ways. The so-called forces of nature do the rest. Men plough the ground, sow the seed, and harvest the crop, but without the germinating principle in the seed itself, and the nourishing influences of sun, rain, and soil, the united labors of the whole human race could not avail to produce a grain of wheat.

In some cases the work of production consists more obviously of moving things than in other cases. In the production of beef, for example, it is only by an effort of thought that we perceive the exact nature of men's contribution to the product. But in the case of producing coal, lumber, fish, ice, and the like, we perceive it very readily. The reason is that in the latter case nature's work is, so to say, completed before man's part begins; whereas in the other case man's work and nature's work go on simultaneously, and men easily take credit to themselves for more than they actually accomplish.

CHAPTER V.

WHY NATURAL WEALTH, ORIGINALLY A GIFT TO MEN, CANNOT ALWAYS BE OBTAINED FREE OF COST.

1. The Supply of Natural Wealth.—Different kinds of natural wealth differ very much in point of copiousness of supply. Some forms of it are found in practically unlimited quantity in every part of the habitable globe: the air is an example of this. Other kinds are found in abundance in particular neighborhoods, while in other places little or none is found: coal, petroleum, and most of the metals are examples; also the distinctive natural products of particular zones of the world. Still other kinds of natural wealth are found in but few places and in but small quantities: of these gold and silver, diamonds and other precious stones are examples.

Again it usually happens that not all portions of the supply in any given region are equally desirable. In some cases the differences relate to quality, in other cases to ease of access or convenience in use; in still other cases some portions of the supply combine several kinds of superiority over other portions. There is usually, therefore, a descending scale of excellence from the best to the poorest in the case of each species of material wealth in any given region. Further, the best and really desirable portions are in most cases very limited in supply as compared with the less desirable portions.

These facts are most clearly seen in the case of Land, one of the most important parts of natural wealth. The whole area of land in the world is very great, but different portions of it differ very much in point of fertility, convenience of situation, nearness to the great centres of population, etc. Further, the amount of really excellent land, excellent in all respects, is very limited in comparison with the amount of indifferent and distinctly poor land. Between the two extremes, the best and the utterly useless, there is an infinite variety in lands, one piece differing from another by a very slight balance of advantages.

2. **The Demand for Natural Wealth.**—The demand for natural wealth in any region depends partly on the number and partly on the character of its inhabitants. The demands of a civilized people are very different from those of a savage one. In one sense at least the savage has a larger demand for natural wealth than the civilized man. He must have a wide range of territory for his hunting and other crude pursuits, otherwise he cannot find a subsistence. His demand is, so to say, a wasteful one: he must have much more natural wealth than he uses. He remains poor and squalid in the midst of overflowing natural wealth.

The civilized man, on the other hand, has a stronger demand for material wealth than the savage. There is no known limit to his demand for natural wealth, except his physical ability to make use of it. His demand is, however, much more intelligent than that of the savage. He seeks out all the various resources of his region, and endeavors by labor to turn all the best of them to account. A civilized community may, therefore, live and flourish in a region where a savage community one-tenth as numerous would perish of want.

Given the character of the inhabitants of a country, we may safely assume that the demand for natural wealth will increase with the increase of population. The more persons there are to be supplied, the greater the amount needed to satisfy them. This does not mean that the demand for each kind of natural wealth must increase in the same proportion: trade between different regions and countries modifies the particular direction of the demand in each case. England, for example, draws her supply of wheat largely from the United States. This increases in our country the demand for wheat-growing lands, and diminishes the demand for the sources of materials needed for the production of the things we get in exchange for the wheat. In England there is a lessened demand for wheat-growing land, and an increased demand for the natural wealth needed for the production of the articles she gives us in exchange. Still, it is clear that an increase of population involves, in every country, an increased demand for some form, and usually for all forms, of natural wealth.

3. Natural Wealth is gratuitous while the Supply exceeds the Demand. — Natural wealth is originally a gift to the human race. The first owner, whether a government or an individual, gets it in all cases for the mere trouble of taking it. So long, in any region, as there is enough of any particular kind of natural wealth to satisfy the whole desire of everybody for the possession of it, that particular kind can be obtained free of cost by everybody. No man would pay a price for a given portion of it, if other portions equally desirable were still to be had out of nature's free supply. Therefore natural wealth that is found everywhere in unlimited quantity and of uniform quality, — air, for example, — can never cost any man anything. There are, no doubt, special circumstances in which men find themselves cut off from the natural supply of air, in which, therefore, laborious contrivances have to be used for conveying fresh air to them. But fresh air in a crowded hall, or in a mine, or in a diving-bell, is brought there by the use of labor: is, in fact, a product of labor quite as truly as coal in our bins or ice in our refrigerators is a product of labor. The contrivances for conveying it cost something; but the air itself required for the purpose costs nothing.

4. Natural Wealth acquires a Price when Demand exceeds Supply. — Natural wealth that is limited in supply can also be obtained free of cost wherever the supply, though limited, exceeds the demand. But so soon as, owing to increase of population, the demand for any given kind of natural wealth becomes greater than the supply, that particular kind passes into the list of things for which a price must be paid. Those who wish to get it must induce some holder of it to part with his holding, by the offer of something else in exchange.

It may seem, in such a case, that the cause of the price is the fact that certain persons hold the whole supply and refuse to part with it without payment. But the true cause is the greatness of the demand. If the whole supply were again thrown open to everybody free of cost, or were shared equally among all seekers, the article would still command a price, because (on the supposition that the demand exceeds the supply) there would still be some persons desirous of getting more than the equal sharing would give them; and they would be ready to pay something to other holders for their share.

Since most kinds of natural wealth are found in varying degrees of excellence, only the better grades or specimens of each have a price at first. So long as the next inferior grade exceeds the demand for it, it will remain gratuitous; and the price of the better grade will be limited to the value of the difference between them.

Since the population of most parts of the United States is increasing, we find, as we should expect to find, that many things which could formerly be obtained free of cost, or at a merely nominal price, are now no longer so obtainable. Also since the ratio of population to natural wealth differs greatly in different parts of the country, we find that some forms of natural wealth which cost little or nothing in one part, have a considerable price in other parts.

Of course in the case of transportable things, this difference of price could not ordinarily exceed the cost of transportation. But the cost of transportation is itself considerable, especially in the case of bulky and heavy articles such as make up so large a part of natural wealth (*e. g.* coal, wood of all kinds, building-stone, metallic ores, etc.). Again some kinds of natural wealth are not transportable. Land, for example, cannot be carried from regions where it is cheap to places where it is dear. It therefore happens that land, especially land for building purposes, may have a very high price in one place and a very low one in another. A single square yard of land in the central parts of New York, or Chicago, costs more than a square mile in some parts of the world.

5. Some Exceptional Cases. — There are a few forms of natural wealth that never acquire a value in exchange, however far the supply of them may fall short of satisfying the demand. In certain cases this is because the nature of the thing is such that many persons can use it in common without interfering with each other, and the laws of civilized countries give the right of use to everybody free of charge: harbors and navigable rivers are examples. In the remaining cases the failure to acquire exchange value is due to the fact that the nature of the things themselves renders it impossible for them to be bought and sold. Rain, for example, would bring a high price in some countries at almost any time, and in every country at particular times. But rain is a form of natural wealth that cannot be transferred or diverted from one man's fields to those of another, or from one region to another. The same is true of all other elements that go to form the climate of any region. Those who would have the benefit of them must go where they are found, and found only as gratuities of nature.

Though harbors, rivers, climate, scenery, and the like have no exchange value of their own, it is obvious that they may affect very much the value of other kinds of natural wealth, — especially that of land. It is well known that land lying near to harbors and navigable rivers has a higher value than land, equally good as land, which is remote from such facilities. In the same way a good climate, including regularity and sufficiency of rainfall, tends to attract men to the regions enjoying those advantages. The resulting increase of demand for the natural wealth of those regions must, of course, tend to raise the value of such parts of it as can have exchange value.

6. The Rising Value of Natural Wealth no general

Gain.—When a useful thing, formerly without exchange value, acquires a value in exchange by reason of an increase of demand, it is well to observe that the community as a whole gains nothing by the change. The persons who own the existing supply of the article are benefited, but their gain is at the expense of the rest of the community. The change implies, in itself, no increase of the actual things owned and enjoyed by the community as natural wealth. There is simply an increase in the number of persons wanting those things, with the result that there is less for each than there was formerly.

If the circumstance that causes any kind of natural wealth to acquire an exchange value be a lessening of the supply, it is obvious that the community is not only not richer, but is even poorer by reason of the change. It has, so far as this portion of its wealth is concerned, a smaller stock of useful things than before. The individual owners of the remaining supply may gain by the change. Their gain, however, is at the expense of other men. If, for example, the supply of fresh water should become so reduced as to acquire a considerable exchange value, the owners of ordinary springs might be enriched; but the general body of citizens would be poorer than before.

When the natural wealth that has been lessened in supply is not private, but public, property, nobody gains by the change. For example, the diminished productiveness of the fisheries has been attended by a rise in the value of fish. But this rise is only sufficient to compensate the fishermen for the increased labor required in catching a given quantity. The diminished yield is a simple loss to everybody. The same principle applies to the present scarcity and consequent high value of game, forest-trees, fur-bearing animals, etc., as compared with early times.

This last remark suggests the fact that some kinds of natural wealth are unavoidably diminished by the progress of civilization. The destruction of the forests, together with the game and other products of wild nature, is necessary in order to fit the land for agriculture; and it is needless to say that the farms are more useful and a greater wealth than the forests they have displaced. But it is none the less true that the loss of the forests is in itself a loss of wealth. If land could be tilled without interfering with the growth of trees, we should all be richer, not poorer, than we are. Trees for fuel and for building purposes could then be obtained, in most places, for the mere trouble of cutting them down on the nearest hill-side; whereas at present they have a very considerable exchange value in all settled regions.

CHAPTER VI.

OF LABOR AND ITS PRODUCTIVENESS.

1. Productive Labor. — Natural wealth, as we have seen, is the basis and source of wealth produced by labor. Any human exertion devoted to procuring or preparing natural wealth for the uses of men is called Productive Labor.

Productive labor is of many kinds. First and most obviously, it includes all the manual labor of preparing tools, implements, buildings, and machinery needed in production; of preparing the natural agents (*e. g.* land) and procuring the raw materials; of working up these raw materials into the various commodities of civilized life; and of carrying on the exchange of products between the various sets of producers, — including herein the necessary labor of transportation.

Productive labor includes, secondly, all mental efforts whose aim is the production of material wealth. Strictly there is a mental effort involved even in manual labor of the simplest kind. But there are some kinds of productive labor in which the exertion is more distinctly that of the mind. This is true of the labors of merchants, bankers, book-keepers, inventors, managers, and all others whose task lies in planning and directing the work of production and exchange. Such labors are necessary in order to carry on production effectively, and are as truly productive as is the labor of those who come into actual contact with the things produced.

2. Non-productive Labor. — The greater part of the world's labor is directed to the production of wealth. But we have many needs besides those that material things can satisfy. In infancy and again in old age we need nursing and care. In sickness we need also the help of a physician. Born ignorant and with many evil propensities to overcome, we need much careful training, instruction, and (on our own part) study, in order to become enlightened and useful men and women. As members of civilized society we need the labors of legislators, judges, administrators, and other guardians of law and civil order. These and many other sorts of labor we need not as producers, but as men and as citizens of a civilized country. We should need them even if the material commodities we require were supplied to us without effort or exertion on our part. These kinds of labor we shall therefore designate as non-productive.

Incidentally non-productive labor may help in the production of wealth. When a teacher reclaims a vagrant youth and converts him into an honest laborer, or a physician cures the ailment of a producer and restores him to his work, or the civil authorities repress public disorders, the act has in each case the effect of increasing production. But this effect is undesigned, or at most secondary. Besides it would be difficult, as well as useless, to distinguish, among acts of this character, those that are indirectly productive from those that are not so. We shall, therefore, understand Productive labor to mean labor whose immediate object is the production or exchange of wealth. All other labor we shall regard as Non-productive.

3. The Productiveness of Labor. — The circumstances which determine how great an amount of wealth a man may produce by his labor, are too numerous to admit of complete enumeration. They are, however, reducible, for the most part, to three general classes:

(*a*) The working capacity of the man himself, his diligence, energy, intelligence, and endurance, go far to determine the product. These are points in which men differ very much; this is true not only of individuals but to a considerable extent of whole nations and races. The people of the United States are pre-eminent for their efficiency as laborers. They are drawn mainly from those branches of the human family that excel in all the qualities that give success in the production of wealth. Further, the original settlers were, in a way, picked men of the nations to which they belonged, since none but men of courage and capacity would face the dangers and hardships of the long voyage and of the pioneer life that it brought them to. Of the subsequent migration of Europeans to our country, the same remark holds true to a very considerable extent. The more capable and enterprising are those most ready to come; the sluggish and shiftless usually stay at home.

(b) The productiveness of a man's labor depends largely on the character of the natural wealth he has free access to. If that be rich and copious, and all the natural conditions be favorable to his industry, his product will be large for a given outlay of labor. The people of the United States are highly favored in these respects. We have ample areas of fertile soil; for the most part we have a favorable climate; we have almost every material and natural facility for production. Compared with the extent of our natural wealth of all kinds, our population is small, so that there are comparatively few places in which very good resources may not be obtained at a low cost. In these respects our producers have great advantages over the inhabitants of older and more crowded countries.

(c) The productiveness of labor in a country depends much on the advancement its people have made in the arts of production, that is to say, in the discoveries and inventions by which the great forces of nature are made to aid in the work of production. There are some industries, such as the manufacture of cloth, in which it is probable that modern machinery enables men to produce a hundred times as much as they could produce by the old modes of hand-manufacture. In every sort of production skilful devices may do much to add to the product, or improve its quality. Here again the people of the United States have shown great capacity for the invention and use of machinery, and for the discovery of new methods of production. The intelligence and ingenuity of our laborers have been stimulated into great inventive activity by our Patent Laws, which secure to every inventor the exclusive right to manufacture his device for a limited number of years.

In addition to these general causes affecting the productiveness of labor, the capacity of a nation for properly organizing and managing its industries deserves to be mentioned. The industrial system of a civilized country is highly complicated, and calls for great skill on the part of those who arrange its details. How best to divide and subdivide the work among different sets of laborers; what grouping of the various sets is most advantageous; how the various local resources may be turned to best account; how large a scale of production under a single management gives the best results,—these and many similar questions must be solved before the labor of a country can reach its full capacity for production of wealth. Wise and skilful management turns every advantage to the best account, prevents waste of labor and materials, and thus gives us every commodity for the least possible exertion.

4. Well-being of the Laborer.—There is one other general remark to be made regarding the productive capacity of laborers, and that is that the productiveness of labor depends much on the state of comfort and contentment in which the laborers are maintained. A certain degree of comfort is necessary in order simply to keep them in physical vigor. But that is as true of dumb animals as it is of men. Men are much influenced by their state of mind as well as by their state of body. It is, therefore, wise, on purely economic grounds, to do what may be done without injustice to others, to remove real or fancied grievances on the part of any class of laborers. Men who are satisfied with the conditions under which they work, will produce more and better results than men who are chafing under a sense of wrong, or have abandoned themselves to despair.

For this reason, as well as on higher grounds, slavery is to be condemned. It deprives the laborer of everything which could spur him to exert his powers. For this reason also every other unfair or oppressive treatment of laborers is contrary to the general interest. Cheerful and willing workers are those who produce most wealth.

CHAPTER VII.

THE NATURE AND NECESSITY OF CAPITAL.

1. Contrast between Savage and Civilized Industry. — Wherever laborers and natural wealth exist, production of some sort is possible. In those parts of the world, where, without the aid of human labor, the earth bears copious supplies of wild fruits, nuts, and edible roots, men may find a rude subsistence without other tool or implement than their hands. The production carried on by savage races, consisting as it does, for the most part, in merely gathering or capturing the spontaneous growths of land and water, requires but few implements, and those of the simplest character.

If we compare the production carried on in civilized countries with crude production of this kind, we find (in addition to other differences) these striking points of contrast: First, that civilized production requires a large outfit of tools, machinery, buildings, and other appliances. Secondly, that civilized production requires large quantities of materials, meaning thereby not only things in their natural state, but also things that have had labor bestowed upon them, — things that have passed through one or more stages of production. Thirdly, that civilized industry, being carried on by division of labor, needs to have large quantities of finished commodities always on hand, for purposes of exchange.

We see, then, that in order to carry on civilized production and exchange the producers must have the use, at any given moment, of the results of much previous labor. To these results of past labor used in present production and exchange the general name of *Capital* is given.

2. Three Forms of Capital. — The capital of a country consists of three parts, answering to the three needs spoken of above. In order to obtain clear views as to the nature and uses of capital it will be necessary to consider each of these portions separately.

(*a*) The plant of production. This includes the buildings, implements, and machinery of all kinds used in production and exchange. Under this head we include also many things which would not ordinarily be called machinery; such as railways, ships, canals, piers, and the like. Also we include money, since it is a product of labor used in the exchange of products. Also we must include the changes wrought by labor in the land in order to prepare it for use in production. The land itself, in its natural state, is not capital, because it is not a product of labor. The capital used in agriculture includes, besides buildings and implements, everything by which a farm differs from a forest. That is to say, the improvements in land are capital, though the land itself is not.

(*b*) Secondly, materials of production on which, or for which, labor has been spent. This brings us again to the fact that the production of a commodity is in most cases not a single act, but a succession of acts. To make a table includes cutting down the tree, sawing it up, drying the boards, dressing the pieces to the required shapes, and finally fastening them together in the form of a table. To make a coat involves raising the wool, combing and spinning it, dyeing the yarn, weaving it into cloth, fulling the cloth, and finally making it up into the desired garment.

Now, under division of labor, we must have all these operations going on at once. The saw-mill must have logs on hand; the drying establishment must have boards on hand getting dried; and the cabinet-maker must have a supply of seasoned stock on hand to select from. The spinner must have wool on hand; the dyer must have yarn in his vats; the weaver must have an assortment of dyed yarns; the fuller must have unfulled cloth on hand; and finally the tailor must have a supply of various kinds and patterns of cloth to draw on in order to suit the tastes of those who want coats.

If anybody doubts that these products of past labor are necessary in order that the labor of to-day may go forward, let him imagine how things would stand with the cabinet-maker, if he had to wait till the tree, cut down this morning, should be ready for making up into tables; or how it would fare with the tailor and the man who wants the coat, if they had to wait for the cloth to be woven, and the weaver had to wait for the yarn to be spun, and the spinner had to wait for the wool to be grown.

As all producers are to work every day, each, except the first in each series, must have a supply of his proper material to work upon, and this supply must have been prepared for him by previous labor on the part of those performing the earlier stages of the work. It is obvious also that in all cases where other things are needed besides machinery and the material operated on, these too must be provided in advance. The most common example of this is fuel for the engine.

Materials on which, or for which, no labor has been expended, are not capital. Coal in the furnace-room of a mill is capital, but not so coal in its native seam. Logs in the timber-pond are capital, but forest-trees are not. The crop growing on a farm and the cattle on a ranch are capital; but the fishes in our rivers and lakes and the wild animals in our forests are not.

(*c*) Capital in commodities seeking exchange. — The third form of Capital is connected with division of labor. It consists of commodities awaiting exchange. The difficulty of selling products has already been spoken of. We are not here concerned merely with the labor it involves, which is greater in many cases than the labor of actually producing the articles. The chief point to notice at present is that, in order to carry on exchange of products, we need to have great masses of commodities of all kinds continually on hand in the stores and warehouses. These commodities are capital, products of labor used in exchange. Production cannot go on without them.

Inventions have done much to cheapen the production of things; but beyond diminishing the cost of transportation, little has been done to cheapen exchange. In fact, considering the tendency of recent times to erect very costly buildings for use as stores and shops, and to multiply the number of them everywhere, we may fairly question whether exchange has been cheapened at all.

Just how great a number of shops, and how great supplies of finished commodities displayed in them, may be necessary for carrying on exchange in the most economical way, it would be impossible even to conjecture. It is only evident that we need here a large accumulation of products of past labor, and that the more the community is willing to pay for convenience and sumptuousness of service in its buying and selling, the more numerous and costly and fully stocked the stores and shops will be.

3. **Production in Progress.** — Viewing now the productive system as a whole, and at work, we may think of its results as a stream of commodities flowing day by day into the reservoirs of trade, and through these into the homes of the people. This stream is made up of many smaller streams,—

each industry contributing its quota to the flow. Continuing the figure, we may say that each of these lesser streams has at its fountain-head the laborers who draw the original materials from the earth; the other laborers in the industry, each in his place, are engaged in forwarding and transforming these materials, stage by stage, towards the final form in which they are to be received by the consumer.

Out of the reservoirs of trade every man receives the reward of his exertions,— the daily food, clothing, and whatever of other comforts and luxuries he may have earned. The larger the stream of products the more the community will have to divide and enjoy,— for everything in it goes to somebody. How each man's share is determined, we shall consider later.

4. Capital is Consumed.— It follows from the nature of the uses Capital is put to that it is perpetually undergoing transformations. The portion that consists of materials is in a constant state of change until it eventually is carried as finished commodity into the stores and shops; from here it sooner or later passes into the hands of the consumer and ceases to be capital. But it is replaced, in the natural course of production, by new materials and new products coming forward all the time by the action of the producers. Once provided with capital and started on its present basis, production itself keeps up the stock of capital, so far as the portions consisting of materials and of commodities awaiting exchange are concerned. We could not produce the kinds of commodities we do produce, and use division of labor, without creating these forms of capital, even if they did not exist before. This is simply putting in other words the proposition that capital is necessary for civilized production; it is in fact inseparable from it.

As to the other portion of capital, which consists of machinery, buildings, railways, and the like, the case is somewhat different. This form of capital is also consumed, but more slowly than the other portions. The machinery wears out, the buildings and ships decay. These, however, are not inevitably and, as it were, unconsciously replaced by the mere course of production itself. A portion of the labor of the country has to be diverted from the work of directly producing commodities, to the work of providing the tools, machinery, and other equipment designed to assist that production.

Fixed and Circulating Capital. — The greater lasting power of machinery, buildings, etc., has led economists to distinguish this portion of Capital as Fixed, the remainder being designated as Circulating Capital. The latter includes all parts of capital that are consumed at a single use: *e. g.* the wool used by the spinner, the grain used by the miller, the fuel used for the engine, etc. On the other hand, all tools and implements belong to Fixed Capital, on the ground that they are not used up at a single use. The distinction is not important except so far as it bears on the law of wages, and for this purpose it is far from covering the whole principle with which it is connected, viz., the element of Time in production.

CHAPTER VIII.

CAPITAL REPRESENTS INDUSTRIAL IMPROVEMENTS.

1. The Capital of To-day a Legacy. — The present generation inherited from the one just preceding it a productive system equipped with materials and machinery. The same is true of every other generation of men since the dawn of history. Each inherited capital from its predecessor. The proportion of capital was undoubtedly smaller in early times than it is now; but our ancestors, as far back as we know anything of them, had industrial knowledge and capital for turning it to account. As men's knowledge increased, and improved ways of using the productive forces were invented, additions have been made to the world's capital, until it is what we find it. To those who already have capital, increase is comparatively easy. With the old tools new ones can be made. But how did the progenitors of our race produce their first capital?

2. The Beginnings of Capital. — The only answer we can give to this question is to consider briefly the circumstances in which a community would naturally become possessed of capital. We must suppose some member of the community to have discovered a new and better way of getting food, clothing, or some other needful thing, — which new way promises larger returns for labor, but at the expense of waiting longer than hitherto for the finished product to appear. Without this knowledge there would be neither motive nor room for the existence of capital. In the second place, we must suppose the community, or some of its members, to have spare time and strength left over after providing for their daily necessities; otherwise they could produce no capital, since the production of capital requires the expenditure of labor in some way that promises no immediate result good for human use. In the third place, they must be diligent and enterprising enough to use this spare time in the manner their new discovery suggests, for the sake of the future benefit it promises.

Given these conditions, capital will inevitably spring into existence.

3. Capital may be created by working for the Future. — As to the precise mode of creating capital in such a case, there would be several alternatives open. It may help to clear up our notions regarding the nature of capital, if we consider these alternatives briefly. Taking as primitive a case as possible, let us imagine a community that has subsisted hitherto on roots, nuts, berries, and such varieties of fish and game as can be captured without laborious contrivances of any kind.

Supposing now that a member of this community, by happy accident, discovers the superiority of some particular root, say the potato, when grown in loose soil, in an open place where it has plenty of sun and no weeds to retard its growth, over the same plant grown in the hap-hazard way of wild nature. To make use of this discovery will require much preliminary labor in clearing the ground, gathering good specimens for seed, planting them and protecting them while they grow, weeding, etc.

This is a case in which, I think, the work would naturally be done little by little, in the spare time left over after providing for daily wants.[1] It would naturally be tried on a small scale at first, in order to be quite sure that the discovery was a real advantange, — worth the labor of putting it into practice. As each successive crop showed more and more conclusively the value of the discovery, a larger area would gradually be cleared and planted, until finally the raising of potatoes became a regular source of food supply. In this case the improvement of the land, the necessary seed,[2] and, in its season, the growing crop, would be capital.

If, instead of an agricultural discovery, the new idea

[1] We may suppose the daily consumption to be reduced in order to gain time for the new work, — if such reduction be possible.

[2] The land itself, as already stated, is not Capital, — not being a product of human labor. By the "improvement of the land" we mean the changes made in or upon it by labor, with a view to production: for example, the removal of trees, levelling the hillocks, plowing, fencing, etc.

happened to be the construction of a weir for capturing fish by the flow and ebb of the tide, the same mode of procedure would be open. The labor of constructing the weir could be done in whatever time could be spared from getting food and other necessaries in the old way,—partly, perhaps, by stinting the consumption of these things in order to have more time for the new work. The weir would, in this case, be the resulting Capital. Till finished, it would of course add nothing to the daily food supply.

4. **Capital may be created by Saving.**—It is obvious that, in both of these cases, the man making the improvement might proceed differently. He might begin by saving up a supply of food obtained in the old way, by working harder, and perhaps consuming less than usual, in order to be able presently to devote his time entirely to the work of making the improvement. This course, however, would be less likely to be adopted than the other, both because it seems to call for more energy and self-denial than the other; and because the kinds of food accessible in such a case as we are considering, are hard to preserve for any length of time, and always lose something by keeping. If it should be adopted, the store of food and other necessaries would ordinarily be called capital. For, though not strictly used in production, it is accumulated for a productive purpose.[1]

[1] If such a store were used merely as the means of living for a time in idleness, it would not be Capital.

We shall see later that in an advanced state of society, the more common mode of creating new capital is by thus saving the means of support for laborers in advance. But it is never the sole mode.

5. A Third Alternative. — If, instead of a single producer, several producers should unite to make the improvement; or if the single producer should have dependents or slaves to assist him, still another method would be open. Some of those concerned could devote their time entirely to the new work of creating capital, while the rest provided, by the old way, enough of the necessaries of life for the whole number, until the new method of production began to yield its returns. For a time they would have to work harder than formerly, or consume less than formerly, or both, in order to obtain the capital necessary for putting the new discovery or invention into practical use. Thus the creation of Capital implies a present sacrifice for a future gain.

6. Capital facilitates the Creation of more Capital. — If the new contrivance should prove successful, it would presently add to the productiveness of the labor of the community. Its members would have more to enjoy than formerly, without working any harder. They would therefore be in a better position to take advantage of any fresh invention that might occur to them. They could more easily spare the labor required to put it into practice.

Thus, every step in advance makes every succeeding

step easier. This is especially true in relation to mechanical inventions. The making of the first tools and implements ever made in the world must have been a very slow and painful process,—for tools are needed in making tools. Men must have worked longer and harder to make a wretched axe of stone, in the so-called stone-age of the world, than they now work to get a whole outfit of cutting tools made of steel. Not only so, but it must have been infinitely harder for them to spare time from the struggle for daily food, for the purpose of making tools.

7. Civilization and Capital.—We thus see that in every way capital and civilization go together, and grow together. Increasing knowledge of nature and natural laws comes with the experience and observation of successive generations. The ingenuity of men is always ready to suggest contrivances by which the new knowledge may be turned to account in producing wealth.

With rare exceptions, every new contrivance demands a larger outlay of labor without immediate return, than was demanded by the old devices. It demands more waiting or longer waiting after the outlay of labor, as the price of its larger yield. Unless men are ready to bestow labor on these terms, the new idea remains a mere idea. How many happy conceptions have failed to be put into use in the world's history, because no man was able and willing to make the sacrifice of present ease and comfort required for introducing it, we shall never know. But it is more than probable that there have been many such cases.

The many peoples of the world, who are still living in poverty and barbarism, can hardly be wholly ignorant, all of them, of the better ways of production developed by the nations of Western Europe and America. They lack the energy and self-denial, rather than the knowledge, required for the creation of Capital.

8. Two Sets of Helpers. — From all this it follows that two sets of men have conferred great industrial benefits on their fellow-men: first, the inventors and discoverers who have suggested new and better ways of production: secondly, those who, by their willingness to labor and wait for their return, or to accept future instead of present commodities, have furnished the means of putting these improvements into actual operation. The work of the inventor — the idea — goes first: the labor and waiting required for putting it into practice come later. Both are necessary in order to give us the blessing of easier and better ways of producing wealth.

It may perhaps seem strange to some of my readers to call such things as a weir, or an axe, or the cultivation of the land, an "improvement in production." But unless we are to believe that men were created with a large knowledge of productive devices, there must have been a time when the very simplest and commonest parts of our present knowledge came as a new discovery or invention.

CHAPTER IX.

TWO CLASSES OF PRODUCERS: EMPLOYERS AND LABORERS.

1. Comparatively Few Men own Capital.—Nothing has been said hitherto about the familiar division of producers into the two classes known as Employers and Laborers. For the sake of simplicity, I have spoken as if every producer supplied the capital requisite for carrying on his industry. We must now consider the highly important fact that the enormous capital used in production and exchange belongs, in the main, to a comparatively small number of persons.

We have already seen that for the production of capital, labor must be spent in ways that promise no immediate return. Capital is the result of labor and waiting. Now we know that people differ very much in the power and willingness to wait for good things. To the eager and passionate, such waiting is much more irksome than it is to the cool and sedate. Some are by nature careless and improvident, ready to "let the future take care of itself"; others are naturally thrifty, anxious to increase their possessions, always willing to forego present enjoyment for the sake of future advantage.

The nature of production puts these qualities to the test. Those who are not willing to work for a distant object, decline to fulfil the conditions on which alone large returns can be obtained for their labor. They doom themselves in advance to a life of rude poverty, such as that led by our native Indians, or to a life of dependence on whatever other men may offer in exchange for labor, as is the case with so many laborers in all countries.

On the other hand, those who have the foresight and strength of will to meet fairly the whole burden of civilized production, who are ready not only to labor but to wait as long as need be for the enjoyable results, are able to win the largest and best rewards for their exertions. Not only so, but they are enabled, by the possession of capital, to make gain by hiring their less provident neighbors to work for them. Once possessor of enough capital to employ even a small number of laborers, a man is usually able to gain a livelihood without further manual labor on his own part. His task becomes that of directing and controlling the labor of other men. The possessor of large capital is even able to relieve himself of the trouble of managing industry; he can live in comfort on the interest of his capital by loaning it to employers.

The familiar differences between men as regards care for the future are therefore •of great consequence, socially and economically. They must be relied on chiefly to explain the fact that some men have capital while others have none.

Of course men have not at the present time, perhaps they have never had, equal opportunities for acquiring capital. Some have inherited wealth, while others have inherited nothing. In this, as in other respects, the shortcomings of the fathers are visited upon the children. The man who has inherited even a little can add to it more easily than the man who has nothing can acquire the beginnings of capital. It is the first steps that are hard.

Yet we may safely believe that, apart from misfortune, the cases are rare in our country, in which diligence and thrift would fail of winning some amount of capital. The chief obstacle is lack of will, the natural inclination of most men to consider the present rather than the future, and to work only in such ways or on such terms as promise speedy returns. Though well aware that, by adding the sacrifice of waiting to the sacrifice of labor, they might presently increase to an indefinite extent the rewards of their industry, they make no attempt to avail themselves of the opportunity.

Let us be clear, once for all, that the richest man is under constant temptation, just as the poor man is, to spend his whole income in immediate enjoyment instead of turning it into capital. It is only by resisting this temptation that anybody, rich or poor, has ever acquired or maintained capital. Those who resist it successfully are our capitalists.

2. Distinction between Savings and Capital. — The fact

that the mass of laborers work for wages rather than for the final products of their labor, has an important effect on the mode by which those who desire to have capital may set about obtaining it. The presence of laborers ready to work for wages makes it possible to acquire working capital in return for mere savings, — *i. e.* for finished commodities, or the means to buy finished commodities. This is therefore the course usually followed in practice. The person desiring to possess capital saves his income, or borrows other men's savings, and uses the amount so obtained in paying wages to laborers for producing the desired capital.

For this reason it is common to speak of savings as capital. But capital is the equipment for producing and exchanging commodities; it is the necessary means for effective industry. Savings, on the other hand, are the completed results of production and exchange, — commodities (or the means to buy commodities) which the owner chooses not to consume but to spare for hiring laborers. When turned over to the laborers, these commodities are not used to assist production; they are consumed by the laborers and their families just as they might have been consumed by the original owner.

To say that savings are capital, or are a necessity of production, is to look on industry solely from the point of view of the employer; is to regard the laborers not as men but as mere animals for use in production, and needing to be fed and clothed by other men, in order that they may be able to work effectively. No man can be an employer, in the present sense of the word, without the use of savings. But capital, as we have already seen, can be produced without the necessity of some men saving in order to pay other men wages.

It is, strictly, only for the payment of wages in advance of production that savings are necessary. In order that some men may have wages, other men must save the means of paying them. In other words, if some men must have a reward for their labor sooner than production yields it, then other men must postpone the enjoyment of their reward beyond the point at which production yields it. One man's wages can only come from another man's savings.

But there is surely no necessity or reason in the nature of production, why the burden of the necessary waiting should be borne by different persons from those who perform the labor. That is rather a consequence, originally, of the very unequal degrees in which men are gifted with the readiness to work for future advantage, — partly also, now, a natural consequence of the existing inequalities of wealth.

As capital is, in practice, usually provided through the savings of the few, no serious error is likely to arise, except in treating wages, from confounding savings with working capital. It is customary to speak of "saving capital," and we may safely enough follow the general usage, understanding the phrase as a short expression for "saving the means to pay laborers for producing capital."

3. **Incidental Results of Wage-paying.**—It is of course in the nature of working for wages that the product of the labor belongs to the employer. That is the basis of the bargain. Yet some persons talk and write as if the laborer had still a reserved claim upon, or a right of some kind in, the product of his labor. All such assumptions are foolish and vain,—as foolish and vain as it would be to argue that the person selling a commodity has a right both to the thing sold and to the thing he receives in exchange for it.

Under the system known as "Profit-Sharing" there is a right expressly reserved to the laborers of sharing in any profit that may be made beyond a certain fixed rate. But this is not a simple case of working for wages. The manager, in profit-sharing, agrees to pay in advance a certain amount, presumably less than the current rate of wages, and a further sum, greater or less, at the close of the year,—the precise amount to depend on the success of the business in the meantime. This arrangement does, by inference, give the laborers a reserved claim upon the product,—a right, for example, to object to any course that should lessen its value. But in the ordinary case of hiring for wages there is no such right.

A second result of wage-paying is that the employer bears all the pecuniary risks of production. The laborers get their wages whether the enterprise turns out well or ill. For the employer there is always some risk of losing his savings, — especially so in the production of things that are at all subject to sudden change of taste and fashion. He may find that he has produced the wrong article, or the wrong variety of it, and may find no buyers for his product except at a loss.

There is a further risk of loss to employers by the overproduction of any particular commodity. A few producers of any article have the power to bring embarrassment and loss on all producers of it by reckless increase of the supply.

Under the system of producing only to fill orders, which is common in some branches of manufacturing, these risks are assumed by the capitalist, merchant, or dealer, who gives the order. The risk under this plan is probably lessened, since the dealer has better opportunities for watching the tendencies of the market than the manufacturer has. But the risk can never be wholly done away until a plan is devised by which things may be produced only in response to orders from consumers. It is needless to say that such a plan is very unlikely to be devised.

Apart from the general risks attending all production under division of labor, some industries have special risks of their own. In farming, for instance, there are dangers from unfavorable weather, the attacks of destructive insects, etc. In mining there is danger from fire, exhaustion of the deposit, etc. In the manufacture of gunpowder there is constant danger of loss by explosion. These risks, so far as they affect property, are borne by the employer.

4. Advantages of the Wages System. — As the employer bears the pecuniary risks of production, and owns the product when completed, it is natural that he should have complete direction of the business. Wherever the laborers, even if supplied with capital, are too ignorant to manage the work of production, or to choose efficient managers to act for them, the control of a wise employer is undoubtedly an advantage for all concerned. It prevents waste of labor through short-sighted and inefficient modes of production. In those industries that need the joint action of large bodies of laborers, the managing rights of the employer are particularly important. Laborers have not always had the education and training that would qualify them even for choosing wise directors in such industries, — to say nothing of their ability to pronounce on difficult questions of general business policy. It may therefore be taken for granted that, so far as regards the mere question of management, the wages system has been generally favorable, in the past, to wise and efficient direction of all large industrial enterprises.

Again, the regularity and certainty of the reward for labor under the wages system is a clear advantage. For persons whose income must, in any event, be small, it is important to know exactly how much they are to receive, and when they are to receive it. They can then arrange their scale of expenditure on a safe basis. Any risk of delay in receiving their earnings, or any uncertainty as to the amount to be received, is burdensome in such cases.

Another great and obvious advantage of the wages system is that it provides the whole labor force of the country with abundant capital. The amount of capital available for each laborer is made as great, not as the laborer himself would have made it, but as those would have it who are most able and willing to save. The labor of the man who owns no capital is thus supplied with a full equipment of the most effective devices for increasing production.

The resulting increase of product goes mainly to the hired laborer himself. The gains of the employer are easily reckoned, being the difference between his payments and his receipts. But the laborer who has no capital of his own is the great gainer by the wages system, though his gain is less easily measured than his employer's, and is often quite forgotten.

In order to tell how much the laborers of a civilized country are benefited by the savings of other men, we should need to know how much they could produce, with little or no capital, if thrown entirely on their own resources. We can only be sure that, in comparison with even the lowest wages, the amount would be small. The whole excess of wages above what could be so produced is a clear gain to the laborers from being hired. It is a benefit accruing to them from the presence of capital which they have done nothing towards accumulating.

5. Some Disadvantages of the Wages System.— On the other hand, it must be admitted that production by hired labor has some serious drawbacks. On the side of the laborer it is unfavorable to efficiency. The hired laborer has no direct and personal interest in the product of his labor. Any immediate gain from improving its quality, or increasing its quantity, goes to the employer. The same is true of the benefit arising from any saving in materials or needless wear and tear of machinery and buildings. The hired laborer lacks the personal incentive to make the best use of his labor and to turn everything to the best account.

While, therefore, the wages system has undoubtedly been favorable to efficiency and far-sightedness in management, it depends too much on the presence and watchfulness of the manager. The "hireling" has always been proverbial for slackness in his work. Men, as a rule, work with a will only when the product of their labor is to be their own. The eye of the overseer cannot be everywhere; and even if it could be, it is a very poor substitute for the active spur of self-interest, urging the worker who looks to his product as his reward.

The adoption of "piece-work," or payment according to results, acts to some extent as a corrective of this evil. But this plan puts the workman under a strong temptation to do his work in a poor and hasty manner. Except in the few industries where defects of workmanship are readily observed, this plan is unsuitable. Like the system of paying by the day, it depends too much on the eye of the manager. The workman has no personal interest in the goodness and value of his product, nor in economizing the materials and machinery used in producing it.

Since the employer owns the product he at least is interested in having it as great and excellent as possible. But it is another defect of the wages system that even the employer's interest in production is not of the simple and stimulating kind that sees in the product a reward for the labor of producing it. For him the product is not a reward of labor, but a return for savings paid out in getting it made. His motive is to make profit, not to get wealth produced. Take away the chance to make profit, and he will cease to carry on production.

Now the employer's chance to make profit depends, at any given time, on the price at which he can sell the product. A fall of the price may cut off his profit and thus leave him no motive for going forward. When this happens production comes to a standstill, unless the laborers are willing to work for less money. As they commonly are not willing to do this, strikes and lockouts follow,—with resulting loss and bitterness for all concerned. These disastrous interruptions of industry, instead of decreasing with the spread of education among the masses, seem rather to increase in number and intensity as time goes on. No device has yet been discovered for preventing them. They are an evil common to all forms of wage-paying.

It will be convenient to defer our discussion of wages and profits until we have considered the principles governing the value of commodities in exchange.

QUESTIONS AND EXERCISES.

1. How do you show that the business of merchants is to manage the exchange of products?

2. In what sense is it true that all wealth is *useful?* Should you give the name of wealth to rum? to quack medicines? to dime novels?

3. Should you give the name of wealth to a good voice? to a talent for acting on the stage? to great physical strength? Why?

4. What is Natural Wealth, and how is it related to wealth produced by labor? Give examples of each kind of wealth.

5. Show that increase of knowledge tends to increase natural wealth. What illustrations can you give?

6. What is meant by Production? Can you always tell by the mere name of a thing whether it is a product of labor or not? For example: if you were asked whether a tree, or a flower, or a berry, or a parrot is a product of labor, could you answer without knowing particulars? How as to books, coats, houses, and pictures?

7. In what circumstances does any kind of natural wealth acquire a value in exchange? Is a nation enriched by the fact of its natural wealth acquiring an exchange value? Suppose, for example, the lands, coal mines, etc., of the United States became twice as high in value as they are at present, would this of itself add anything to the wealth of the people?

8. Is it possible for any person to grow richer by reason of the destruction of natural wealth? If so, what is the precise source of his gain?

9. Did President Lincoln's proclamation of freedom for the slaves make any class of persons poorer than they were before? If so, did it diminish the wealth of the United States?

10. Why does land differ more in value in different places than cotton cloth does? Do you see any reason why timber should differ more widely in different places than silk? Any reason why green vegetables or fresh fish should differ more than tea or sugar?

11. Why have rivers and natural harbors no exchange value, whereas canals and artificial harbors have a value in exchange? Would it be true to say that streets and highways have exchange value, as streets and highways? How as to railways?

12. Are mortgages and railroad bonds to be regarded as wealth? How as to railroad stocks? When a man buys a railroad bond, or a share of railroad stock, just what does he buy? Suppose a railroad pays no dividends, is it wealth? Is a banknote wealth?

13. Illustrate by example in your own neighborhood the distinction between Capital and other wealth.

14. What three classes of things constitute the capital of a community? Give examples of each kind.

15. A watchmaker's stock of watches are part of his capital: does it follow that all watches are capital? Is there any kind of wealth that can never be capital? Any kind that is always capital.

16. Explain the remark that "Capital is perpetually undergoing transformations."

17. If you were asked whether *paper* is capital, why could you give no definite answer? Should you have the same difficulty if the question were asked in reference to coal? Pig iron? Racehorses? Printing paper? Mill machinery? Unimproved lands?

Ploughs? Turnip seeds? Could you answer with certainty in any of these cases? Why?

18. What circumstances determine the productiveness of labor? Why is American labor more productive than that of most other countries?

19. Illustrate the distinction between Productive and Non-productive labor. Mention some kinds of labor that are neither wholly productive nor wholly non-productive. To which class should you assign each of the following labors: nut-gathering; building toy-boats; making fire-crackers; fishing for sport; exercising in a gymnasium; playing base ball; the study of music; the study of architecture; the study of drawing; the labor of a bank-teller; of a tailor's apprentice; of a merchant; of an inventor; of a doctor; of a policeman; of a jailer? Is the fact that labor is paid for a proof that it is productive?

20. In what ways may capital be created? How do you distinguish between Savings and Capital?

21. How does the possession of some capital facilitate the creation of more?

22. Why are the Indian tribes of the West usually so poor?

23. How do you account for the fact that comparatively few men own capital?

24. Mention the chief industrial consequences of the fact that the mass of producers work for *wages*.

25. The profits made by hiring laborers can be accurately measured. Can the gain of the laborer be measured? How should you express the laborer's gain from being hired?

26. Can wages change without any change in the amount of money the laborers receive?

27. Explain the remark that "The more a nation saves, the more it can produce." Do you think of any limit to the increase of production through increased saving?

CHAPTER X.

OF VALUE IN EXCHANGE.

1. The Distinction between Value and Price. — We must now consider the principles governing the value of commodities. The first thing to be done is to make sure that we see clearly what is meant by the value of an article, and how its value differs from the price of it. The price of a thing means the amount of money it exchanges for: the value of it means the amount of any and every other commodity it exchanges for.

The value of a thing, therefore, includes the price of it. The price is simply one example or instance of its value; the instance that, by frequent use, is most familiar and expressive to us. In speaking of value we compare each commodity with all other commodities; in speaking of price, we compare it with the one commodity, money.

Money gives us a convenient and ready standard for expressing the value of things. For all practical purposes men naturally prefer to speak of price rather than value. Even when they use the word value, they often mean only the price. In political economy it is necessary to keep in mind the distinction, and to observe it very carefully. For example, the price of a thing may rise, without any change taking place in its value: the price of every other thing may rise at the same time. If, for example, all prices rise ten per cent., money is the only thing whose value is affected: the value of money is lowered.

All prices may rise or fall together, but it is impossible for all values to rise or fall together. If some things rise in value, other things fall. If beef rises in value as compared with tea, tea falls in value as compared with beef. It would be impossible for a pound of tea to become worth more beef, and a pound of beef to become, at the same time, worth more tea. To speak of a general rise or a general fall of values is to use a contradiction in terms, since to say that some things have risen in value is the same as saying that other things have fallen in value. In other words, value is purely a matter of comparison; there is no absolute standard for measuring it. We simply compare one commodity with another. As all the runners in a race cannot simultaneously gain on each other, so all commodities cannot simultaneously rise or fall in value.

We shall find that the price of every commodity is subject to two very different kinds of change. In the first place, it may rise or fall without a corresponding rise or fall in the prices of other things. In this case the value of the commodity is affected. It becomes worth more or less of other commodities than it was worth before.

In the second place, all prices may change together, and equally; that is to say, the exchange value of money may rise or fall. In this case, leaving money out of the account, the exchange value of other things, compared among themselves, remains unaltered. The difference between the two cases is highly important.

Since a change in the price of an article may or may not imply a change in its value, it would be safest always to speak of value, rather than price. But we can hardly avoid speaking of prices. Whenever, in the following pages, a rise or fall of price is spoken of, it is to be understood as a rise or fall confined to the commodity named: implying therefore a corresponding change in the value of the commodity.

2. Exchange Value and Intrinsic Value.—It is necessary also to guard against confounding the value of which we speak in political economy with the intrinsic value or usefulness of things. The value of which we speak here relates simply to buying and selling. The full name for it is value in exchange.

It is true, of course, that nothing can have value in exchange unless some persons consider it a good thing to have. Things that have no intrinsic value for anybody have no exchange value either. But, beyond this, there is no connection between the exchange value of commodities and their intrinsic utility. I suppose we should all agree that bread is intrinsically more useful than diamonds; yet one little diamond has more exchange value than many tons of bread.

If the world should be overtaken by a famine, the exchange value of bread and diamonds would be changed. In either case, the value of the bread or of the diamond is the amount of other things to be got in exchange for it.

3. Value depends immediately on Demand and Supply.—We are all aware that when the supply of a commodity coming forward for sale falls short of the demand for it, the price is usually raised. Those who have it for sale find that they can charge more for it than before, and yet dispose of their whole stock. Since business men are on the alert to make all they can, they ordinarily raise the price at once. Even if for any reason they fail to do this, the stock will presently become exhausted, and the buyers, eager to get more, will offer a higher price for it.

On the other hand, when the salable supply of a commodity exceeds the demand for it at the existing price, those who have it for sale find themselves obliged to lower the price in order to tempt people to buy more of it. If they fail to do this a portion of the supply will remain unsold on their hands and they may lose more thereby than they would lose by lowering the price.

Thus much we could safely say, even if all sellers worked in perfect harmony and strict combination with each other. But it is extremely rare that all sellers act in harmony,—they are usually more or less in the attitude of rivals. Each acts for himself; and when it becomes clear that the commodity is not selling as fast as it is produced, some dealer is pretty certain to offer his stock at a lower price than before. In such a case, the action of one dealer is usually followed by others, and finally by all. Any dealer who declines to follow, does so at the risk of selling little or none of his stock. We have in this a case of the competition of sellers.

4. Equilibrium of Supply and Demand. — The natural aim of trade is to make exchange keep pace with production, — to sell things as rapidly as they are produced.

When people buy any commodity faster than it comes forward from the producers, the price is raised. The rise of price causes people to buy less of it. The price goes on rising until the demand is brought to a rough equality with the daily production.

In the reverse case, when a commodity does not sell as fast as it is produced, the price is lowered in order to tempt people to buy more of it. The price goes on falling until the purchases of consumers come to be roughly equal to the daily production.

Thus the value of everything tends to be such as to make the demand equal to the supply. But changes of value react on the supply of things as well as on the demand for them. On the side of supply we come to the source of commodities, namely, production.

When the value of a commodity rises, the production of it becomes more profitable than before. Those who produce it are stimulated to produce more of it; new laborers are called in, more capital is devoted to the work, and the production is increased.

On the other hand, when the value of a thing falls, those who produce it find their industry less profitable. This will tend to make them produce less of it.

But the process of increasing or diminishing the production of most commodities is necessarily somewhat slow. Production, as we have already seen, requires time, especially where much machinery is needed, or long processes of growth and manufacture have to be waited for. Again, once men have engaged in producing a given commodity, it is not easy for them to withdraw from it. Even a temporary stoppage implies great inconvenience and loss both to employers and laborers. Men usually abandon an industry only when they are forced to do so.

It follows that the rough equality between supply and demand is maintained, from day to day, rather by affecting the demand through changes of value than by affecting the supply through changes of production. A high or low value acts at once on the demand, checking or stimulating it into equality with the existing supply, until production can adjust itself to the situation.

The connection between value and production will be considered more fully in the next chapter.

CHAPTER XI.

COST OF PRODUCTION AS THE ULTIMATE REGULATOR OF VALUE.

1. Cost of Production to the Employer, or Money Cost. — There are two ways of looking at cost of production. We may, in the first place, regard the matter wholly from the stand-point of employers of labor. For them the cost of producing a commodity is the amount they pay out for materials, machinery, etc., and in wages to their laborers. This is a natural and convenient view of cost of production as a matter of practical business. It is, in fact, the only view that could find expression in book-keeping. It gives the employer a basis for reckoning how much he gains by selling his product at any given price. The question of cost for him has reference only to his profits. Of course, the more cheaply he can get the requisites of production, including productive labor, the greater his profits will be.

But in several ways this view is inadequate for scientific uses. First, it is too narrow, since it applies only to production carried on by hired labor. It gives us no definition for the cost of production where those who do the labor provide the capital too, — as is the case, for example, with many hunters, fishermen, tailors, shoemakers, small farmers, and others. In fact, it relates not to production in and of itself, but to the terms on which some men can hire other men to labor for them in producing things. It views the hired laborer as a productive machine whose services cost men something, rather than as himself a man equally interested with the employer in getting commodities produced at a low cost. The true cost to men of producing the things they need must be the same, whether some work as hired laborers for others, or all work for themselves. We therefore need a broader definition that shall not view production solely as an opportunity for employers to make profit.

Secondly, even where production is carried on by hired laborers, this view of cost of production exposes those who adopt it to very serious errors and misconceptions. The payments an employer has to make in getting an article produced are liable to change for reasons that have no real connection with the production of the article. For example, four hundred years ago an employer's accounts showed very much smaller payments for wages and other things than they do at present. Men could be hired for from ten to fifteen cents a day; wheat could be bought for eighteen cents a bushel; beef for less than a cent a pound; butter for a cent; and other things in proportion.[1] In those days money had ten or twelve times more value than it has now. If, therefore, we should hold the view

[1] Thorold Rogers, *Work and Wages*, p. 539.

that the cost of production of things is measured by the money payments of employers, we should have to say that it is greater now than it was four hundred years ago: the fact being that inventions have very much lessened it.

Those who compare the cost of producing things in different countries at the present time, using the money payments of employers as a basis of comparison, are liable to the same error. The value of money differs very considerably in different countries and even in different parts of the same country. This is especially true in the case of countries and regions between which trade is impeded or prevented. For example, in the early days of gold mining in California, before facilities existed for trade with other parts, money had a much lower value than it had in the rest of the country.

2. True Cost of Production. — We need a broader and truer definition of cost of production than the one just considered, a definition that shall apply to all production under whatever conditions carried on, and shall be free from liability to error on account of fluctuations in the value of money.

Such a definition we gain by looking simply at production itself, rather than at the accidental and more or less artificial arrangements made between men in regard to it. It is no necessary feature of production that a few men should own the capital and should hire the rest with a view to making profit.

It is, however, necessary that men should labor; and it is equally necessary, owing to the nature of production, that most of the labor needed for producing enjoyable commodities, should be expended long in advance of receiving them as its reward.

These two sacrifices of our ease and present enjoyment, first the burden of labor and then the burden of waiting for our reward, are demanded by the very nature of production, and constitute for men the true cost of everything they produce. Men who, having the requisite knowledge and natural wealth, are able and willing to labor and to wait for the reward, are in a position to produce for themselves whatever it is possible for men to produce. We may therefore define the cost of production of every commodity as the quantity of labor and the amount of waiting necessary in order to produce it. (See Appendix, page 387.)

This definition applies equally well whether those who perform the labor receive wages or wait for the natural reward of their labor; if they receive wages, then the burden of waiting is assumed by another. It also avoids all danger of error on account of changes in the value of money.

As thus defined, cost of production is affected only by changes that appear in the act of production itself,—changes that make the production easier or harder than it was before. Inventions that lessen the necessary labor, and the discovery of new and more fruitful sources of materials, lessen the cost of production. On the other hand, if the best and most convenient sources of materials should become exhausted, the cost of production would be increased.

But changes of wages have no effect on cost of production as here defined. The labor and the waiting required to produce any article are the same when wages are high as when wages are low. Changes of wages, as we shall see presently, affect only the profits of employers.

Again, according to this definition the exertions of the employer himself are part of the cost of production, since the labor of planning and directing the work is a necessary part of the labor of producing things. The view that finds the cost of production in the employer's payments, makes no account of this: it ignores the employer's own share in production.

Since, however, the business man's view of the cost of production is not likely to be abandoned, we may distinguish the two definitions by calling the first, Employer's Cost or Money Cost, and the other, Economic Cost or Real Cost. In this way we may hope to avoid misunderstandings. The two, as we shall see more fully later, relate to very different things.

3. Labor as an Element in the Cost of Production. — The chief element in the cost of production is labor. We include, in each case, all the labor, whether of hand or head, which contributes in any way to the production of the commodity. The mental labor of planning the work and of directing and overseeing the workmen, is part of the cost of production as well as the exertions of the workmen themselves.

It is to be remembered that the labor of producing an article includes all the labor from the beginning, not merely the last stage of the work. For example, the labor of making cotton cloth includes the labor spent in raising and transporting the raw cotton, as well as that spent in making it up into cloth at the mills. Also, it includes the labor of producing all the secondary materials needed in the production, such as, in the case of cotton cloth, starch, dyes, chemicals, fuel, etc.

In the industries requiring skill or training, the labor of acquiring this skill is also included in the cost of production.

The labor of producing a commodity also includes the labor of making the requisite tools, machinery, and appliances of all kinds for carrying on the work.

But here we must remember that the machinery, buildings, etc., are not used up in producing a single specimen of the commodity. The labor of making the machinery must be regarded as belonging, in part, to every specimen it helps to produce until it is worn out. Thus, if a sewing-machine stitches ten thousand shirts before it wears out, only one-ten-thousandth part of the labor of making it is chargeable to each shirt. In the same way, in the case of all other apparatus of production and exchange, only a proportional part of the labor of making it belongs to the cost of production of any given quantity of each commodity.

4. How Labor is Measured. — The term "quantity of labor," as used in defining cost of production, needs some explanation. The quantity of labor required for producing a commodity is not measured simply by days or hours, though the length of time occupied must always be the chief factor in the case. We must include, with the length of time, every other feature of the work that tends to attract or to repel producers.

A day's labor in an industry that is disagreeable, or dangerous, or exhausting for those engaged in it, is a greater quantity of labor than a day's work in a pleasant, safe, and easy occupation. The standard, however, for judging the character of different occupations in these respects, is the opinion and behavior of the laborers concerned, — which may or may not be entirely in harmony with the actual facts. What they think hard or dangerous or disagreeable is, for our present purpose, hard or dangerous or disagreeable; what they think easy and pleasant is easy and pleasant.

The product of an industry that the laborers are reluctant to enter must have a higher value than a product made in the same length of time in an in-industry which they regard as attractive, — enough higher to correspond with the greater sacrifice made by the laborers who engage in the distasteful industry.

If, for example, workmen think two days' labor in a coal-pit as great a sacrifice as three days' labor in the fields or in the forest, then so far as cost of production is concerned, two days' work in a coal-pit is as great a quantity of labor as three days' labor in the fields or in the woods. In such a case, other things being equal, the coal produced by two days' labor will ordinarily have the same value as the amount of wheat or of lumber produced by three days' labor.

5. Of Waiting as an Element in Cost of Production.— I have said that labor is the chief element in the cost of production. But since labor does not result at once in a commodity good for human use, and since it is burdensome to wait for good things after we have labored to get them, this necessity of waiting must be included in each case as part of the cost. It is a sacrifice as real as the labor itself, though of a different kind.

The period of necessary waiting differs much, as we have already seen, in different industries. For example, a quarter of beef and a load of building stones may have cost the same amount of labor; but their values are not for that reason the same. The labor that produced the building stone may have been for the most part quite recent; whereas, by the necessity of the case, the labor of raising the beef must have been spread over several years. The labor spent in the early stages of producing the beef has to go long without its natural reward. Therefore, the beef, when at last it is ready for use, must have a value enough higher than that of the stones to reward this longer waiting. Otherwise men would avoid industries, such as the raising of beef, in which long waiting is necessary, and would flock into those occupations that yield their products most quickly.

The waiting element in cost of production is connected, as we see at once, with the capital used. Capital at any moment represents the labor put into production without receiving, as yet, any enjoyable return. Somebody is, of course, entitled to receive Nature's reward for that labor in the future. The man who actually performed the labor may have been relieved of the waiting, may have parted with his right to the future reward by receiving wages instead of it; but this only transfers the burden of the waiting to another. Capital always implies a deferred reward for labor.

A large part of capital consists of machinery. The natural reward of the labor spent in making machinery, comes by small installments, day by day, in the enjoyable products the machinery helps to produce. The sustained waiting for these products to appear constitutes a substantial part of the cost of producing them. When machinery is introduced into an industry previously carried on by hand, the cost of production is not lessened to the same extent as the quantity of labor is lessened. The making of the machinery involves new waiting, since the natural reward of the labor that makes it will be very slow in coming. If the new mode of production should give us the commodity for half the old quantity of labor (counting in the labor of making the machinery), the value of the commodity would not fall to half of the old value. If it did, there would be nothing to reward the new waiting for the reward of the labor that makes the machinery. On these terms no man would devote labor to the making of machines.

How much the value of a commodity that requires long waiting shall exceed the value of one made by the same amount of labor but with less waiting, depends mainly on the character of the people who have to be looked to for the capital needed in production. If these regard waiting as a great sacrifice, the value of things requiring long waiting will be high in comparison with things requiring little waiting, — the amount of labor being the same in both. If, on the other hand, they regard waiting as a slight sacrifice, then the waiting element in cost of production will count for comparatively little in determining value.[1]

In other words, there is no standard for measuring how great a sacrifice waiting is in itself; we can only take the judgment of those who submit to it. Their opinion regarding it is roughly indicated by the average

[1] It follows that, as a community becomes more willing to make the sacrifice of waiting, those products which demand longest waiting decline in exchange value.

rate of interest on loans. In a country where the people readily submit to waiting, the rate of interest is usually low; whereas in countries where waiting is regarded as more burdensome, the rate of interest is usually high.

6. Cost of Production is made up of many small parts. — If now we should try to analyze the cost of production of any commodity, we should find it to consist of many small bits of labor, each followed by its own period of waiting. The number of persons who contribute, in one way or another, to the work of producing and exchanging even the simplest commodity, is surprisingly large. The production of a book is probably not more complicated than that of most other commodities; yet if I were to begin here a full account of all the separate contributions made by different persons to the production of this little book, I think the book itself would hardly contain the list of them.

Let us look for a moment at the cost of producing the paper on which it is printed.

The cost of manufacturing the best printing-paper, and of transporting it to the place of use, is made up of the items given in the following list: The figures are for a quantity costing $10,000, and are taken from the actual accounts of a New England paper-mill for the year 1887. They represent, of course, what we have called the Employer's, or Money, Cost, since this is all that the manufacturer's books are concerned with.

Cost of Production the Regulator of Value.

Buildings [1]	$200	Bleach	$103
Machinery [1]	516	Lubricating Oil	21
Fuel	360	Lights	17
Wood Fibre	3,753	Lumber	91
Cotton Rags	1,388	Wrappers	64
Linen "	142	Marline	73
Papers	158	Freight and Cartage	562
Soda Ash	11	Horse and Carriage	24
Alum	49	Sundries	48
Clay	125	Insurance [2]	90
Lime	75	Taxes [2]	46
Rosin	6	Wages (including manager's	
Oil of Vitriol	2	salary)	1,974
Colors	14		
Starch	88	TOTAL	$10,000

It may seem at first sight that only about a fifth of the whole money cost of manufacturing paper consists of wages. But a little study of the matter enables us to see that the sums paid for machinery, materials, etc. are in fact mainly payments of wages in disguise. These sums replace (with a profit) to other employers the wages paid for the production of the machinery, materials, etc. In this respect the division of labor among employers makes no difference; in the end it is as if one employer carried on the whole business. As the true cost of production is always, at bottom, made up

[1] Of course these figures represent not the total cost of the buildings and machinery, but the proportion of that cost assignable to the given quantity of paper. (See p. 91.) The buildings and machinery are in fact worth many thousands of dollars.

[2] In regard to insurance as an element in cost of production, see the note on "Risk" at the end of this chapter. Taxes are strictly not a part of the cost of production; they are rather to be regarded as a portion of the product taken by the government for public purposes.

of labor and waiting, so the employer's cost is always at bottom made up of payments for labor and waiting.

If now we should attempt to analyze the cost of production of any commodity into all the parts or particles of which it is composed, the task would prove to be very long. Whatever is used in the production of the buildings or the machinery, or the wood-fibre or the alum or anything else named in the above list, is in fact used in the production of paper. Its cost of production is therefore part of the cost of producing paper. In analyzing the cost of production of paper we should have to analyze the cost of each of these,— which would give us for each of them a list of items about as long as that given above for the paper itself. Again, each article named in these new lists, would have a cost of production needing, in turn, to be similarly resolved into its parts; which would give a new and very numerous set of items; and so on until we should bring in every article that comes into play, directly or indirectly, in the production of paper. We should find, in this way, that the labor of making paper is resolvable into many hundreds, perhaps thousands, of parts; some of them perhaps too small to be stated, but all of them necessary to the final result. The sum of all these labors, together with the aggregate of all corresponding periods of waiting for reward, constitute the true or economic cost of production.

This reminds us of the wonderful extent to which civilized men have carried division of labor. The industries of a nation are closely interwoven with each other, forming in reality one great system of co-operation. Each producer depends on the help of thousands of others, whom he has never seen. The situation, along with the great advantages it brings, obviously imposes a grave duty on all concerned. Any interruption or disturbance at any part of the system is certain to work injury for the whole body of producers.

7. Market Value tends to Conform to Natural Value.— The Natural Value of every commodity is that which corresponds to the cost of producing it. Things exchange for each other at their natural value when for a given quantity of any particular commodity, the seller can obtain as much of every other commodity as is produced by the same quantity, or equivalent quantities, of labor and waiting. Thus the law of natural value is simply the just rule of equal rewards for equal sacrifices.

This is, however, a rather ideal standard to which the actual values of things at any given moment seldom or never exactly correspond. The actual or market value of every commodity is acted on, as we know, by every change of demand or of supply. These disturbances are temporary in their effects, but they are constantly occurring. The result is that the market value of every commodity is commonly somewhat above or below its natural value.

But we can safely say that, except in special cases to be spoken of in a later chapter, when the market value of any commodity is above or below its natural value, the rule of equal rewards for equal sacrifices will tend to bring it back to that level. When the business of producing any commodity is more profitable than the production of other things, new labor and capital will be attracted into producing it, and the resulting increase of supply will cause the market value to fall; when it is less profitable, the reverse will happen.

We now see how, under division of labor, each man knows what to produce and what to avoid producing, though he has never seen the persons who are to use his product. These changes of value are messages of a very effective sort from the consumers, telling when too much or too little of any article is produced. Without them, production by division of labor would be reduced to hopeless guessing.

8. Improvements in Production. — It is important in considering the effect of improvements, to bear in mind that it is the comparative, not the absolute, cost of production that governs the values of things. If by a universal improvement we could lessen by one-half the cost of production of all things, the value of every commodity would remain unchanged. The ratio of the cost of each to that of every other would be the same as before, and it is obviously on this alone that values depend, since value is simply a comparison.

The only effect of a general and equal cheapening of all things would be to increase the rewards of labor and waiting. Wages and profits would be higher. Things would be cheaper in the sense of getting more of them for our work, but not in the sense of getting more of one commodity for another.

Improvements do always, in practice, affect values when they are introduced, because no invention is universally applicable. Coming as they do, in single industries, they have the effect of lowering the values of the commodities whose production they make easier than it was before. It is to be observed that they also increase the rewards of all producers who use the cheapened articles. The fall of value is obviously the process by which improvements in single industries extend their benefits to the whole community. Every improvement that lessens the labor of producing any article in general use, adds to the general prosperity.

Since, in the long run, improvements are made to some extent in every industry, it follows that to some extent the effect of improvements in the long run, is rather to raise wages and profits than to lower the values or prices of commodities. Perhaps a better way to express it is to say that, in the long run, improvements raise wages and profits without lowering values or prices.

It used to be thought necessary to show in political economy, that labor-saving improvements are not injurious to the laborers. There was formerly among the laborers of the old world a strong dislike of machinery, on the ground that it took the place of men, and deprived laborers of the opportunity to earn wages. There is no doubt that, temporarily, the introduction of machinery on a large scale may give rise to hardships until things adjust themselves to the new situation. But when necessary changes are made, every labor-saving contrivance is a benefit to the community. The displaced laborers soon find other employment, and the community as a whole has a greater return for its labor than it had before. I think that in America machinery needs no defence.

Of Risk in Production.—It is usual to name risk as an element in cost of production, but it does not seem to me that risk is an element distinct in kind from the necessary labor and waiting. Personal risks to health, etc. incurred by the producers are included in the quantity of labor required. [See p. 98]. Risks to the capital employed are no burden in themselves. The real burden is, in part, the labor of taking precautions against the danger, and in part, the labor of repairing the damage when loss occurs. The burden of risk is therefore resolvable into labor; it simply adds to the quantity of labor necessary on the average for accomplishing a given result. The business of insuring against loss by fire, shipwreck, etc. is simply a useful device for distributing the actual losses among all who incur the risk: a small payment by each of them is ordinarily sufficient to make good the losses, and leave a profit for those who conduct the insurance.

The risk of loss to individual employers and dealers by a fall in the value of their goods, is strictly no part of the burden of production, since it affects only the comparative earnings of particular individuals, and not the general result for the whole community. What one man loses by a fall of value other men gain, since they get that particular commodity more cheaply than they could naturally have hoped to get it. These risks involve a chance for gain as well as a danger of loss.

CHAPTER XII.

EXCEPTIONS TO THE GENERAL LAW OF VALUE.

1. The Value of Natural Wealth. — The general law of value considered in the preceding chapter applies only to wealth on which labor has been bestowed, since that alone has a cost of production. Things that have come to mankind as simple gifts of the Creator acquire an exchange value, as we have seen in Chapter V., when the demand for them as a gratuity exceeds the supply.

The value of natural wealth of any kind, at any particular place, is wholly under the control of the demand. The supply being fixed, whenever the demand, at any given value, exceeds that supply the value rises. In every place where population is increasing, this rise of value is usually progressive. It is the process by which the demand for the natural wealth of the region is kept down to an equality with the fixed supply.

There are two checks on this local rise in the value of natural wealth. The first of these is the power of men to move away to other places where there is less crowding. The second is the continual cheapening in the cost of transportation, which enables men to bring the materials of production from regions where the local demand is small to places where it is great. Of course things so transported cease to be strictly natural wealth and become wealth produced by labor, their value being regulated by the cost of bringing them. But in the place to which they are brought, the materials of production serve the same purpose as if they had been procured on the spot. The additional supplies obtained from other places keep down the value of the home supply.

Such things as do not admit of transportation may rise indefinitely in value in the crowded portions of the world. As already noted, land for building purposes is the most important article of this character. Yet even the value of building land is greatly affected by the cheapening and quickening of transportation. In one sense the demand for building ground in the cities is diminished by the facility with which men, whose business is in the city, are enabled by the railroads to have their homes in the country. But, on the other hand, the railroads enable vastly greater numbers to congregate in the cities than could find subsistence there without them. The result is that cheap transportation tends powerfully, in the long run, to raise the value of city lands.

2. Products that cannot be increased in Supply. — There are a few products of human labor which cannot be increased at will. Old pictures and statuary, old furniture, and all relics of by-gone times are of this nature. The value of all such articles is governed by the demand. As the supply is fixed, when the demand for them at any given price becomes greater or less than this supply, the price rises or falls so as to restore the equality.

Works of art even by living masters have their value determined in the same way. Though subject to increase, they cannot be indefinitely increased, since only one person in each case has the gift of producing them. In practice it is nearly as if the supply of such works were absolutely limited. The demand for the productions of real artists is always greatly in excess of the supply, except at values far above that of other things having the same cost of production.

The inventor of any new article is given, by the laws of most countries, the exclusive right of manufacturing the article for a limited term of years (in the United States seventeen years). An article covered by a patent may be classed, as far as the general body of producers are concerned, with things that cannot be increased in supply at will. Yet, in practice, such articles are produced freely in answer to the demand. The effect of the patent is to enable the owner of it to obtain an extra profit or royalty on the manufacture. In other words, it enables him to hold the market value somewhat above the natural value,— that is, if his invention should meet with a ready demand.

There is a constant effort on the part of producers and traders to obtain, as regards ordinary commodities, a similar advantage by the use of trade-marks. Where trade-marks enjoy legal protection, they enable the producer of any commodity to keep exclusive control of the market for his own particular brand or "make" of the article. The primary effect of trade-marks may be to serve as a guarantee of quality for the consumer. They save the consumer some trouble of investigation at each purchase. But for this very reason they may enable the possessor of an established brand to obtain more for his product than other less-known producers are getting for the same quality.

3. Products of Skilled Labor. — The value of products requiring special skill or long training on the part of the producers, is not fully controlled by the cost of production. Such products are permanently higher in value than ordinary products made by the same quantity of labor and waiting.

The reason is two-fold. First, the need of skill limits the number of persons who are able to make these articles: the general mass of laborers are effectually barred out from the business by lack of this essential qualification. Secondly, the demand for these products, if they were offered for sale at their natural prices, would far exceed the supply which this limited number of laborers can produce. The high value is caused by this large demand acting on a restricted supply.

But why do not more of the laborers learn the necessary skill? The answer to this is that it is costly to acquire skill; further, the outlay is for a somewhat distant object. The same reasons which prevent the mass of laborers from acquiring capital, also prevent them from acquiring skill. Few among them are able and willing to save from their slender incomes the means whereby they themselves, or their children, may acquire the training necessary for the higher grades of productive labor. The young laborers, partly no doubt from necessity, partly however from eagerness to earn quickly something of their own, turn to industries in which little or no preliminary training is needed.

Thus it happens that the number of men in the skilled trades is never large enough to supply all the products of skill that would readily sell at their natural value. The resulting high market value is the premium constantly paid by the community to induce laborers to make the sacrifice necessary for obtaining skill.[1]

This is obviously a case of defective competition among producers. The rule of equal rewards for equal

[1] Of course all the actual labor and waiting demanded in acquiring skill are included in the cost of production. The point is that the value of skilled products is ordinarily considerably above that of other things costing the same amount of labor and waiting. The labor of the skilled occupations is, in itself, usually lighter and more agreeable than that of the unskilled. Yet, day for day, its products are always a good deal higher in value, in some cases two or three times higher. It is, of course, possible to maintain that the reluctance or inability of common laborers to strive for skill is a part of the cost of production in these cases; and that the natural value here, as in the case of unskilled products, is a rough average of the actual market value. In this view the only peculiarity in the case of skilled products is the fact that a considerable part of the waiting necessary in producing them, has to be borne by a class of men who find long waiting very burdensome.

sacrifices, which keeps market value in touch with natural value, takes effect only where men ordinarily choose the industries that, all things considered, offer best returns for the sacrifices demanded. If the producers, especially those who are beginning life, customarily neglect their best opportunity in any direction, the full and direct control of natural value over market value is to that extent defeated.

It is not, however, even in these cases, wholly prevented. The market value of skilled products is always above the natural value; but the interval between them is not a matter of mere accident. It depends on the amount of inducement required in order to make parents and young laborers willing to face the cost of acquiring skill. At this interval, the market value is held in check, in the ordinary way, by the cost of production. Competition is obstructed; but, with an allowance for the obstruction, it works as in other cases.

4. Exchange between Distant Places. — A similar obstacle to freedom of competition among producers is found in the case of men in different countries, and even in distant parts of the same country. Any two places are distant from each other in the sense here intended if there are serious impediments to the free movement of laborers from the one to the other.

The impediment may be difference of language, or of religion, or of social customs, or of climate; or it may be mere national prejudice, or love of home and friends, or the difficulties and cost of the journey.

Exceptions to the General Law of Value. 115

When a trade exists between two places distant from each other in any of these ways, the active principle that keeps exchange on the basis of cost of production is lacking. The only reason why we can say that market value, in any case of exchange, tends to conform to the cost of production, is the fact that producers may ordinarily be counted on to choose among their home industries those that offer best returns. The difficulty, in trade between distant places, is that they are largely prevented from doing this. In the exchange of commodities between countries, it is therefore possible that the products of the one shall have regularly a higher value, as compared with those of the other, than the cost of production on either side would suggest. For example, the United States, in trading with Brazil or with China, may ordinarily obtain for the product of two days' labor here, commodities that cost five days' labor in the other country.

Further discussion of this very interesting portion of our subject will be found under the head of International Trade.

5. Things having a Joint Cost of Production. — We have thus far spoken as if every commodity were the result of a separate and independent outlay of productive labor. In point of fact very many products are coupled in production with other products, so that the one is never produced without the other. The production of wheat is also the production of straw; the production of wool involves that of mutton; the production of beef that of hides and tallow, etc. Nearly every sort of production has some by-product or products of more or less commercial importance.

It is to be noted that men cannot in these cases regulate the proportions in which the several associated articles shall be produced. Nature fixes the ratio for us. In order to increase or diminish the supply of beef we must also increase or diminish in the same proportion the supply of hides, horns, hair, tallow, etc.

The natural value of the whole group of products resulting from the raising of an ox is, of course, determined by the cost of raising the animal. The relative value of each separate product in the group depends on comparative supply and demand. The stronger the demand for each product, in comparison with its quantity, the higher its relative value.

Suppose that, at the existing prices of beef, hides, and tallow, the demand for beef increases, without increase of demand for the other products. The price of beef will rise. This makes the raising of oxen more profitable than before: the production of beef will be increased. But this brings also an increased supply of the associated products; and since there is no increase of demand for these, the price of them must fall in order to create more demand. In the end, what is gained by the rise in the value of beef is lost by the fall in value of the associated products,—the combined value of the whole group tending always to conform to the cost of producing the animal from which they are made.

6. Arbitrary Exceptions. — There is a further class of exceptions to the general law of value, arising from intentional interference with the free course of industry.

An example, now fortunately much rarer than in former times, is seen in the case of things produced by slaves. Slave labor is not adapted for any but the crudest occupations; usually it is confined to a few industries. It is not open to the slaves to leave these industries when the products fall below their natural value; nor is it for the master's interest to withdraw them. The result is, that the value of slave products may be permanently below that of other things made in the same country by an equal quantity of free labor.

In some cases men who trade in several commodities single out one of them for exceptional treatment, — setting the price of it rather with a view to drawing customers than to making a profit. The commodity selected for the purpose needs to be one in common use, as to the usual price of which there is general knowledge, so that the buyer may recognize a good bargain when one is offered to him. In such cases the dealer counts on making up for the lack of profit on his decoy, by increasing his sales of other things.

The result is sometimes, however, to establish for a time, a low price for the article at all the competing shops. It is commonly understood, for example, that retail grocers in most parts of the United States have not been making any profit by the sale of sugar for a number of years past. They have had to compensate themselves, of course, by charging higher prices for other things.

7. Combinations, Trusts, etc. — In some cases those who have a commodity for sale are able to combine to keep up the price of it. At the time of writing these pages, there is much talk of "trusts" and other combinations for raising the prices of various articles. If a commodity be produced in a few places only, or by a few large establishments only, its price may be fixed by agreement between the producers rather than by competition.

In order that the price may be kept much above the natural price, those who make the combination must be able to prevent other men from entering the business. This they can do in the long run, only by gaining control of most of the available sources of supply.

A combination controlling the whole supply of a commodity might extort from the consumers any price it chose. But even in such a case the monopolists might discover that it would not be for their own advantage to charge much more than the natural price. A high price lessens the demand for any article. There are few things which are absolutely necessary, and for which no tolerable substitute can be found. Mostly, therefore, any attempt to extort an unreasonable price for an article would only result in loss to the monopolists. They would have to limit their production very much in order to find a market. It is probable that the most advantageous price for the producers of all ordinary articles is, in the long run, the one that corresponds most nearly to the natural price.

Yet it is undoubtedly true that a combination among the producers, or even the chief producers of a commodity, may succeed for a time in raising the price of their product. This is especially true where large plant is required for the production. The mere time necessary for starting a competing establishment may be considerable. Further, the greatness of the outlay required, and the risk of loss in facing a competition with the combination, may deter outsiders for a considerable period from embarking in the business. To that extent the community is always exposed to injury at the hands of a combination.

Our best protection against monopolies has hitherto been the difficulty of forming and maintaining effective combinations. Where the means of production are widespread and producers are numerous, effective combination is probably impossible. Even where the sources of production are limited, it has yet to be shown that effective combination can be made permanent. No monopoly has in the past succeeded in maintaining itself for any length of time unless sustained by force of law. In a country where the laws allow perfect freedom of industry, I think there is no serious danger to be apprehended from "trusts" or other combinations to interfere with the natural course of production and exchange. In the end every such attempt is likely to bring loss rather than gain to those who make it.

It must not be inferred from the space devoted to exceptional commodities in this chapter, that they constitute a very large proportion of all the things bought and sold, or that their value departs very widely from the ordinary rule. Compared with the great mass of exchanges subject to the ordinary rule, they are very small in amount: and the extent of their departure from the common law of value is not often great.

QUESTIONS AND EXERCISES.

1. Explain the distinction between Value and Price. Show that the price of a thing may change without a change of its value.

2. Remembering that every article may fall in value, show whether all things may fall in value together.

3. How does a change in the value of money show itself? Has money a price?

4. What is meant by the "equilibrium of demand and supply"? How is it maintained from day to day?

5. What do you understand by the Natural Value of any commodity? What may cause it to change?

6. When the market value of any commodity is above its natural value, what ground is there for anticipating a fall? Should you expect the fall to come equally soon in all cases? Compare, for example, apples, beef, coal, and paving-stones.

7. Are there any products whose market value is always above their natural value? Any always below? Why?

8. Explain carefully the distinction between employer's Cost of Production, and the true or Economic Cost.

9. Show that the employer's cost of production may change without any change in the true cost.

10. How should you proceed to analyze the economic cost of producing a woolen coat? What account should you make of the loom on which the cloth was woven?

11. Explain the term "quantity of labor" as used in defining cost of production?

12. If two articles are produced by equal quantities of labor why can we not assume, without further knowledge about them, that they will ordinarily have the same exchange value?

13. Explain the remark that "the law of natural value is simply the just rule of equal rewards for equal sacrifices." How is the rule put in force?

14. If one should argue that the invention of reaping-machines has benefited farmers only, how should you answer him?

15. How is the value of building land determined? What products of labor have their value determined in the same general way, and why?

16. Suppose a machine invented that gives us, for half of the previous labor, an article formerly made by hand; should you expect the value of the article to fall to half of its old value.

17. Is there any connection between the value of products of skilled labor and their economic cost of production?

18. How is the value of wool determined? Suppose the demand for mutton should increase without increase of demand for wool, how and by what steps would the value of wool be affected?

19. In what cases are "trusts" likely to succeed in maintaining high prices? What is necessary in order to insure permanent success?

20. Supposing it were possible for all producers to combine effectively, what effects should you anticipate from a universal system of trusts?

21. How do you explain the fact that a diamond necklace is worth so much more than a barrel of flour, — seeing that bread is so much more necessary than jewelry?

22. Suppose a man loses $1,000,000 by a fall in the price of wheat, show whether the world is poorer by that amount.

CHAPTER XIII.

OF PRICES, OR THE VALUE OF MONEY.

1. Importance of Changes in the Value of Money. — The value of money is expressed by the general level of prices. When the value of money rises the change is shown by a general fall of prices, and *vice versa*. Money has itself no price; a dollar is always worth a dollar, whether the exchange value of money be high or low; but every change in the general level of prices makes each dollar worth more, or less, of other things than it was worth before.

So far as the mere exchanging of products is concerned, it obviously makes no difference to the exchangers whether the prices be all high or all low. If, for example, a man has a hundred bushels of wheat to exchange for cotton cloth, it makes no difference to him whether the wheat be a dollar a bushel and the cloth ten cents a yard; or the wheat five dollars a bushel and the cloth fifty cents a yard. It is only comparative prices that tell in simple exchange. If the price of wheat should change, the price of cloth remaining stationary, that would affect the values of the two articles.

But though the general level of prices is immaterial in simple exchange, it is highly important in some other ways. Much of the business of the world involves agreements to pay money in the future. All loans, especially loans for long periods, such as are represented by city, state, and national bonds, are of this character; also all contracts for the future delivery of goods at set prices. If the value of money change in the meantime, evidently the basis of the agreement is disturbed to the disadvantage of one of the parties to it.

Again, the wages of laborers (including salaries of all grades) are agreed upon in money. Every general rise or fall of prices lowers or raises the real wages of all persons who work for hire. Of course the wage agreements may be revised; but they are never revised at once, and for mere temporary fluctuations of prices they could hardly be revised at all.

2. Market Value and Natural Value of Money.—True money is always a product of labor. Every nation has the power to choose the product of which its money shall consist. In past times there was a good deal of diversity in the money of different peoples; some used cattle, some iron, some bronze, and some silver; others used shells, others salt, and still others, tea. In modern times all civilized nations agree in using gold and silver. The essential qualities of true money are that it shall have a value of its own, that it shall be convenient, and that it shall be as little as possible exposed to fluctuations of value.

True money being a product of labor, it has, like all other products, a natural or normal value depending on the cost of producing it. Also it has, like all other products, a market value depending immediately on supply and demand, but tending in the long run to conform to the natural value. There are, however, some notable peculiarities in the case of money which call for a special discussion of its law of value. In the present chapter we shall confine our attention to its market value alone.

3. Meaning of the Supply of Money. — The supply of money, like the supply of every other article, is the amount of it offering in exchange for other things. But the supply of every other article is kept down by the constant drain made upon it by the purchases of consumers. The amount of it in the market at any time consists mainly of newly-made specimens. In the case of money there is little or no buying for consumption. We buy it (*i.e.* give other things in exchange for it), not intending to keep it, but to pay it away again for other things. The supply of money consists, therefore, mostly of old pieces. The same old money is paid again and again for goods, until it becomes so worn as to need recoining.

Now every time a piece of money is used in making an exchange, it counts in the supply of money quite as effectually as if it were a new piece. It follows that in order to ascertain the supply of money in a country, we should have to do something more than merely to count the number of dollars or pounds in its currency; we should have to take into account the number of times each dollar is used in exchange in a given period. This is called the Rapidity of Circulation of money.

The rapidity with which money circulates in a country depends partly on the business arrangements and partly on the temperament of its people. We shall have occasion to discuss the subject fully a little farther on.

4. Peculiar Character of the Demand for Money. — The demand for money is also marked by two notable peculiarities. The first of these is its remarkable steadiness. Money being the medium for making exchanges, the demand for it is as great as the demand for all other things put together; the demand for every other thing presents itself first in the form of a demand for the money wherewith to buy it.

Putting the same fact in another way, the demand for money consists of all the things offering for sale, or needing to be sold. Evidently, therefore, it depends on the total production of things, and this, as we easily see, must be slow to change. It follows that the demand for money has greater steadiness than the demand for any other thing. Changes of fashion, so powerful in other cases, have no effect on the demand for money since they imply no change in the total product of labor.

Again, merely anticipated changes of supply, owing to changes in the conditions of production, can have but little influence on the demand for money. If the wheat crop threatens to be deficient, the demand for wheat increases and the value rises at once. If a new copper mine is discovered, the demand for copper falls off at once: intending buyers will not buy much at the old value, and holders of it must lower the price before a single pound of the new copper is in the market.

But the demand for money does not fluctuate for such causes; it can be changed only by changing the total quantity of things for sale. To give up demanding money would be to give up trying to sell goods. Further, it would be impossible to get more money for goods this year because the supply of money is likely to be greater next year. Prices are as high already as the existing supply of money will allow them to be, on condition of selling things as rapidly as they are produced.

The second peculiarity of the demand for money is that, being in fact a demand for other things, it is satisfied with any substitute or representative of actual money which will answer equally well the real end in view. Now we shall see presently that men have invented some excellent substitutes for money, — together, unfortunately, with some very bad ones. A very small proportion of the payments made for goods in this country are now made with coin. We find mere paper evidences of the right to get gold and silver on demand a more convenient sort of currency for ordinary purposes than actual gold and silver coins.

The result is that the offer of goods for sale has now become a nominal rather than a real demand for true money. It is in practice a demand for the mere right to get true money in case of need, but with a practical certainty, in most cases, that the seller will find the mere right itself entirely sufficient for his purpose. In fact, then, the real demand for money is limited to such a sum as may enable the banks and the Treasury to pay coin to every holder of the right to get coin, who chooses to exercise his right.

I shall not wait in this chapter to discuss the various substitutes for money, and the peculiar effects of each. Our present task is to consider the operation of supply and demand in determining the market value of money, or the general level of prices at any given time. For the moment we shall regard as money everything that the people accept as money. Since true money and all the honest substitutes for it rise and fall in value together, we run no risk of falling into error by temporarily treating the whole currency, whatever its amount and composition, as if it consisted wholly of true money.

5. How the General Level of Prices is Fixed. — The problem of the value of money, or the general level of prices, is one of considerable difficulty. In order to master it, the student must consider carefully every point in the case.

In the first place, it is to be remembered that things must be sold as fast, on the whole, as they are produced;

otherwise the markets become glutted. The efforts of the producers and dealers are directed towards obtaining for all articles the highest prices at which the whole product will sell. The producers are especially interested in having the price as high as possible. The dealers, however, must take care that the goods on hand shall move off as rapidly as new goods come forward from the producers. If they find products accumulating on their hands they must, in self-protection, set the prices lower, both when they buy and when they sell.

Now, in order that exchange may keep pace with production, it is necessary that the amount of money demanded for the whole product of industry shall be roughly equal to the whole supply of money offering for goods. In other words, if you add together the prices of all the goods needing to be sold each week, the sum of them must be roughly equal to the amount of money the buyers are able and willing to spend in the purchase of goods each week.

If, for example, the aggregate of the prices asked for the week's product be one hundred and two millions, and the people have only one hundred millions to spend in buying, it is clear that about two per cent. of the goods must remain unsold. In this situation prices must fall; that is to say, the value of money must rise.

If, on the other hand, the prices asked be ninety-eight millions, the supply of money being a hundred millions, the stocks on the hands of the dealers will get sold faster than new goods can be found to replace them. In this case the prices must rise, that is to say, the value of money must fall.

Since, however, buying and selling are only the separated halves of the general exchange of products, the prices paid are on the whole identical with the prices received. It may seem therefore that the buyers may pay as much as they receive, and that there is really no limit to the prices that might be charged and paid.

This would be true if product were exchanged directly for product, using the price of each simply as a means of comparison. But where money of any kind has to be used, there is at once a question of the sufficiency of the supply of it to carry on the exchanges at a given scale of prices. No part of the money can be in two places at once. Everywhere that a payment is being made, there must be money enough to make it; and the same money cannot be used in making another exchange until the receiver, or somebody else receiving it from or through him, uses it again in buying goods.

This brings us back to the two things which determine the supply of money; the quantity of it in circulation and the rapidity of its circulation. The quantity being a simple question of the number of dollars in use, it is not likely to perplex the student. We shall consider in the next chapter the circumstances on which the quantity of money depends. The circumstances determining its rapidity of circulation are equally influential in fixing the general scale of prices, and are at the same time much less simple. We must therefore try to gain some clear ideas regarding them.

6. The Movements of Money. — The movements of money in detail are exceedingly intricate, but there are certain great currents of circulation which are created and determined by the business arrangements of each country. These are not hard to follow, and they are sufficient at least to explain the meaning of "rapidity of circulation" in its bearing on prices. In studying them the following hints may be helpful.

(a) It is most convenient here to confine our attention to prices at retail. Though these are not uniform, not being fully under the control of competition, nevertheless it is at retail that the true exchange of products is effected. The transfers of goods from the producers to wholesale merchants, and from these to the retail merchants, look towards the final sale to consumers and are designed to facilitate this. For our present purpose, prices at wholesale may be regarded as conforming to prices at retail, with an interval sufficient to give the retail merchant the ordinary rate of profit. In the same way the prices at wholesale may be regarded as conforming to the prices the wholesale merchants pay to the producers; these latter, in turn, depend on the employer's cost of production, and this, as we have seen, on money wages.

(b) When money has once been used in the purchase

of goods for the buyer's consumption, it cannot be similarly used again until, in the course of business, somebody again receives it in payment for labor or waiting, and chooses to spend it in that way. If the receiver should choose to save it for paying wages to productive laborers, or to spend it in paying for non-productive services of any kind, the circulating period is likely to be longer than if he should buy goods with it himself. Again, if the receiver of the wages should in turn save it for use in hiring another man, instead of buying goods with it for himself, the circulating period is likely to be still further lengthened.

(c) After each use of money in buying goods for the buyer's own consumption, the business arrangements of the country may require it to make a considerable circuit before it can reach the person who is next to use it in similar buying. The money that pays for goods at retail must find its way back through all the channels by which the goods, and the materials for making them, come forward in the course of production and exchange. Some of it must go to each person whose labor or waiting aids in producing goods or in conveying them to the consumer. The number of hands through which it must pass in reaching the next man to spend it, and the delay at each stage of its passage, determine the length of time that must elapse between each use of money in paying for goods at retail, and the next similar use.[1]

[1] It may be well to state that these principles relate, not to particular pieces, but to *sums* of money. Each dollar being the precise

(d) It is evident at once that the circulating period is not the same for all parts of the currency. The sellers at retail spend a part of the money they receive in buying things for their own use and that of their families. The money so used returns quickly to become again part of the supply acting on prices: it makes the shortest circuit that is possible. Very different is the circuit made by money which is used by the retail merchant in buying goods at wholesale, and then by the wholesale merchant in buying goods of the manufacturers, and then by the manufacturers in buying materials, and then by the producers of materials in paying wages to their laborers. It is clear that a sum of money always taking the short circuit could do much more buying at retail than an equal sum that should always take the long one.

(e) To all except the last receiver (the one who spends it) the money may represent savings to be used in business with a view to profit. This usually requires some consideration and planning. Even if this were not so, every business man needs to keep some money by him to meet unforeseen calls. Each must therefore hold the money he receives long enough to keep his reserve of cash up to the required limit. In fact, at any given moment, the money of the world is mainly held by

equivalent of every other, the individual pieces of money may exchange places freely without affecting the result. In fact, the very form of currency used in retail transactions differs from that chiefly used in wholesale trade. In the former, notes and coins are used for the most part, whereas the larger transactions of wholesale trade are settled by the use of bank deposits.

business men, either as savings awaiting investment (or re-investment) or as reserve funds to meet emergencies.

Even those persons who ordinarily spend their whole income do not part with all the money they receive the very day they receive it. They must ordinarily reserve some part for current payments, until they can count on receiving more.

(*f*) It is to be noted that money has two distinct functions to perform in its circuit, the one as a medium of exchange, the other as a vehicle for transmitting un-invested savings and for paying wages. It is highly important to keep the distinction in mind.

The consumer who pays money for goods, uses it simply as a medium of exchange. The dealer, in his turn, uses in the same way whatever part of it he spends. For him, however, the sale of the goods is the close of an investment. The money represents savings, now in the free or uninvested state. Much the greater part of it he must use over again in his business. If he pay it as wages, his act is clearly not one of exchange. If he use it to buy new goods at wholesale, this again is a case of investment rather than of economic exchange. He gives free savings in return for invested savings. The same is true when the wholesale merchant buys goods of the manufacturer. By these transfers the savings released from investment by the consumer's purchases at retail, are transmitted to the producing employers, by whom they are embarked in new investments through payment as wages. In the hands of the laborers the money received as wages becomes again a mere medium of exchange.

7. Diagram illustrating the Circuits made by Money in the ordinary course of production and exchange.

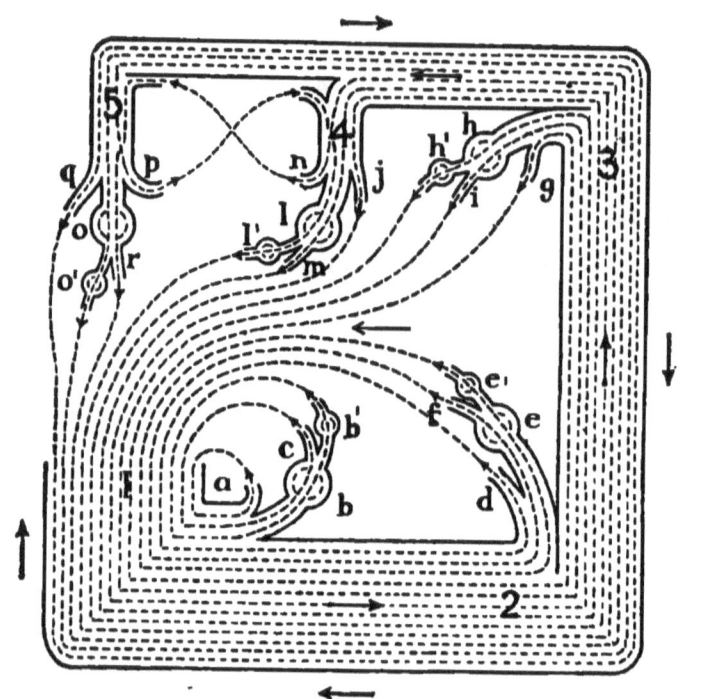

EXPLANATIONS. — At 1 the money is paid for consumable commodities at retail; at 2 it is paid to the wholesale dealers; at 3 to the producers of finished commodities; at 4 to the producers of materials; and at 5 to the producers of machinery. The dealers and employers spend the portions of a, d, g, j, and q, in buying commodities at retail, and pay as wages the portions b, e, h, l, and o. (The latter include salaries, fees, and payments for nonproductive services as well as savings paid to productive laborers. Money paid as wages passes through a bulb.) The recipients of the wages spend the portions c, f, i, m, and r, in buying commodities at retail, and save or pay as wages in other ways the portions b', e', h', l', and o'. The producers of materials pay the portion n

for machinery; and the producers of machinery the portion p for materials.

Everything is a finished commodity in the sense here intended when it has reached the condition in which it is to be used and enjoyed as a reward of labor or waiting. For example, coal for house use is a finished commodity, even though coal for use in a factory is only a material. The arrows outside of the figure are intended to indicate the return movement of products of labor, for which the money is paid, — thus the one at the top indicates the movement of materials and machinery to the producers of finished commodities; the one at the right the movement of finished commodities from the producers to the wholesale dealers, etc.

The diagram makes no pretence of giving a complete picture of industry, or of including all the movements of money. For example, speculative trading in stocks, bonds, land, etc., makes a considerable demand on the currency; but it may be regarded rather as keeping a certain amount of money out of use in production and exchange than as constituting a part of the true circulation. Again, no attempt is made to separate payments for transporting goods and materials from other payments; though they do not exactly coincide in point of time with any other set of payments, we may perhaps regard them as included in the disbursements at wholesale. Again, no account is made of the lessening of industrial incomes by taxes. These undoubtedly lessen somewhat the rapidity of circulation of the money drawn into public treasuries; but unless taxes be excessive, or the proceeds be held unduly long, the proportion of the general circulation absorbed by them is small, and may be ignored.

It is assumed in the diagram that all commodities pass through the hands of one, and only one, wholesale merchant. In fact, of course, many products are sold directly to the retailer by the producer, while others pass through the hands of several wholesale dealers. Perhaps the two errors may be regarded as offsetting each other, so far as the rapidity of circulation of money is concerned.

8. Application of the Foregoing Principles. — Let us now suppose the currency of a country to consist of $150,000,000, distributed among the circuits of our diagram as indicated in the following table. Assuming for simplicity that each receiver of money holds it for a week, we group together circuits of the same length.

Returning at	Amount circulating.	Circulating period.	Corresponding supply of money for purchases at retail each week.
a	$10,000,000	1 week.	$10,000,000
c and d . . .	24,000,000	2 weeks.	12,000,000
b', f, and g . .	27,000,000	3 "	9,000,000
e', i, j, and q .	40,000,000	4 "	10,000,000
h', m, and r . .	25,000,000	5 "	5,000,000
l' and o' . . .	18,000,000	6 "	3,000,000
n and p . . .	6,000,000	5, 6, 7 "	(say) 1,000,000 [1]
	$150,000,000		$50,000,000

The weekly output of consumable commodities offered at retail in the country must, under these conditions, bear an aggregate price of about $50,000,000. This will determine the general level of prices in the country. The relative cost of production of each commodity will, of course, determine the *relative* price of each, *i. e.*, its value.

If the amount of money in circulation should be increased to $200,000,000, distributed in the same way, the aggregate price of each week's product would be

[1] Divided between j, l, o, and q.

raised from $50,000,000 to $67,000,000. If each receiver of money should come to hold it, on an average, one day longer, the aggregate price would have to fall from $50,000,000 to about $42,000,000.

If, the supply of money remaining unchanged, the aggregate production of commodities should be increased say ten per cent., the price of each article would have to be lowered roughly ten per cent. in order to sell the whole product.

The money transactions of a commercial country are of course much less simple and uniform than our diagram and this hypothetical case may seem to imply. But whatever their complexity, they are governed by the same general principles as the simple case; the supply of money offering for goods has the same dependence on the quantity of money in circulation, and the rapidity of circulation of the different portions.

A study of our diagram may also help to make clear the two functions of money (p. 133), and the resulting connection between the payment of wages and the exchange of commodities. If anything occurs to check the payment of wages at $b, e, h, l,$ or o, it is easy to see that the supply of money offering for goods at 1 must fall off in consequence. In fact, the lessened sales to laborers constitute the real lessening of wages in such a case. The situation is that known under the name of "dull times," or a depression of business.

9. Deficiency of Money looks like an Excess of Goods. — The popular explanation of a business depression is usually that too many commodities are produced. The appearance of the markets certainly favors this view. There is an apparent surplus of every commodity; a real surplus, if one can be imagined, could hardly look differently.

But those who regard this as a case of general overproduction are misled by mere appearances. They forget the masses of people who, in times of business depression, suffer for want of these very things that seem to be in excessive supply, and would gladly give their labor in return for them.

The real trouble, at such a time, lies in the hesitation of business men as to the investment of their savings. The money and substitutes for money that are ordinarily paid for labor as rapidly as new money is received, are partly allowed to lie unused in the banks. The result is that those who live by wages are unable to buy as freely as usual. The circulation of money is checked.

Just why business men are more perplexed and slower to invest at some times than at other times is a question we cannot now attempt to answer,—it is in fact a most difficult question. Usually these periods of depression follow periods of strong confidence and prompt investment. The change from brisk times to dull times usually begins with the failure of some ill-judged ventures of a speculative character, carried on by means of borrowing and other forms of credit. The losses caused by these failures often involve sound business houses in disaster. In consequence of them trade becomes embarrassed, and wide-spread distrust takes the place of over-confidence.

Excess of Money looks like a Deficiency of Goods. 139

The real trouble, in the period of depression which follows, is not a general excess of commodities but excessive caution in the hiring of laborers. Business men do not invest their savings in new enterprises with accustomed promptness and energy; the result is that many laborers are unemployed, and others work only half-time. The aggregate money income of those who live by wages being reduced, a corresponding reduction takes place in their usual purchases of commodities. Goods lie unsold on the hands of the dealers. There are not too many commodities, but there are too many commodities unsold. There is a deficiency of purchasing power on the part of the usual buyers.

The true remedy would be, not to lessen the world's supply of good things (of which we always have too few), but to restore the purchasing power of the wage-earners. This could be done either by restoring to the old amount the payments of money to laborers; or by reducing the prices of commodities in the same ratio as the money income of the laboring class has been diminished.

But the first remedy is out of the question until the congestion of the market shows signs of lessening; and the second is naturally resisted by holders of goods, since it seems to involve a loss of their profits. A business depression is therefore an awkward dilemma. It lasts usually until, partly by fall of prices and partly by restricted production, the aggregate prices of the goods for sale come to match the money in circulation.

10. Excess of Money looks like a Deficiency of Goods. — When for any reason the supply of money exceeds the demand for it, we have the opposite effect to that just considered. The readiness of most persons to buy is limited only by their means of purchase. In the case we are now considering the money income of the mass of men has been increased. Their purchasing power exceeds, at previous prices, the forthcoming supply of commodities. The stocks of commodities for sale become daily lessened, because people buy faster than new goods are produced. There is apparently a deficient production of all things.

This situation lasts but little time in comparison with that in which money is deficient. Men are slow and reluctant to lower their prices, but they are very prompt to raise them when opportunity offers. When the supply of money is increased its value soon falls. This case attracts little attention because it is of brief duration. It regularly appears after a depression of business, when the money and substitutes for money that have been held back during the "dull times" are once more put into active circulation by being used in hiring laborers, or in purchasing products of labor from those engaged in production. It also appears whenever new discoveries of gold add to the local supply of money, and when additions are made to the bank currency of any country.

CHAPTER XIV.

PRODUCTION OF THE PRECIOUS METALS.

1. Dependence of Prices on Quantity of Currency.—All that now remains to be done in order to complete our study of prices, or the value of money, is to consider how the quantity of money in circulation is determined. The goods needing to be sold constitute the demand for money. The supply depends on the quantity circulating, and the rapidity of its circulation. We have seen that the business arrangements and habits of each country determine the rapidity of circulation of its money. Our remaining question, then, is, What determines the quantity of money?

The question of quantity brings us at once to the source of money. The gold and silver of which all our true money consists, are products of human labor. The quantity of them produced must therefore depend in the long run on the principles laid down in Chapter XI.; that is to say, men can be counted on to produce as much of them as there is a demand for at the natural value.

But here we are met by a familiar fact which makes the application of ordinary principles much less obvious in the case of money than in any other case. The demand for money being at bottom a demand for other things, it is satisfied with any representative of true money that will answer the real object in view. We all know that, in point of fact, people in this country use hardly any gold coin in ordinary business, and not much silver beyond the amount necessary for small change. We use instead mere promises to pay coin, and rights to demand coin, supplied to us by the banks and by the Treasury of the United States.[1]

So far then as our prices depend on the quantity of money in circulation, they depend on the quantity of this Bank Currency, as we may conveniently call it. This exceeds very much the total quantity of coin in the country. Yet each dollar of it purports to represent a dollar of true money; it gives the holder an unquestioned right to get a dollar of coin if he wishes it; so that its quantity must stand in some definite relation to the quantity of coin.

2. Nominal and Real Demand and Supply of Money. — The fact is that, in the case of money, there is a nominal demand far exceeding the real demand, and a nominal supply far exceeding the real supply. The nominal demand consists of all the goods needing to be sold; the real demand is limited to the amount requisite for maintaining confidence in the bank currency with which in practice exchange of products is mainly carried on. On the side of supply, the nominal stock of coin is as great

[1] For the present purpose we may regard the Treasury as simply a great bank issuing promises to pay coin on demand.

as the whole mass of coin and rights to call for coin which constitute the active currency; the real stock is the far smaller amount held as reserves for redeeming the bank currency, plus the coin in actual circulation.

The question of prices, then, so far as it is a question of the quantity of money, has two distinct branches: first, What determines the actual stock of coin? and secondly, What settles the proportion between bank currency or the nominal stock of coin and the real stock? The first of these questions relates to the production of the money-metals. The second involves some elementary principles of banking. Both must be studied in order to understand how the value of money is governed.

3. **The Value of the Precious Metals not due to Coining.** — It is necessary to observe at the outset, that gold and silver have other uses besides serving as money. They have long been highly prized by all nations as material for jewelry and other ornaments, plate, watch-cases, etc. In fact, it was the high value attached to them for these purposes that made them specially suitable for use as money. No substance could be generally used as money if it were not generally regarded as useful or desirable in itself. In payments between men of different nations it would not be accepted. Further, even for use in any one country, it would be defective as money, because it would lack one of the most important influences in steadying the value of gold and silver; any decline of their value calls out an increase of demand for them in the arts, thus checking the fall.

Gold and silver were used as money before mints and coining were introduced, and before there were any laws on the subject of money. It is still one of their chief recommendations that their value as coin is independent of the mint-mark they bear. The mere coining adds nothing to their value. The coins may be defaced or even melted back into bullion without loss of value. In fact, coins are constantly melted down for use in the arts, just as if they were mere bullion.[1]

In old times gold and silver passed by weight. The name of the English "pound" sterling, although it has now become a mere name, is a standing reminder of the way in which our early ancestors used silver as money. One is apt to forget that the money-metal of our own day still passes by weight, though we seem only to count it as dollars. The weighing is done once for all at the mints. The name and other marks stamped on each piece are merely ready proof that it contains a certain quantity of metal. This is the advantage of coining, that it saves us all trouble as to weighing, and gives us the gold and silver in pieces of uniform size, thus avoiding troublesome fractions in the reckoning.

The coinage laws of each country fix the weights and names of its coins. As to the exchange value of the eagle, or the sovereign, or the franc, after it is coined,

[1] These statements assume unrestricted coinage. Of course, no silversmith would think of using our present silver coins as mere silver; he can buy the silver contained in a dollar piece for about seventy or seventy-five cents. They are all mere "tokens," and the coinage of them is strictly limited. See Chapter XVI.

that is a matter over which the coinage laws can have no control, since it depends on the prices of goods, and these no statute attempts to regulate.

4. The Production of Gold and Silver. — The production of the precious metals seems to be in some respects different from ordinary industries. The labor required in the production of all minerals is largely that of mere search for the natural deposits of them. This seems to be specially true of gold and silver. They are seldom found in very extensive deposits, as, for example, coal and iron are found. They are found rather in scattered washings, veins and "pockets," often of great richness, but usually of limited extent. The search for these is always more or less of a lottery, and as a result the output at any one source is more variable than in other mining industries. Where so much depends on luck and on chance discovery, it may seem unreasonable to speak of any connection between the value of the precious metals and their cost of production. Yet there is undoubtedly a connection. It is the high value of gold and silver that impels men to search for them. Every fall of their value abates something of the zeal in discovery; every rise increases it.

Again, although the result of one man's labor for a day or a week is very uncertain, the average product of the labor of many men is less so. Much depends on chance "finds" from day to day, but apart from great discoveries these average themselves in the general result for periods of considerable length.[1]

[1] Notwithstanding local variations, the total yearly product of gold for the whole world has been remarkably steady of late, being esti-

Men go into the production of gold and silver as they go into fishing and other uncertain pursuits, because they think that, taking good and bad luck together, men do as well in that as in other things. Even allowing much for the spirit of gambling, which undoubtedly plays an active part, there is enough of business principle in the production of gold and silver to keep their value roughly under the control of ordinary rules. When the profits of gold and silver mining are on the whole high, men will be attracted into the industry; when they are low, men will seek other industries in preference.[2]

There are two sets of changes occurring from time to time in the cost of producing gold and silver, and therefore changing the quantity of them produced. The first of these relates to the sources of the metals. The discovery of new and more productive mines may greatly increase the yield for a given amount of labor. When

mated at a little less than five million ounces. The production of silver is much less steady, and is estimated to be about twenty times as great as that of gold, — one hundred and one million (101,000,000) ounces in 1886. Much of the silver is obtained as a by-product in the mining of lead, copper, and some other metals.

[2] It is necessary to bear in mind the precise way in which a general rise or a general fall of prices changes the earnings of the gold-miners. The money-metal of a country has itself no real price. If coinage be unrestricted, an ounce of the metal will always sell for the amount of coin it will make. But when the product of the mines is coined, it is obvious that the quantity of ordinary commodities the miners can get for their labor will depend on the general level of prices. A rise of prices, therefore, makes it harder to get commodities by digging gold.

discoveries of this kind are made on a great scale, as happened in the case of gold in 1848 and 1849, and in the case of silver in 1875, the annual output is enormously increased. On the other hand, the exhaustion of a part of the known sources may diminish to an indefinite extent the current production.

The other set of changes are connected with the mode of extracting the metals from the foreign substances with which, in their native beds, they are mixed or chemically combined. The process of extraction was formerly laborious, and therefore costly. It has now been much cheapened, and may be further cheapened by new inventions. The immediate effect of these improvements is less striking than that resulting from great discoveries of gold and silver, but in the long run their influence on the product may be as great. They make the output of every mine greater than before. They make it possible to resume the working of mines that were formerly abandoned as unprofitable: of such there are many in different parts of the world. Even the refuse of former mining is now, in many cases, worked over again with a profit.

5. The Stock of the Precious Metals slow to Change. — While the production of gold and silver is subject to greater variations than that of most other things, the total available supply of them is much less variable than that of most other things. This is a fact of great importance in relation to the value of money. It is due primarily to the good care men take of gold and silver, especially the former. Gold is not put to rough uses as the baser metals are, and worn out or destroyed; it is mostly treasured and kept.[1]

The result is that the world has now accumulated a great stock of gold, — in comparison, that is, with the amount produced from year to year. A good part of the gold on hand at present was produced centuries ago; comparatively little of it is of recent production. It is estimated that the stock on hand is at least a hundred times as great as the average yearly product.

It follows that the fluctuations of the yearly product have little effect on the total stock. If all the gold-mines in the world were closed for a year, there would be no unusual scarcity of gold. If they should all double their yield for a year the increase of gold would hardly be appreciable. The difference, either way, would not exceed one or two per cent. of the total quantity on hand.

In the case of most other things the whole stock on

[1] Of course gold is not wholly exempt from destructive uses. Watch-cases, jewelry, etc., are subject to some wear and tear, although the gold they contain is mainly saved and used over again. The gold used in gilding and plating, dentistry, etc., is almost wholly lost to the supply. The wear and tear of gold in the coinage is very slight. As used in the United States, to form reserves for the Treasury and the banks, there is no reason why gold coins should not last thousands of years.

Silver, being only about one twentieth part as costly as gold, is applied to rough and destructive uses much more freely than gold, and is accordingly consumed much more quickly. Even in the form of coin, silver, being used as change, is put to a rougher use and is worn out more quickly than gold.

hand is of recent origin, partly because they are in themselves perishable, but more commonly because they are put to uses that destroy them, or soon wear them out. If the production of iron, or of coal, or of wool were to cease for a year, there would be a dreadful dearth of it; if the production were doubled the stock for sale would be doubled also. We can readily see that the effect of the change on the values of these products would be vastly greater than the effect of a similar change in the production of gold on the value of that metal.

CHAPTER XV.

BANK CURRENCY.

1. Bank Currency More Convenient than Coin.—Gold and silver coins are highly useful and even necessary, but they are inconveniently heavy for carrying in one's pocket.[1] It was natural that civilized men should invent a plan for using mere titles to coin, or ready evidence of ownership in coin, while keeping the actual gold and silver stored in a few safe places where they could be readily obtained by any person holding the right to call for them. Sensible men would have been glad to pay something for the advantages of such an arrangement.

It is the great discovery of modern Banking that a very admirable arrangement of this kind can be supplied to us free of charge, while those who perform the gratuitous service make a handsome profit from it.

The secret of banking profits is that, for ordinary purposes, people like the right to get coin better than coin itself. We need only a simple way of passing the right from man to man just as we should pass coin. Bankers have supplied us with two very simple devices for doing this, namely, Bank Notes and Checks. The two differ in several important respects, but they are alike in this es-

[1] Two hundred dollars in gold weigh nearly a pound (Troy); the same amount in silver dollars weighs over fourteen pounds.

sential point, that the effect of each when used in making a payment, is to transfer from one person to another the right of demanding coin from a bank. Their differences arise from a difference in the form of holding the right.

2. Two Forms of Bank Currency: Notes and Deposits. — A bank-note is itself a proof of the holder's claim upon the bank, as well as an instrument for transferring it. The holder of a deposit has no such ready evidence of his right. His name, with the amount of the deposit standing to his credit, is written in the ledger of the bank; but he has in his own hands no evidence of the fact. If he wishes to transfer any part of his right to another in payment for goods or services, he must write out an order, called a check, directing the bank to make the desired payment on his behalf.

The receiver of the check has no guarantee, except the character of the giver, that the deposit exists. For use between strangers, therefore, and between persons who have not confidence in each other's honor, the depositor's right is much less convenient than the note-holder's. The same is true of persons living at a distance from banks.

The note circulates as readily as coin wherever the rights given by the bank issuing it form part of the currency. For these reasons the note is much more used in retail trade than the deposit, since in retail transactions the buyer and seller are seldom acquainted with each other. Besides this, the transactions are mostly too small in amount to make it worth while to write out checks.

On the other hand, it is much safer to have a deposit to one's credit at a bank than to keep bank-notes in one's pocket or drawer. Notes are exposed to all the risks that coin would be exposed to: they may be lost, or stolen, or destroyed by fire, and the loss of the note means the loss of the right it gave. The deposit is safe from these and all other dangers except the failure of the bank. For men whose money transactions are large this is a decisive point in favor of the deposit rather than the note. The deposit liabilities of the banks in this country are several times greater in amount than their outstanding notes.

It is important to see clearly that the proportion of bank currency held in each form is purely a matter of convenience for the holders, and is entirely in their control, unless hampered by legal restrictions. The holder of notes can at any time convert his right into the other form by simply "depositing" them to his credit. The retail merchant does this daily with the notes received for his goods.

The holder of a deposit can with equal readiness exchange it for notes by simply presenting his check and taking notes in "payment." In fact, the two forms are freely interchanged day by day to suit the convenience of individual holders. In ninety-nine cases out of a hundred, what is popularly called "getting a check cashed" consists in getting a depositor's right to demand coin converted into a note-holder's right to do the same thing. To the bank it is a matter of indifference which form of right the holder chooses. The effect on prices, or the value of money, is also the same in either case.

When a check is presented for payment, the person presenting it usually wishes not so much coin as pocket-money. For this purpose well secured bank-notes have everything to recommend them; they are, in fact, the pocket form of bank currency. The admirable notes of our own national banks are as readily current as coin in every part of the Union. No person would think of declining them in payment of a check, unless he happened to need money for use outside the limits of the United States.

In the home trade of a country, such notes answer perfectly well as a reserve for paying deposits. So long as they are convertible into coin, on demand, the whole currency is kept on the coin basis. It has therefore been thought advisable, in most countries, to guard carefully by law the issue of notes; whereas, the use of deposits and checks has been left without legal restriction, except in the case of our own national banks.

3. The Source of Banking Profits. — The profits of banking are due to the fact that very few of the persons who get the right to demand coin ever exercise their right. The mere title to coin being the most convenient currency for practical use, the banks can safely count on having but few calls for actual coin. So long as there is general confidence in their ability to meet all their liabilities promptly and fully, they can safely bind themselves to pay on demand a much larger amount of coin than they have actually on hand.

This is the reason why bank-notes and deposits affect the value of money. By using these as currency, each dollar of coin, while itself reposing in the bank-vaults, is made to do the work of several dollars. The active supply of money offering for goods becomes in effect as great as the supply of these rights to call for money. The rights are for the most part purely nominal no doubt: any attempt to enforce all of them simultaneously would show this; but their effect on prices is just as great as if each dollar of them were a dollar of real money.

If the banks were required to keep always on hand as much coin as they bind themselves to pay on demand, notes and deposits would have no effect on prices, and there would be no profit in banking. The gold and silver "certificates" issued by our Treasury furnish a good illustration of this: the full amount of coin they represent is required by law to be kept in the Treasury for redeeming them. The issuing of them is therefore a burden rather than a source of profit; and they add nothing to the volume of the currency, since they only take the place of the same amount of coin.

On the other hand, the United States notes (or greenbacks) are, in this respect, a true bank currency. There are three hundred and forty-six millions of dollars ($346,000,000) authorized to be issued, and the amount of coin required by law to be kept for redeeming them is only one hundred millions.

4. The Limit of Bank Currency. — Banks are primarily great lending institutions. Their profits come to them in the form of interest on loans made to business men. They lend, not actual money, or coin, but the right to call on them to pay coin. The borrower is credited with a deposit to the amount of his loan (or takes the bank's notes if more convenient), and the bank receives interest on that amount quite as if it had given him real money.

Of course every such loan increases the bank's liability to pay real money. The loan at once becomes currency, for the borrower soon turns over his deposit-right (or the notes) to other men, some of whom may find actual coin more convenient for their purposes than the right to call on that particular bank for coin. The bank must therefore be on its guard against giving men the right to demand coin more freely than the amount of coin it has on hand clearly warrants. Any overstraining of its credit, any whisper of a doubt as to its ability to meet all calls promptly and easily, would be quite sure to injure its business and might even cause a "run" on the part of those holding rights to demand money from it.

The limit of safety for the bank itself is therefore the only necessary limit to its power of swelling the currency by the issue of notes and the granting of loan-deposits. But what is the limit of safety for the bank?

This is a question to which no very definite answer can be given. There is no one rule good for all cases. Much depends on the nature of the bank's business, the character of the people who hold rights against it, and especially on the strength of the public confidence in the management of the bank's affairs. Each bank must therefore judge by its own experience where the danger-line begins.

The most common occasion for the demand of true money instead of bank currency is connected with the external trade of each country and region. Bank currency has a limited area of circulation, particularly the part of it that consists of deposit-rights to demand money. When any holder of such a right wishes to use it in making a payment at a distance, there is always a strong chance that real money will have to be sent.

Now an increase of bank currency in any region causes an increased demand for goods. More things than usual are brought in from other places, and money has to be sent out to pay for them. The banks are called on for coin, in such a case, by those holders of bank currency who have the outside payments to make. For this reason the banks at the great centres of foreign trade in each country need to carry a strong cash reserve.

5. Bank Currency of the United States. — We have now four kinds of circulating notes in use: 1. United States Notes or Greenbacks (known also as legal-tender notes, from the fact that they are "lawful money and a legal tender;" the other notes have not this quality). 2. Gold Certificates. 3. Silver Certificates. 4. National Bank Notes.

The first three of these classes are issued by the Treasury. They differ in that the notes are simple promises made by the United States to pay to any person presenting them for redemption, the amount of money named in each; whereas the certificates certify that the amount of gold or silver named in each has been deposited in the Treasury, and will be paid to any person presenting the certificate and demanding delivery of the coin. The notes, as stated above, are supported by a reserve of one hundred millions in gold; the certificates, as their form implies, are covered, dollar for dollar, by gold and silver coin on deposit in the Treasury.

For the circulating notes issued by the national banks no specific reserve is required by law. They are amply secured by a pledge of United States bonds deposited in the Treasury by the banks, and each bank is required to keep the Treasury supplied with lawful money to the extent of five per cent. of its outstanding notes. Out of the fund thus provided, the Treasury pays lawful money (*i. e.*, gold, silver dollars, or greenbacks) for all national bank notes presented for redemption.

As to the deposit portion of our currency, the Acts of Congress draw a distinction between national banks in the leading cities and those in the rest of the country. City banks are required to limit their deposit liabilities to a hundred dollars for every twenty-five dollars of lawful money held as reserve; whereas the so-called "country-banks" are allowed to owe depositors a hundred dollars for every fifteen dollars they hold as reserve.[1]

Taking the bank currency of the United States as a

---

[1] It ought to be added that the country banks make little or no use of their special privilege. They keep, on the average, about as strong reserves as the city banks.

whole, but omitting private and state banks, we find that at the middle of the year 1879 (the first year in which our present system existed on a coin basis) the proportion of bank currency to coin was a little less than eight dollars for one. In 1887 the ratio had fallen, by reason of the increase of coin in the Treasury and the national banks, to about six dollars for one. But the aggregate bank currency of the country is rapidly increasing, and seems likely to reach, before many years, a proportion to the coin reserve not much below that of 1879.[1] The note circulation, it is true, is decreasing; by reason of the high price of United States bonds, which have to be placed in the Treasury as a security for notes issued, the banks find the issue of notes less profitable than the

[1] The figures for the years 1879 and 1887 were as follows, — not including notes in the Treasury and in the banks:

1879

Net Gold in the Treasury. $135,000,000	U. S. Notes in hands of public. $265,000,000
" " " Nat. Banks. 21,000,000	Nat. Bk. " " " " " 295,000,000
	Deposits of Nat. Banks . . 650,000,000
TOTAL $156,000,000	
	TOTAL $1,210,000,000

1887

Net Gold in the Treasury. $188,000,000	U. S. Notes $250,000,000
" " Nat. Banks . . 152,000,000	Silver Certificates 150,000,000
	Nat. Bank Notes 250,000,000
TOTAL $340,000,000	Deposits of Nat. Banks . . 1,350,000,000
	TOTAL $2,000,000,000

I include the silver certificates among the circulating notes, but do not include in the coin reserve the two hundred and twenty million of silver dollars ($220,000,000) in the Treasury. The reason is that thus far the silver dollars have strictly nothing to do with the value of the certificates. See Chapter XVI., § 9.

granting of the right to call on them for money by check. Accordingly, deposits increased from about six hundred million dollars ($600,000,000) at the beginning of 1879, to one thousand three hundred and fifty million dollars ($1,350,000,000) at the end of 1887. In the same period the note issues of the national banks decreased from about three hundred million dollars ($300,000,000) to about two hundred and fifty million dollars ($250,000,000).[1]

There are many banking institutions in the United States which have not come into the national system. The "Finance Report" for 1887 gives statistics for 2,472 private banks, loan and trust companies, and State banks other than savings' banks. These institutions are prevented from issuing notes by the heavy tax (ten per cent. a year) imposed on such notes by Act of Congress; but they can lend the right to demand money by check with entire freedom. Their deposits payable on demand are returned at seven hundred and eighty million dollars ($780,000,000). So far as regards the volume of our currency, this amount must be added to the one thousand three hundred and fifty million dollars ($1,350,000,000) similarly payable by the national banks, making the total deposit currency of the country for the year 1887, two thousand one hundred and thirty millions of dollars ($2,130,000,000).[2]

[1] It may be well to observe that the silver certificates issued by the Treasury have more than supplied the place, in the ordinary circulation, of the retired bank-notes.

[2] The returns from private banks are very incomplete. There are in fact about four thousand of them in the United States.

If we add to this sum the circulating notes of all kinds in the hands of the public, we find the total bank currency of the United States to be about two thousand seven hundred and fifty millions of dollars ($2,750,-000,000). This rests on a basis of gold in the Treasury and in the banks amounting to about four hundred millions of dollars ($400,000,000), or somewhat more than one dollar of gold for seven of bank currency.

In other words, if all persons having a right to demand true money of the banks and the Treasury should suddenly and simultaneously demand payment, not much more than one dollar in seven could be paid in gold; yet every dollar of the whole mass is doing the work of a gold dollar and (with the exception of the silver certificates) is convertible into gold at any time, at the option of the holder.

6. Effect of Bank Currency on Prices.—Though prices in the United States are obviously six or seven times higher than, without the aid of banking, our present stock of gold would make them, yet it would be a mistake to suppose that our prices are six or seven times higher than they would be if bank currency had never been invented. The stock of coin itself would have been greater than it is, if its value had not been kept down by the introduction of bank currency. How much greater we cannot tell, because we do not know how great the difficulty would have been of adding a given quantity to the annual product; nor do we know how much the higher value would have checked the consumption of the precious metals in the arts. But it is certain that much more would have been produced year by year, and that a smaller amount would have been used in making watches, jewelry, etc.

Of course, if the whole world had changed suddenly from the use of coin in all payments to a system of bank currency such as we now have in the United States, the immediate effect on prices would have been to multiply them by six or seven. But the introduction of banking has been gradual,—it is still but slightly developed in many parts of the world.[1] Moreover the period of its introduction has been one of enormous increase in the demand for money, owing to the great increase in the production and exchange of commodities.

Coming at such a time, and expanding gradually, bank currency has had for its chief effect the prevention of a great fall in prices. The world's stock of coin could not have been increased as rapidly as the goods to be exchanged have been increased in the past hundred years. Even with the great increase in the production of the precious metals since 1848, and the steady expansion of banking, the general level of prices is not much

---

[1] Deposit-banking can hardly be said to exist outside of the English-speaking countries. Circulating notes are used extensively in most countries; but where circulating notes are preferred to deposits, many are likely to prefer coin to the notes. In France, for example, the whole volume of bank currency is not supposed to be equal to the amount of coin in the country. Obviously, the chief effect of a disproportional expansion of bank currency in any one country must be to send a part of its coin away to countries where banking is less developed.

higher now than it was a hundred years ago. Had it not been for the growth of bank currency prices must have fallen very much.

The most important effect of bank currency in the long run is the saving of labor it makes in providing the medium for exchanging commodities. It is essentially a labor-saving contrivance. By means of it the labor of one man is made to yield as much circulating medium as the labor of six or eight men without it. Thousands of men are thus released from the work of producing mere counters for making exchanges, and are employed, instead, in adding to the general stock of enjoyable commodities.

The value of money, with as without banking, tends in the long run to conform to the cost of producing the money-metal. The difference is that, with banking, the real demand for the metal at its natural value, is made much less than it would be without banking, and thus the production of it is confined to the most fertile sources of supply. Its value, therefore, corresponds to the cost of producing it where production is comparatively easy. If the whole demand for money had to be met with actual coin, less productive sources of gold would have to be resorted to, and the value of it would be permanently higher than it is.

7. The Volume of Bank Currency Variable. — The use of bank currency introduces an element of unsteadiness into the circulating medium. The volume of it depends very much on the mere will of the bankers. There is a constant temptation to expand the issue of it, because every addition brings additional gain to the banks. A currency consisting wholly of coin could not be thus increased at will.

In times of business prosperity there is a strong demand for loans, and when business men are succeeding well, it seems safe to lend to them freely. The banks at such times expand greatly the deposit portion of the currency,—the loans being given in the form of credits on the bank books, just as if the borrowers had actually deposited the sums borrowed. These credits become at once part and parcel of the bank currency acting on prices.

As a result, we have periods of expanding bank currency and rising prices. Such periods are times of great activity and seeming prosperity in business. Not only is the volume of currency increased, but its rapidity of circulation is quickened. The result is a steady and often rapid rise of prices, *i. e.*, a fall in the value of money. Every rise of prices seems to bring gain to holders of commodities and to furnish a basis for new loans from banks, with consequent further increase of bank currency.

The movement goes on until the banks reach the utmost limit of their lending power. The arrest of the expansion is usually attended by business failures. Men who entered on speculative enterprises, counting on continued loans from the banks, are forced into bankruptcy when new loans can no longer be obtained. A panic begins a period of contraction in bank currency. The banks are always heavy losers by business failures: when these begin, they scrutinize sharply all applications for loans and reject those that are in the least doubtful. Further, the changed condition of affairs causes men of undoubted credit to have less desire for loans than they had while business was prosperous. The result is a general shrinkage of bank currency. There is at the same time a lessened rapidity of circulation. A gradual decline of prices is the necessary consequence.

These changes in the value of money would probably happen to some extent, even if bank currency did not exist. I think they are primarily due to the fact that savings intended for investment, whether directly or by loan, are always in the form of money. When savings are promptly and fully invested, the currency, whatever its character, is kept completely and actively in circulation. When savings accumulate, unemployed, in the hands of those who make them, the supply of currency offering for goods is necessarily diminished.

The circumstances that cause banks to enlarge or to curtail their loans in bank currency, would cause them to enlarge or to curtail their loans, if they had nothing but coin to lend. The use of bank currency simply intensifies the evil very much by giving a wider scope for enlargement and contraction of loans.

CHAPTER XVI.

QUESTIONS BETWEEN GOLD AND SILVER.

1. Contrast between Gold and Silver. — In the foregoing chapters silver and gold have been spoken of together, as if both could be used as money, side by side, on a footing of perfect equality. We must now consider some difficulties that are met in the attempt to use them in that manner.

First, however, we must note an important difference between the two metals. Weight for weight, gold is at present (1889) worth nearly twenty-two times as much as silver. If we compare them by bulk, the contrast is still greater, — a cubic inch of gold being worth nearly forty times as much as a cubic inch of silver.[1]

2. Superiority of Silver for Small Money. — This wide difference in value gives each metal an obvious advantage over the other for one of the uses of money. As material for coins of small value, silver is much more suitable than gold. Dimes made of gold would be almost invisible. Even the one-dollar gold piece, formerly coined at our mints, was found to be inconveniently small, and the coinage of it was given up. Coins so diminutive are

[1] The specific gravity of silver is 10.47 ; that of gold is 19.34.

difficult to handle and are constantly in danger of getting lost.

For small money, then, silver has everything to recommend it over gold. But at the other end of the scale, it must be admitted that silver is subject to a very serious drawback. Even so small a sum of it as ten dollars makes an awkward package for carrying in one's pocket. A million dollars' worth of silver, at its present value, weighs nearly forty tons.

3. Superiority of Gold for Large Transactions. — For large transactions, gold is vastly more convenient than silver. The labor of transporting a given sum in gold is less than one-twentieth part as great as in the case of silver. The space required for holding it is only one-fortieth part as great. Any one who has had experience in guarding valuable articles, knows how much the difficulty increases with increase of bulk. It is many times harder to make a large "strong box" than a small one.

Now the financial affairs of a great commercial nation require the constant care and handling of large sums in coin. In the movement of such amounts as are daily passing about in the settlement of accounts between banks, and in the operations of the national Treasury, the difference in favor of gold amounts in the course of a year to a very considerable sum.

Nor is this a matter affecting the bankers alone, or even chiefly. The saving by the use of gold rather than silver is a gain to the whole community. Like every other labor-saving contrivance, it lightens the work of production and exchange by supplying a more convenient, instead of a less convenient medium. It gives precisely the same advantage as the use of silver, rather than copper or tin, gives in the case of our smaller coinage. The benefit accrues to all who have occasion to use money, that is to the whole community. Whatever makes banking difficult and costly, is sure, in the long run, to increase the cost to the community of the services which the bankers render.

4. **The Double Standard.**—All men agree that both silver and gold are needed as money, since each serves a purpose for which the other is much less suitable. But when we come to the question of the best method of obtaining the use of the two metals in coinage, we find ourselves at once in a region of doubt and controversy.

It was once supposed that a nation wishing to have the use of the two metals as money, needed only to coin both of them freely. But experience has clearly proved this to be a mistake. Every country that has tried it has found that the result is to give the use of one metal only.

The reason is clear. The adoption of two sets of coins as full money, is in fact an attempt to have two standard units for measuring value. The two may indeed be accurately adjusted at the start, so that a dollar of the one sort shall have precisely the same value as a dollar of the other sort,—comparing them simply as (what they are in truth) pieces of metals produced by labor.

But the difficulty is that each is produced independently of the other, and the cost of production of the one may change without a corresponding change in the cost of the other. When this happens (and it is constantly happening in the case of gold and silver) the two sets of dollars become unequal in natural value; the country acquires in consequence two different standards or measures of value. Hence the name of Double Standard applied to this arrangement.

Now to set up two different measures of value would be as absurd and inconvenient as to adopt two yardsticks of unequal length, or two bushel measures of unequal capacity. The law, where the double standard prevails, attempts to keep the two kinds of money equal in value by providing that each kind shall be lawful money and a legal tender to any amount. This does indeed cause the two kinds to have equal value (*i. e.*, market value) so long as both continue to circulate: but the effect, in the end, is to drive one of them out of use as money. It is the fatal weakness of the double standard that, while in theory it is a plan for giving us the use of both gold and silver as money, it is in practice a plan that limits us to one of the two.

5. Double Standard in the United States. — The practical working of the double standard may be readily seen by studying the history of it in our own case. Our first national coinage was made under an Act of Congress passed in 1792. Under this act gold and silver were coined free of charge for all persons sending in the necessary bullion, — one pound of gold being made into as many dollars as fifteen pounds of silver. Coins of either were made a "lawful tender in all payments whatsoever."

The ratio of $1 = 15$ was approximately correct at the date of the Act. But silver was at that time slowly declining in value as compared with gold, owing to increased production of it in Mexico. By the year 1800 one ounce of gold was worth $15\frac{1}{2}$ ounces of silver.

In this state of things men ceased to carry gold to our mints to be coined. They even found a profit in sending out of the country the gold already coined. For fifteen thousand dollars in gold one could buy silver enough abroad to make fifteen thousand five hundred silver dollars, thus gaining five hundred dollars by the operation. As a result the gold coin of the United States disappeared from circulation, and the country was left with silver alone.

In 1834 an Act of Congress was passed to restore the use of gold. By this Act it was ordered that a less quantity of gold should be used in making the gold coins thereafter. In the new arrangement one ounce of gold was coined into as many dollars as sixteen ounces of silver.[1]

[1] The amount of pure gold in the eagle was cut down from $247\frac{1}{2}$ grains to 232 grains. The quantity of pure silver in the silver dollar was and is $371\frac{1}{4}$ grains. $23.2 : 371\frac{1}{4} = 1 : 16 -$. Our standard gold and silver contain one part alloy for nine of pure gold or silver; the weight of the silver dollar-piece is therefore $412\frac{1}{2}$ grains ($371\frac{1}{4}$ of silver and $41\frac{1}{4}$ of alloy).

Just before the passage of the Act silver had fallen to about 16 = 1, but it rose again and remained, in the markets of the world, above our coinage valuation. There was, therefore, in the new adjustment, the same reason for exporting our silver coins to pay for gold, as there had been in the previous adjustment for the reverse operation.

The consequence was that all full-weight silver coins presently disappeared from circulation, and their places were taken by the new gold coinage. Even the small change disappeared with the rest, excepting the pieces that were too much worn to be sold as silver. By 1850 we had a coinage consisting almost exclusively of gold, with worn Mexican silver for change. New silver pieces were coined from time to time by the Government, but they disappeared as speedily as they were issued.

6. Gold Standard with Subsidiary Silver. — In order to remedy this evil, an Act was passed in 1853 which provided that the smaller silver pieces to be coined thereafter should contain about seven per cent. less silver than the former issues.[1] This device was adopted in order that the new issues might be worth less as mere silver than as coins of the United States, and should therefore always stay in circulation. In other words, the amount of silver in the half dollar, the quarter, the dime, etc., was known and intended to be worth less than the sum the coin was to pass for.

[1] One dollar of the new silver change contains only 384 grains of standard silver, whereas the silver dollar-piece weighs 412½ grains.

The new coins were not made a legal tender for sums exceeding five dollars. The privilege of getting silver coined into these pieces was conferred on the Treasury alone, in order to guard against excessive production of them.

These light-weight silver coins, of limited legal-tender quality, are called a subsidiary coinage. The result of the Act of 1853 was to give us, in practice, the single gold standard with a limited supply of silver coins for small payments.[1] The arrangement worked well, and remained in operation until the over-issue of inconvertible currency during the Civil War drove all sorts of metallic money out of use. It is, so far as experience goes, the only plan that succeeds in giving a country the use of both metals.

Since the Resumption of Specie Payments at the beginning of 1879 we have again had in practice the single gold standard, with the subsidiary silver coins provided by the Act of 1853. Unfortunately, however, we have also some peculiar enactments regarding the silver dollar which are likely, unless repealed, to bring us again into the troubles of the Double Standard.

7. The Silver Act of 1878. — After the change of ratio in 1834, owners of silver ceased to get it coined into dollars. In the year 1873 the right of getting it so

---

[1] It was still the right of any person having silver bullion to get it coined into dollars of 412½ grains standard silver. But 412½ grains of standard silver could be *sold* for more than a dollar; so no man cared for the privilege of getting it coined into a dollar.

coined was abolished.[1] Shortly after this was done the value of silver began to decline. By the year 1876 it had fallen so much that 412½ grains of silver could be bought for ninety cents in gold.

The primary cause of the decline was the discovery of new and very productive mines in Colorado and Nevada. The effect of the great increase of production that followed was intensified by the cessation of silver coining by Germany, France, and Italy. The mints of those countries had previously absorbed a considerable part of the current product. By the stoppage of most of the coinage demand for new silver, the metal in the uncoined state ceased to have its value steadied as the value of money is steadied. It became possible for the value of silver bullion to fall indefinitely below the value of the same quantity of silver in the form of coin. In a word, silver bullion could fall, and did fall, in value, just as copper or iron fall when the production is increased.

The producers of silver in this country were naturally clamorous to regain the right of converting their product into money. They were joined in this demand by many unthinking persons who imagined the increase of silver

[1] The Act of Congress authorizing the coinage of the trade dollar contained the clause, "The silver coins of the United States shall be a trade dollar, a half dollar or fifty cent piece, a quarter dollar, etc." The old silver dollar (412½ grains) was omitted from the list. The trade dollar was intended for use in the Oriental trade; its weight was made 420 grains, in order to match the currency already in use in that trade.

money would be a good thing for the whole community. The agitation led to the passage, in 1878, of an Act of Congress providing for a renewal of the coining of silver dollars.

The Act requires the Secretary of the Treasury to buy silver at the market price, and coin not less than two millions, nor more than four millions, of silver dollars each month. Private owners of bullion are not entitled to have it coined at their pleasure, as they were previous to 1873.

Upwards of three hundred millions of silver dollars have already been coined under this Act (close of 1888). For the most part these coins remain on the hands of the Government; they are stored in the Treasury and Sub-Treasuries. Yet we go on coining them. In the whole history of the United States, from the opening of our mint down to the year 1878, the total number of silver dollars coined was only eight millions. Now we coin that number every four months.

This is a foolish waste of the public revenue. It benefits nobody except the proprietors of silver mines; these are no doubt glad to have so good a market for two millions of their product every month. But there is no reason why the nation should single out the producers of silver for this benefaction, rather than the producers of tin or copper. The only interest of the nation in the matter is to keep its currency on a sound basis: and this is not accomplished by the compulsory purchase and coinage of two millions of silver dollars each month, to be stored away in the vaults of our national Treasury.

8. Our Currency Tending Towards the Silver Standard. — Thus far our national money has suffered no serious harm from the Act of 1878. The restriction on the coinage of silver has saved us from descending to the silver standard. But if the Act remains unrepealed, it must end in causing our stock of gold to leave us and in bringing down the standard of our dollar to the market value of $412\frac{1}{2}$ grains of silver.

The process will be comparatively slow. The issue of additional silver certificates, month by month, goes to swell our currency and tends to lower the value of money, *i. e.*, to raise prices. This will attract increased importation of goods from other countries, and will at the same time check the exportation of our products. The balance which we shall owe to other nations in consequence will have to be paid in money, and gold will be the money sent to pay it.

So long as any considerable quantity of gold remains in the country, the currency will keep on the gold basis. But when the gold has been drained off, the further increase of silver certificates will not be offset by a decrease of any other sort of currency. The result will be that it will gradually sink in value until a dollar of it will just buy $412\frac{1}{2}$ grains of standard silver. Supposing no further decline in the value of silver to occur in the meantime, this would give us a currency in which each dollar would be worth, at most, seventy-five cents of our present money.[1]

In order to restore the circulation of gold we should then have to coin a new supply of gold pieces, lighter than the present ones, — just as the present ones are lighter than those coined before 1834. The change, however, the debasement, would have to be much greater in the new case than it was under the Act of 1834. Every successive stage in the vain struggle to keep two money-standards in use side by side, involves a recoining of one metal or the other, and a continuous debasing of both standards.

The present law is drawing us slowly but surely towards a currency based on silver alone. If the nation desires such a currency, it is clearly entitled to have it. But the present law is a most wasteful and extravagant mode of accomplishing the object. We have already coined and stored in the Treasury enough silver dollars to answer as a reserve for a thousand millions in circulating notes, — that is, for some hundreds of millions more paper money than we have ever used in the past. And yet the Act of 1878 requires the Secretary of the Treasury to add two millions of new silver dollars to

[1] The London price of silver has fluctuated of late between 42d. and 44d. the ounce. This is for English standard silver, 37-40ths fine (*i. e.*, thirty-seven parts silver to three parts alloy). The ounce therefore contains 444 grains of pure silver. Our dollar piece of 412½ grains contains 371¼ grains of pure silver, the American standard being 9-10ths fine. At 44d. for the English ounce, our silver dollar is worth 74¼ cents in American gold.

the stock every month. This is simply a waste of the public revenues. If the object be to bring our currency upon a silver basis, it ought at least to be done on an economical plan.[1]

Some persons seem to assume that the country is under a moral obligation to coin all the silver that may be produced. Our only obligation in the case is to keep the currency of the country on a sound basis; especially to avoid, as far as we can, every act that tends to cause needless fluctuations in the value of our money.

9. The Silver in the Treasury not a Strict Reserve.— It has been stated (Chap. XV., § 5, note) that the silver dollars in the Treasury have strictly no part in maintaining the value of the certificates issued in respect of them. The grounds of this statement are now obvious. There is not the least likelihood of a call for silver dollars. Whenever a demand for specie arises, whether for exportation or any other purpose, it is certain to be a demand for gold. The issue of the silver certificates,

---

[1] The chief use made of the silver dollars hitherto has been to issue upon them an equal amount of silver certificates. But coin certificates are a very costly form of circulating notes. They were originally intended, not for general circulation, but for use in payments between banks and other moneyed institutions, — as the gold certificates are for the most part still used. Three quarters of the coin held against the present issue of silver certificates might be spared, even if it were a true reserve, without in the least endangering the convertibility of the certificates. The number of silver dollars in the Treasury at this date (close of 1888) is roughly two hundred and sixty million ($260,000,000); the amount of silver certificates outstanding is about two hundred and forty million dollars ($240,000,000).

by swelling the currency, tends to create such a demand. The situation would not be essentially different, in this respect, if we had an addition to the United States notes equal in amount to the silver certificates issued, and the silver in the Treasury were still in the bowels of the earth.

If ever our currency is allowed to depreciate to the silver standard, the case will be different. The silver dollars will then become a true reserve. As a somewhat early preparation against that time, the store of silver in the Treasury may have some importance. But, for any present relation to our currency, it might as well be a store of bits of iron or leather bearing the mint-marks of the United States, and declared by law to be legal tender. The immediate danger of any general presentation of the certificates for redemption would be precisely as great in the one case as in the other.

The whole stress of our currency, as regards its true reserve, falls on the gold. Even if the Treasury and the banks should cease to pay gold on demand, there would be no call for silver dollars, so long as the volume of the currency is kept within its present limits. Nothing but inflation and consequent fall of value will cause the stored silver of the Treasury to fill the place of a coin reserve for any part of the note circulation.

10. International Bimetallism. — A movement has recently been set on foot aiming to bring the chief commercial countries into a general agreement regarding the use of gold and silver as money. The advocates of this plan contend that, if the chief nations should agree to coin both metals freely, all using the same mint ratio of values, both metals would remain permanently in circulation in each country.

They argue that the failure of the Double Standard hitherto has been due to the want of uniformity in the treatment of the two metals in different countries. They point, for example, to the fact that when the United States, under the Act of 1792, found it impossible to keep gold in use as money, our coinage laws placed the ratio at 1:15, whereas France used the ratio 1:15½. In that situation the gold, they say, went to France simply because that country set its coinage value higher in terms of silver than the United States did.

The bimetallist theory, briefly stated, is that if the great commercial nations should agree on a common ratio for gold and silver, and should all adopt the double standard on that basis, the two metals would remain permanently in circulation everywhere, with the relative value agreed upon. There can be no doubt that such an arrangement would prevent wholesale interchanges of gold and silver between countries. But it does not follow that it is the only, or even the best, solution of the coinage question.

The general adoption of the single gold standard, with subsidiary silver coins, would equally cut off the motive for mere interchange of coins between countries.

11. Weakness of the Bimetallic Theory.—The bimetallist contention that two metals with full legal tender quality are better than one, or are in the least necessary, has not been successfully maintained. Two variable standards expose us to two sets of variations in the value of money, instead of one. The argument that there is not enough gold to suffice for all countries, ignores the fact that the modern way of using metallic money, makes a dollar go as far as seven or eight dollars went two hundred years ago. The age in which metallic money is passing out of use as active currency, and into use as a mere reserve for the active currency, is a time when gold may safely be adopted as the single standard for large payments. Bank currency based on gold may far exceed the total supply of both gold and silver.

The proposition that the comparative value of gold and silver may be permanently controlled by international agreement, is one that can hardly be admitted without better evidence of its soundness than has yet been supplied. No man would maintain the same doctrine with reference to any other two products of labor, even in cases where the one is largely a substitute for the other: *e. g.*, beef and mutton, corn meal and rye meal, tin and zinc. It is the common mark of all foolish schemes for "improving" the world's currency, that they set out by falsely assuming a fundamental difference between money and all other products of human labor. Any scheme is sure to fail in the long run, if it undertakes to put the material of our money under other control than that to which the value of all other products of labor are subject, namely, the cost of its production.

The bimetallic theory holds that the value of gold may be made to follow the cost of silver, and the value of silver the cost of gold, simply by the force of laws and treaties.[1]

If the governments of the leading countries should attempt to fix the comparative value of tin and zinc by international agreement and force of law, we readily see that this would not be enough to ensure success. The agreeing governments would have to undertake the duty of keeping the market supplied with each metal at that value, or run the risk of having the supply of one or the other fall short of the demand, or even fail entirely.

It has not been shown that international bimetallism could be counted on to give us a desirable proportion of each metal, or indeed both metals in any proportion. The

[1] The advocates of the theory lay much stress on what they assume to be a powerful check against the withdrawal of either metal from use as money, owing to a fall in the value of the other. The withdrawal of gold from use as money would cause an increased supply and a decline of its value, as a material for use in the arts: on the other hand, the increased demand for silver as money to take the place of the gold withdrawn, would cause a rise of its value. Thus, they hold, the two metals would tend to keep the relative values imposed on them by the international league. All this may be admitted so far as temporary changes are concerned; but it does not touch the fundamental question of the permanent supply of both metals, especially that proportional supply of each which may best serve the public convenience.

If, for example, international bimetallism had been adopted when the ratio was 1 = 10, does any person suppose that gold would now be in use as money at that ratio unless the governments of the various countries should have kept up the supply of it at a loss to themselves?

agreeing countries might, in the long run, find themselves limited to the use of one metal, unless their governments should assume the burden of keeping up the coinage supply of both at the agreed ratio, in case private producers of either metal should cease to offer it for coining.

12. The Nations not likely to Agree in restoring Silver.— Finally, there is little prospect of any international compact on the subject of bimetallism. There have been several conferences of delegates from the chief commercial countries, but no progress has been made towards a general agreement. Great Britain and Germany are unwilling to abandon the gold standard, and without their co-operation, a bimetallic league would have poor chances of even temporary success.[1]

Meantime all countries (except the United States) that desire to have the use of any gold as money, have closed their mints to the further coinage of silver. The value of silver has now fallen so far, and its production has increased so much in spite of the fall in value, that it would be an act of daring rather than of statesmanship to propose, whether with or without an international agreement, a restoration of unrestricted coinage at the old European ratio of $1 = 15\frac{1}{2}$.

[1] If the nations ever make general agreements on the subject of money, it is to be hoped that they may adopt a common unit of coinage as well as a common treatment of gold and silver. What could be more inconvenient or absurd than the present confusion of monetary units? One dollar of United States money = 4s. 1¼d. English money = 5.18 francs of French money = 4.2 marks of German money = 2.6 florins of Dutch money, etc.

CHAPTER XVII.

INCONVERTIBLE LEGAL-TENDER NOTES.

1. Character of Inconvertible Notes.—There is a squalid imitation of bank currency known as "inconvertible" or "irredeemable" notes. These differ from true bank-notes in the one point that makes the latter acceptable: they give the holder no title to coin. No provision is made for paying coin to such as may desire it: hence the name of this species of currency.

Inconvertible notes are usually issued by needy governments as a way out of financial embarrassment. They are declared by law to be "lawful money and a legal tender;" that is to say, the offer of them in payment of a debt is to be regarded by the courts as if it were an offer of real money. This provision gives them a forced circulation. Though everybody knows that they give the holder no real title to coin or to anything else of value, yet the fact that they can be used in paying debts makes everybody willing to receive them.

If the issue of such notes were kept somewhat within the amount the community would naturally use of redeemable notes, no great harm would be done. The trouble is that no government has ever resorted to the issue of inconvertible currency without carrying it far beyond this limit. Our own country suffered much from the evil before and during the Revolution, and again during the Civil War.

2. Effects of Inconvertible Currency on Prices. — In considering the effects of inconvertible currency, it is necessary to distinguish two cases, or stages. When the issue of inconvertible notes is begun in a country, the first effect is simply to increase the general currency, and raise all prices. The rise of prices causes a change in the external trade of the country; fewer goods are sent abroad and more goods are brought in. To pay the balance thus accruing, the coin and notes convertible into coin are drawn on, — the inconvertible notes being of no use for that purpose.

Every addition made to the inconvertible paper is followed by the gradual disappearance of an equal quantity of the sound currency. While any of the latter remains in circulation, the value of the new notes is not affected by their inconvertible character. The new issue simply has the effect of raising all prices and thus lowering the value of all money. The fall is checked by the continual lessening of the good money.

But when the issue has been so increased that all the sound currency has been displaced from the circulation, a new stage is entered upon. Every addition of irredeemable notes after that point is reached, is followed by a corresponding depreciation of the whole mass. If the quantity be doubled, prices will be doubled also, — each dollar becoming worth only half of a real dollar.

In a country that has a depreciated currency of legal-tender paper, the prices of commodities are fictitious rather than real prices. Though the terms of true money continue to be used, they have no reference any more to true money, but to the pieces of stamped paper arbitrarily substituted for money by force of law. In order to discover the real price of any article one must ascertain the price of the currency itself.

For example, in July, 1864, two dollars and a half of United States notes (legal tender) could be bought for one dollar in gold. In that condition of things, the real price of an article selling for twenty dollars in paper was only eight dollars.

3. Injustice Caused by Excessive Issues.—Inconvertible currency, when issued in excess, becomes the instrument of great injustice. For instance, a man who borrowed $1,000 in this country in 1861, when dollars were real dollars, to be paid back in three years, was enabled by an unjust law to discharge the debt in 1864 by paying $400. The overissue of legal-tender notes has the effect of confiscating a part of every outstanding claim. A law authorizing one citizen to defraud another would not be more unjust.

A similar injustice is inflicted on debtors when a depreciated legal-tender currency is restored to the specie standard. Debts which were incurred in the time of depreciation have to be paid off in dollars of higher value than those in which they were incurred. A larger quantity of wealth has to be paid than the agreement really stipulated.

This latter hardship is usually suffered on a great scale by the offending government itself, when it sets about retrieving its affairs in honorable ways. In the first place, it must redeem the depreciated notes themselves in real money, although for all of them issued after depreciation began, it received less than the value of real money. Secondly, a time of overissue of notes is nearly always a time of copious borrowing on the part of the government. The greater the depreciation of the currency, the greater the borrowing has to be; for the price of everything the government has to buy, as well as the wages it has to pay to its soldiers and workmen, are raised by every depreciation of the currency.

In other words, the dollars it borrows and spends are no real dollars, though it is in honor bound to treat them as if they were. The currency which it has itself created, and which it compels private citizens to accept as money, it cannot well decline to receive from those who subscribe to its loans. Its debt becomes swollen in consequence of the depreciation of the currency, far beyond the figures it would have reached if its affairs were conducted on the basis of coin. Each dollar of this inflated indebtedness has later to be paid in real money, when the time for payment arrives. It has been estimated that the National Debt incurred by the United States during the Civil War was greater by eight hundred and sixty million dollars ($860,000,000), than it would have been if the overissue of greenbacks had been avoided.[1]

[1] Bowen, *American Political Economy*, p. 408.

4. No Justification for making Notes Inconvertible. — The evils attending the overissue of inconvertible currency being so great, no wise statesman could advocate the use of so perilous a substitute for money. If a government wishes to issue circulating notes, there is no sound reason why it should seek to escape the obligation of redeeming in coin such of them as may be presented for redemption.

The whole saving effected by making the notes inconvertible is measured by the amount of reserve that would have to be kept for redeeming them. A government, at least one that always makes good its promises, enjoys higher credit than the banks. Banks find a twenty-five per cent. reserve against circulation sufficient to maintain the convertibility of their notes. It is probable that a government which kept its issue within wise limits, would not need more than a twenty per cent., or even a fifteen per cent. reserve in specie. That for the sake of avoiding this slight burden, any government should subject its citizens to the possible wrongs and injuries of a depreciated currency, is a circumstance not easily explained. The justification alleged is usually a supposed necessity. But whatever momentary advantage a government gains by resorting to inconvertible notes, it gains at the expense of its own citizens. No other form of tax could be more burdensome or unjust.

5. Except in Special Cases, the Value of these Notes depends on the Quantity Issued. — It might be supposed that the value of inconvertible notes would depend on the prospect of their ultimate redemption. This, however, is not the case. Their value would be the same even if it should be expressly enacted that they are never to be redeemed. So long as they constitute the working currency of the country, prices of commodities expressed in that currency are governed by the quantity circulating and the rapidity of circulation, just as in the case of true money.

The prospect of speedy redemption may indeed limit the depth of depreciation. Notes that are certain to be redeemed a year hence cannot fall below the specie standard by more than the current rate of interest. If they did, a part of them would be quickly taken up and held as an investment. The promise of early redemption may thus raise the value of inconvertible notes; but it does so by lessening the quantity of them in actual circulation.

Again, if a doubt should spring up as to the ability and intention of the issuing government to maintain the legal-tender character of its notes; or if, as was the case in the last stages of the Southern Confederacy, the continued existence of the government itself should become doubtful, the notes in circulation may suffer a great depreciation, or even lose all exchange value. The explanation is that merchants and others decline to receive them any more for goods. They prefer to keep their stocks unsold rather than to sell them for notes which may become valueless on their hands.

A somewhat similar case occurs when a serious increase of these notes is in prospect, even where no doubt exists as to the ability and intention of the government to maintain their legal-tender quality. The notes already in circulation may suffer serious depreciation, even before any of the new issue appear. Holders of goods usually raise their prices at once. This rise makes it impossible to sell at once all they ought ordinarily to be selling: the supply of currency is not, at the moment, sufficient to maintain prices at this higher level. But the impending increase of currency will make it possible presently to sell the whole product at the advance; meanwhile it is more profitable to raise prices at once, even at the cost of diminished sales, than to sell the whole stock at the former prices.

These are not exceptions to the general principle of prices. They are rather illustrations of its working under exceptional conditions. Whatever the currency of a country, its prices must, in the long run, conform to the demand and supply of that currency.

6. An Inflated Currency does not promote Industry.— Many persons are led to favor the use of inconvertible notes by a mistaken view as to their effects on trade. These persons start out with the assumption that plenty of money is essential to prosperity. As inconvertible notes can easily be issued in any desired quantity, they hold that this form of currency is superior to every other, and ought to be freely used.

Their argument rests on a very obvious fallacy. "Abundance of money" is a phrase that has two very different meanings. It may mean a large quantity of money in the sense of a great many dollars; or it may mean a large supply of money in comparison with the demand for it, — in comparison, that is, with prices.

Money may be abundant in the first sense without being so in the second. Obviously it is only abundance in relation to prices that can have any stimulating effect on trade. Increase of the currency has, for a little while, the effect of making things sell more rapidly. It creates the situation spoken of in Chapter XIII., § 10. But as soon as prices are raised to correspond with the increase of money, trade becomes as difficult, and money, relatively to the demand for it, as scarce as it was before.

The more dollars we have in circulation the less each dollar is worth. With a currency of ten thousand millions it would be as easy to get ten dollars as, with one of a thousand millions, it would be to get one dollar. But ten dollars in the one case would be no better for a man, would buy no more things, than one dollar in the other case. This is the inevitable result of increasing the currency; it raises all prices.

While the increase is going on, it tends, no doubt, to quicken the sales of goods. But in order to keep up the effect, we should have to be always adding to the issue.[1] This was amply shown in the inflation period of our

[1] It is probable that even this would lose its quickening effect before long. People would soon perceive that the currency was gradually depreciating, and would learn to allow for it in advance.

own greenbacks. Once the prices of things had time to get adjusted to the increased volume of currency, the seeming plentifulness of money ceased. Trade was never duller, money never seemed scarcer than during parts of the period when, measured by the number of dollars, we had a great abundance of currency. Inflation of the currency in the end defeats itself. Besides the ruinous injustice it works, it ends by making all trade more uncertain and difficult than it is on the more solid basis of hard money.

The permanent difficulties of trade are not at all due to scarcity of money. The hard thing is not so much to sell, as to sell at a satisfactory profit. Now the question of profit, as a matter of selling, turns, not on the highness or lowness of prices, but on the relation between prices and money wages. The selling price of each commodity must be sufficiently above the amount paid out in wages in getting it produced, to give the employers and dealers a profit on their outlay. Increase of currency raises prices, but in the long run it raises money wages in the same proportion. It therefore leaves the essential difficulties of the case unchanged.

7. Notes Secured by Pledge of Property. — Another of the erroneous theories relating to inconvertible notes is that they cannot depreciate in value if they are secured by the pledge of property of some kind. It is a favorite notion with currency quacks that every man who owns land or other safe property, ought to be allowed to mortgage it to the government and obtain the issue of legal-tender notes "based" upon this security.

The fatal defect of such notes is that very few of the people who want money want land. Good and useful as land is, it cannot be moved from the place where it lies. Any man wishing to pay a debt in another country could not send land to pay it. If he took some of the land pledged for the notes, and sold it, he could get only notes based on other lands as payment,—which would not help him at all.

Again, notes secured in this way would be liable to indefinite overissue and depreciation. We need in currency notes but a small proportion of the value of our land and other durable property. As soon as the due limit of issue was passed, a general rise of prices would set in,—lands rising in price as well as other things. By the time the issue had reached in amount the original valuation of the lands, these might have risen to five or ten times their original valuation. At this raised valuation each piece of land would become a perfectly good security for a fresh batch of notes. So it would go, until by repeated inflations, the value of the notes became zero.

There is only one safe and useful form of circulating notes, namely those that are in the first place, readily convertible into coin from day to day at the option of each holder, and that are, in the second place, well secured against ultimate failure or neglect on the part of the issuer to keep faith with the public. Many other devices have been tried, but they have always resulted disastrously.

QUESTIONS AND EXERCISES.

1. How do changes in the value of money show themselves? Why are such changes important? How do changes of prices affect the production of gold?

2. How does the supply of money differ from the supply of other things? Wherein is the demand for money peculiar? Distinguish between the nominal and the real demand and supply.

3. When a sum of money has been used in paying for goods at retail, what determines how soon it may be similarly used again?

4. Show that the circulating period is not the same for all parts of the currency.

5. Show that money performs two distinct functions in its circuit.

6. Suppose two countries have the same quantity of currency, and the same amount of products to be exchanged, does it follow that their prices must be alike? Does it follow that they need the same quantity of coin? of notes?

7. What causes the appearance of general overproduction during periods of business depression?

8. What is meant by saying that excess of money looks like a deficiency of goods?

9. How far, or in what respects, is the value of gold an exception to the general laws of value?

10. How is it shown that changes in the current production of gold have little effect on its value?

11. What are the comparative advantages of the two forms of bank currency? Show that the proportion of each is largely a matter of convenience and business habits?

12. What is the source of banking profits?

13. What limits the amount of bank currency in each country? What, roughly, is the proportion of bank currency to coin in the United States? Show that if all notes were abolished, the present volume of deposits could not be maintained. [Consider the increased demand for coin as pocket money.]

14. What provisions are made for redeeming the notes of the National Banks? Is there any security for the payment of their depositors?

15. How does it happen that the silver dollars are equal, in exchange value, to gold dollars, although the silver they contain is worth only seventy and odd cents? Do you think of any other cases of the same kind in our present currency?

16. How is it shown that the silver in the Treasury is not filling the place of a true specie reserve for the silver certificates?

17. Why is the double standard impossible in practice? Illustrate by sketching the history of the double standard in the United States.

18. What are the advantages of using both gold and silver as money? How can both be kept permanently in use in any country?

19. What causes the market value of gold to be slow in conforming to its natural value?

20. Why is it that gold has strictly no price?

21. What is the weak point in the scheme known as International Bimetallism?

22. Explain the present provisions of our laws respecting the coinage of silver, including the silver change.

23. What are the characteristics of "Inconvertible Notes" as currency? How is the value of such notes fixed? What injustice arises from overissue of them?

24. Does the copious issue of inconvertible notes make money plentiful and trade brisk?

25. What is to be said regarding the use of inconvertible legal-tender notes secured by a pledge of property? Could such notes depreciate in value?

CHAPTER XVIII.

WAGES AND PROFITS CONSIDERED AS PORTIONS OF THE PRODUCT OF INDUSTRY.

1. Preliminary Explanations.—We now enter on a new branch of our study. We have seen that productive industry calls for two kinds of exertion or sacrifice, namely, labor and waiting. We have already noted some consequences of the fact that these two burdens are, in the main, borne by two distinct sets of men, known as laborers and employers. We must now inquire how, under this separation of burdens, the industrial rewards of the two sets are respectively determined.

The pay of hired laborers we call wages. The term includes all payments for services of any kind; but, for the sake of simplicity, we shall at first consider only the wages of productive laborers.

Further, the term "wages" is to be understood in the strict sense. We have to do here with hired laborers only. The earnings of those productive laborers who work on their own account (*e. g.* small farmers) are not strictly wages. Such producers have their product, or the things received in exchange for it, as the reward of their labor and waiting. If all producers worked on this basis, we should have no need of a theory of wages.

The term "product of industry" is to be understood as referring only to the final product,—the finished or enjoyable commodities that are desired for their own sake. It does not include machinery, materials, or other things that are useful only as means towards producing enjoyable commodities. In other words, we are to regard industry from the standpoint of its ultimate aim. The labor spent in producing capital is to be regarded as labor spent in obtaining the enjoyable things that the capital helps to produce. Those things, not the capital itself, constitute the natural reward of such labor. (Chap. XI. § 3.)

In our first study of wages and profits we shall consider wages in the mass,—the aggregate wages of the whole body of hired laborers. In the case of profits, also, we consider first the total gains of the whole body of employers. Individual wages and profits we shall discuss later.

The whole product of industry completed from day to day belongs to the employers. Much the larger part of it simply replaces to them the wages paid out in getting it produced. The rest is their profit.

Profits are not, like wages, the reward of a single kind of exertion or sacrifice. Employers could not be employers without a large fund of savings wherewith to pay wages. The whole capital of the country, so far as it has been produced by hired labor, represents savings invested by the employers. Profits are, in part, a reward for the self-denial involved in all this saving. But, secondly, employers are themselves productive laborers of a high order. Industry could not prosper without their services in planning and directing the work. Their profits reward also these personal labors on their part.

How much of the whole mass of profits comes as a reward for the saving, and how much for the personal labors of the employers, cannot be discovered with precision, because there is nothing in the result itself to show this. It is common, however, to give the name of Interest to the portion that rewards the saving, and to assume that the amount of it is shown by the current rate of interest on loans. The portion that rewards their personal labor may be called earnings of management, or personal earnings of employers.[1]

We make no account, for the present, of the fact that the natural advantages for carrying on each industry are rarely quite alike for all engaged in it. Inequalities of opportunity give rise to economic rent, which will form the subject of a later chapter.

2. Wages as a Part of the Current Product of Industry.— Wages, as we all know, are customarily paid in money.

[1] The whole effort to draw an exact line between the two portions of profit is, in my opinion, entirely futile. If employers borrowed their whole investment from another set of men, there would be a basis for exact reckoning in the case. Since no man can be a true employer without some savings of his own, and since employers as a body borrow but a small part of the whole amount they invest, it would seem impossible to make a nice distinction between the two portions of their profit. It is like the attempt, sometimes made, to distinguish, in the products of industry, the portion due to capital from the portion due to labor. Production itself knows nothing of either distinction.

The Source of Wages. 197

But money is no good in itself. The real wages of labor consists of the enjoyable commodities that are bought with the money. Changes of money wages are of no consequence except so far as they imply changes of real wages. The question of wages, then, is what determines the quantity of enjoyable commodities the laborers are able to obtain, week by week, in return for their labor?

Our starting point, in seeking the answer to this question, must be the fact already noticed, that the hired laborers own no part of the enjoyable products of labor awaiting purchasers As a rule, also, they have but little to offer for goods but their own labor. Only the more thrifty among them have saved anything. Some small amounts are ordinarily owing to them as wages; but if against the wages due we set off what they owe merchants and owners of houses, it is probable that the balance in their favor would be but small.

This means that, for their services in producing the good things now awaiting purchasers, they have, as a class, been paid already. If, then, they are to receive any considerable part of these things, it must be for producing, or helping to produce, future commodities. Secondly, it must be by the voluntary action of those who own the existing supply of money and goods. Whatever these choose to consume of the good things already on hand, they have full power and legal right to consume. Only whatever they choose to spare from their own consumption, can be counted on for the laborers. If they consume freely and save little, wages will be low; if they consume little and save much, wages will be high.

3. Wages and the Circulation of Money. — Wages being paid in money, the question how great a part of the current product of industry is to go to the laborers, is decided in practice by the use made of the money employers receive for the things they sell. When a person sells anything, he may use the money received for it in buying commodities for his own consumption, or he may save it for use in business with a view to profit. If he use it in the first of these ways, clearly the commodities he buys are lost to wages: the laborers cannot also have them.

If all who get any part of the money received for goods should suddenly abandon the habit of saving, and should use to the full extent their right of buying things for their own use, there would be nobody to hire laborers any more. Wages would disappear. The whole product of industry would be consumed by the capitalist class.

If, on the other hand, it were possible that all the money received for goods should be devoted to hiring laborers, the whole product of industry would in that case go as wages.

Between these two extremes, whatever proportion of the money received for goods at retail, is saved and applied to hiring laborers, that proportion of the total product of industry is thereby designated as wages of labor. So that the whole matter turns on the question of saving.

Money Wages and Real Wages. 199

The student will find it helpful, at this point, to recur to the diagram on page 134. The money returning to the point 1 through the bulbs, b, e, h, l, o, is the portion of the whole money-supply used in hiring laborers. Whatever proportion this bears to the whole stream of money passing the point 1, that proportion of the total product of industry goes to the laborers as wages. Not, however, it must be remembered, for producing these same commodities, but for helping to produce other commodities that are yet in the future.

The secondary bulbs, b', e', etc., remind us that money received as wages may be saved and become wages over again. The savings thus made from wages by skilled artisans, members of the learned professions, etc., constitute an important fraction of the whole mass saved year by year. Their primary effect on wages is to alter, not the total mass, but the apportionment of the total mass. The wages of the other laborers are greater by the amount that these laborers save. Of course, those who save have their income increased later by the amount their savings bring them.

It is evident from these considerations that the sum of wages, in any community, must depend on two things: first the productiveness of the community's industry; and secondly, the strength of the saving spirit among those members of it who have savable income.

If the productiveness of industry be given and constant, the real wages of the laborers will depend on the second of the two factors; that is to say, on the proportion the total spendings of the capitalist classes bear to their total savings, week by week. Or, stating the same principle in terms of our diagram, the quantity of commodities going to the laborers will depend on the ratio the money passing through the wage-bulbs bears to the whole stream of money offering for goods at 1. For example, in the illustrative case given on page 136, if forty of the fifty millions constituting the weekly supply of money, pass through b, e, h, l, and o, then the laborers receive as wages four-fifths of the weekly product of industry.

4. Savings not Governed by any Strict Rule.—Since wages depend thus directly on savings, the study of wages becomes primarily an inquiry into the practice of saving. If we could discover why just so much is saved, we should have solved the problem of wages. But here the real difficulties of the case begin. The question how the flow of savings has its limits fixed, from week to week, is far from simple.

Many thousands of persons, in every civilized country, save more or less of their income. But the cases are probably rare in which two persons having the same income, save the same precise part of it. Even one and the same person saves a larger proportion of his income at one time than at another. Some save with a definite object in view, such as to provide for their children or for their own old age, or to carry out a specific object in business. Others save with only a general desire to grow richer, and still others because they have a greater income than they care to spend at the moment. It is very clear then that, as saving depends on the free choice of each individual who has income beyond his actual wants, there can be no formula or uniform rule as to savings. We cannot say, for example, that if the product of industry be increased by a given percentage, savings will be increased by the same percentage. Still less can it be assumed that, when the product is increased, the whole increase will be saved. We can only be sure that increase of product causes increase of savings. As to the precise amount of increase, no two persons and no two communities would be likely to behave quite alike in a given case.

5. General Truths Regarding Savings — Yet some general principles may be laid down in regard to the total savings of each community, and the fluctuations to which the total is liable. Some persons save, no doubt, merely in order to postpone the enjoyment of their income. They would save more or less even if thereby they could add to their wealth nothing beyond the amount actually saved. But the amount likely to be saved in that way would fall far short of meeting the needs of the laborers. Their readiness to work for less then their labor eventually produces, gives a chance to make savings a source of income. Most of the savings made in a civilized country are made with a view to taking advantage of this opportunity. Even those who would save something without this inducement, save more because of it.

This being so, we can safely assume that the amount

of savings likely to be made in any given community will depend largely on the rate of profit to be gained by the use of savings. An increase of profits would stimulate those who save, to save more strenuously. A fall of profits, on the other hand, would tend to check their energy in saving.

Again, it is evident that much depends on the character and temperament of those in each community who have savable income. If these be careless about the future, fond of lavish and costly enjoyments, their savings are likely to be meagre. Profits must be high in order to induce such men to save at all. On the other hand, where the richest members of the community are men of energetic spirit and simple tastes, little inclined to luxurious living and costly indulgences, a large proportion of their income is sure to be saved and applied to industrial enterprises. In such a community the rate of profits may be comparatively low without checking the flow of savings. Wages, therefore, may be steadily high in comparison with the productiveness of industry.

6. Bearing of these Truths on Wages.—These general truths form the basis of our reasonings on the subject of wages. It is by means of them that we are enabled to explain the fundamental relation between the wages of hired laborers and the product of their labor.

It follows from them that there is in every community, at any given time, a limit to the amount of savings that will be made for a given rate of profit. If, for any reason, profits should increase, savings may be expected to increase also; if profits decline, savings tend to fall off. Again, if the community should become more eager in the pursuit of riches, more ready to give up present enjoyment for the sake of future gain, savings may be expected to increase without the stimulus of higher profits. If the people should become less thrifty, less energetic in the struggle for wealth, savings would become less in amount even though profits should remain as high as before.

The effect on wages of a change in the volume of savings is too obvious to need remark, seeing that savings must become wages in order to gain a profit. But it is necessary to observe that changes of wages, the productiveness of industry remaining the same, are followed in turn by changes in the rate of profit. The profits of the employers in any given mass of product, consist of its excess over the wages paid out in getting it produced. The less the wages were the greater the profit is. If, therefore, wages should fall, the productiveness of industry being unchanged, profits must become greater than before. Unless those who have savable income have become less ready to save than formerly, this increase of profits must evoke increase of saving and restore wages to the former level. And similarly, if wages should rise without increase of product, the resulting decline of profits would check the flow of savings and thus cause wages to decline again.

7. Normal Wages and Profits.—It follows that we have, in the case of wages and profits, much the same kind of adjusting process as takes place in settling the general level of prices. When, at any given level of wages, the corresponding rate of profit causes men to save more of their income than is needed to pay these wages, the general level of wages will tend to rise, and the general rate of profits tend to decline. On the other hand, when the rate of profit resulting from any given level of wages does not induce men to save enough to pay these wages, the general rate of wages will tend to fall and the rate of profits to rise.

There is therefore for every community, at any given time, a normal level of wages and of profits, to which current (or market) wages and profits tend to conform. Wages are at their normal level when the corresponding rate of profit induces men to save enough, and only enough, to pay these wages. When wages are at the normal level, profits are at the normal rate. Normal wages and profits go together; it is simply a case of equilibrium.

The question whether normal wages shall be high or low in any community will depend, as already indicated, on two things: first, the productiveness of the community's industry; secondly, the strength of the saving spirit among those who own the products of its industry. Both of these factors are subject to change; a change of either would bring a change in the normal level of wages. If, for example, the existing capital of the country should be inherited by a class of men much less inclined to save than the present owners of it, the normal level of wages would inevitably decline. Again, if the laborers should become more diligent, more energetic, and more anxious to make the product of industry as great as possible, normal wages would rise; for increase of product is sure to evoke increased savings.

The normal level of profits depends primarily on the character of those who have savable income. But it also depends somewhat on the amount of income there is which may be easily spared. The larger the fixed capital of a country is in proportion to its population, the lower is its normal rate of profits likely to be. For the greater its fixed capital, the greater, at any given rate, will the total mass of profits be,—the greater, that is to say, will the total income of its capitalists be.

Now it is much easier to save out of a large income than out of a small one. A man who has a very large income can hardly spend more than a fraction of it on himself without a ridiculous and offensive display of his wealth. Great incomes are therefore distinctly favorable to great savings. Even though the rate of profits should be declining, the men whose profits are reckoned on millions of dollars' worth of capital, can easily save enough every year to add greatly to their wealth. Such men have no further need of saving; but they seem to save as eagerly for the mere delight of carrying out great industrial enterprises, as other men do under the spur of actual need. Some of them, we may hope, are also stimulated by the desire to benefit their fellow-men by the intelligent use of their wealth.

The normal rate of profits tends, therefore, to decline as a country grows in fixed capital, especially where this becomes concentrated in the hands of a few men of great industrial ambition. The benefit accrues to the laborers.

8. Wages Influenced by Past Savings. — While wages, at any given time, depend directly on contemporary savings, it is easy to see that they are also greatly influenced by past savings. We have just seen that a high proportion of fixed capital to population is favorable to high wages, by reason of its tendency to lower the normal or necessary rate of profits.

But there is a much more important sense in which such capital affects wages. It adds enormously to the productiveness of industry. It has therefore a double tendency to raise wages: first, by increasing the yield of labor, and secondly, by causing a higher proportion of the total yield to be used as wages.

Now the fixed capital of the present time is mainly a result of the savings of past years. The general body of laborers would probably never have been willing to work for a return so distant as such capital offers. Men who have always spent as rapidly as they have earned, would scarcely have faced the long waiting for reward that is necessary in opening mines, preparing land for tillage, constructing factories, warehouses, ships, railways, etc. Nothing but the offer of wages could have induced most of them to take part in such undertakings.

The great industrial improvements of past years were therefore made possible by the foresight and self-denial of those who supplied the savings necessary to pay the laborers for making them. The great addition these improvements have made to the product of present industry goes mainly to the laborers. Their first effect, no doubt, was to increase the gains of the employers; but the higher profit so gained led to a rapid increase of savings and consequent increase of the total volume of wages.

We see, then, that in any country where the spirit of saving is strong, and has been strong for several generations, two important consequences result from it for the present volume of wages. In the first place, the labor of the country is used in the ways that afford the largest returns; every known device for adding to its productiveness at the cost of longer waiting, is utilized to the fullest extent. In the second place, the stronger the spirit of saving at the present time, the greater is the proportion of this enlarged product going to form the wages of hired laborers.

The effect of sustained saving on the general wealth of a community is too obvious to need extended comment. Saving is, in more ways than one, the mother of riches. The countries that have been notable for the saving spirit of their people are now the wealthy countries of the world. Readiness to save usually goes, no doubt, with a readiness to exert one's self in other ways. The countries where savings are large are generally countries where the people are industrious as well as thrifty. But savings are necessary in order that labor may be used effectively,

Without both industry and thrift a community remains poor, even though surrounded by overflowing natural wealth. On the other hand, dilligence and economy create riches even in the face of great obstacles. New England has but few natural advantages for production. The materials for its industries, and the food for its inhabitants, have very largely to be brought in from other places. But, in spite of these disadvantages, the accumulated wealth of its people is greater than that of many highly-favored countries: and there are few places where the wages of labor are so high. It is a striking illustration of the power of sustained saving, coupled with the industrious spirit.

9. The Rate of Profits hard to Discover in Practice. — The relation of profits to wages is simple enough as a matter of theory. We say that the amount of profit contained in the product of industry completed each day or each week, is the excess of the product over the wages paid out in getting it made. The wages (*i. e.* the real wages) consisted of a certain mass of food, clothing, and other commodities.[1] The product consists of a certain greater mass of similar commodities produced in return for the wages. The difference between the two must therefore be profit for the employers.

This is quite true, and it is highly important to see quite clearly that this excess of product over the real wages paid in producing it is the only source of real

---

[1] These constitute the real cost to the employers of the things produced by hired labor.

profit in business. Yet a little reflection shows us that it would be very hard to discover with exactness how great a part of each week's product is profit, and how much is merely replacement of the savings expended in getting it produced.

The wages paid out by the employers, first and last, in the production of the commodities completed in any given week, were not paid out in any one previous week. The expenditure was, in fact, spread over months and even years. It was so intimately blended, at many points, with the cost of the products of other weeks that no exact separation is possible.

That large part of the employers' cost which consisted of wages paid for clearing land, opening mines, constructing and repairing buildings, machinery, railways, etc., — in a word, the whole industrial plant of the country, cannot be accurately apportioned to any given mass of finished products. Savings expended for the more durable forms of capital are replaced, not in a lump sum, but by a series or stream of small instalments running as long as the capital lasts.

Now the employers can seldom foretell with accuracy how long each part of their productive apparatus is going to last, or what repairs it will need. Any portion of it may wear out sooner, or may last longer, than they can now foresee. Every part of it is liable to be superseded and made valueless at any time, by the invention of better devices or methods. They cannot tell how much more their existing apparatus will eventually yield.

They therefore cannot tell with precision how much of the original labor of making it is chargeable to a given mass of product. It follows that they cannot say with accuracy how much of each week's product of industry is to be set down as replacement of the wages spent in obtaining it. And if they cannot tell exactly how much it has cost them, of course they cannot tell exactly how much their profit is.

The difficulty of ascertaining the exact proportion of profits, in any given mass of completed product, is no reason for doubting whether there be an exact relation between wages and profits. The trouble arises in dealing with limited portions of the product arising from each investment of savings. The account cannot be closed and the balance struck until the investment itself has yielded its whole return. Since, in the long run, nearly all forms of capital do yield their final return, the proportion of profit in each week's product does eventually disclose itself with almost scientific accuracy.

Of course every business man keeps accounts, which are supposed to show how much profit he is making. But the result is only approximate. The reckoning of his profits for any period is based, in large part, on the estimated value of his buildings, machinery, stock, etc., as they stand at the beginning and again at the end of the period. This may answer well enough for practical purposes; but it is only an estimate. It may later prove to have been based on much too high or too low an opinion of the productive power still left in the fixed capital.

10. Wages not Found by Deducting Profits.

— It is obvious, from the facts of the case, how great an error is made by those who assume that wages and profits, as parts of the product of industry, are exclusive of each other, and that if the profits be deducted, the residue will be the portion going to the laborers as wages.

Considered as contemporary portions of the product of industry, wages and profits are not at all complements of each other. They arise from radically different ways of dividing the product.

If from the whole product you take away the part that is profit, the remainder is not wages but replacement of the past savings expended in getting the product made. The complement of your profit is the outlay made in order to gain the profit.

On the other hand, if you take away the part that is to go as wages, the remainder is not profit, but that portion of the product which the capitalist class are to consume in their own enjoyment. The complement of what is saved is what is spent.

The portion wages may therefore overlap the portion profit to an indefinite extent. It does in fact overlap it, whenever a capitalist saves any part of his profit. The sum of wages and profits in any given product may therefore greatly exceed the product. It follows that wages cannot be discovered by deducting profits from the product.

CHAPTER XIX.

WAGES OF INDIVIDUAL LABORERS.

1. Factors on which Market Wages Depend. — Since the whole volume of savings is shared among the productive laborers who work for hire, it is clear that each man's share depends on two factors: first, the amount of savings to be invested, and secondly, the number of laborers to be hired. Any change in either of these factors, without a corresponding change in the other, must raise or lower the general level of individual wages. If the number of laborers be increased, or the flow of savings grow less, wages must tend to fall. If the number of laborers grow less, or the flow of savings increase, wages must tend to rise.

When the number of laborers in a country is increased, the new-comers begin at once to share in the savings offering for labor, but they do not at once add correspondingly to the means of saving. This lies in the nature of production, so long a time being necessary for producing most of the commodities of which real wages consist.

The case is obscured, in practice, by the mingling of the new laborers with the old. If the new laborers were set at work separately, without disturbing in any way the course of industry among the others, then it would be clear that the first use of their labor must be, not to add to the food, clothing, and other commodities available for paying their wages, but to provide the three forms of additional capital necessary for enabling them to produce such commodities.

The mixing up of the new laborers with the old cannot alter this essential feature of the case, though it greatly complicates the study of it. We may be sure that it is still true that the presence of the new laborers involves, as its first effect, the production of increased capital rather than the production of increased commodities. The product of industry cannot be increased in less time than commodities can be produced; the increase must be built up from the foundations. It is therefore a necessity of the case that a considerable period must elapse before the new laborers can add their full quota to the enjoyable products of industry.

In the meantime, whatever they receive as wages must be drawn from the products of other labor, and must be, at least in part, taken from savings that would otherwise have gone to the original laborers. I say "in part," because the general fall of wages resulting from the increase of laborers seeking employment, would open a prospect of higher profits from the investment of savings. This would probably give rise to more strenuous saving on the part of those having spare income, and would thus increase the volume of savings, even before the new laborers began to add appreciably to the stream of enjoyable commodities available for use in paying wages. The consequence would be that wages would not fall in as great a ratio as the number of laborers had been increased.

In the converse case of a sudden decrease of laborers, wages would rise, but not necessarily in the same ratio as the laborers are diminished. The flow of savings seeking investment may be checked because of the lessened chance for making profits. Again the temporary check of investment during periods of business depression, implies diminished earnings for the laborers as a body. On the other hand, when business revives again, wages may rise for a time above their ordinary level: the amounts held back from investment during the depression are then brought forward to be offered for labor, in addition to the current savings of the time itself. These are obviously not exceptions to the principle that wages depend on the ratio of savings to the number of laborers. They are rather illustrations of its working under changing conditions. No circumstance can affect the rate of wages in a community except by first altering this ratio.

2. Classes of Laborers. — The general rule of market wages just given for the general mass of laborers, holds true also for the members of each group or class into which the whole body is divided. The rate of pay for each kind of labor depends on the demand for it as compared with the supply. If the number offering any kind of labor increase, without increase in the amount of savings offered for that kind of labor, the rate of pay for it falls; and *vice versa*. This fall (or rise) in the wages of particular classes or groups of laborers may take place without disturbing the general level of wages.

Probably we should all agree that the fair rule of relative wages would be to make the wages of each occupation proportional to the quantity of labor and other sacrifice it involves.[1] There is, however, no standard for measuring the quantity of labor and other sacrifice involved in each occupation, except the one afforded by the conduct of the laborers themselves in choosing occupations. This brings us to the fundamental principle governing differences of wages in different occupations, namely, the greater or less activity of free competition.

If every laborer, in choosing his occupation, were able to choose it freely, with sole reference to his own interest and desire, differences of wages could not be permanent, except where they correspond to real differences in the character of occupations. For we may safely assume that laborers have at least the wish to do the best they can for themselves; that, therefore, if they had full freedom of choice, they would ordinarily choose the occupations that seemed to offer highest wages in comparison with the whole sacrifice demanded. This would be the state of things known as freedom of competition.

3. Erroneous View of Competition. — It is a common

---

[1] The student must bear in mind the meaning of "quantity of labor." See Chap. XI.

error to regard competition as a force which tends to depress all wages, profits, and prices, and in fact everything that comes under its influence.

If competition had the tendency this view attributes to it, then clearly wages, profits, and prices must long since have been reduced to zero, for competition has always been more or less active among men. This consideration alone ought to be enough to show how mistaken the view is.

The mistake arises from looking only at one side of the case. Competition has no power either to raise or to depress all wages, or all profits, or all prices. In the case of prices we have already seen that its sole tendency is to establish uniformity, to prevent one producer from getting a higher price, or from having to put up with a lower price, than other producers are getting for the same article. How high or low all prices of commodities shall be, depends on the demand and supply of money,—a matter over which competition has no control.

Similarly in the case of wages, competition has nothing to do with fixing the general level. It simply tends to remove inequalities that do not rest on differences in the labor performed. In a state of full competition, laborers would avoid employments in which wages happened to be low in proportion to the labor exacted, and would choose those in which the wages were high. This action on their part would cause wages to rise in the one set of employments, and to fall in the other set, until a condition of equality were reached. The same principle would apply to the case of employers offering different rates of pay for the same or similar kinds of labor; no one employer could obtain laborers except on the condition of paying them as high wages as any other employer was ready to pay them.

Competition tends, no doubt, to lower wages wherever they are above the common level; but it equally tends to raise wages wherever they are below the common level. It is simply the principle of each man's doing the best he can for himself by all fair and honorable means. The laborer acts in free competition when he goes where he can get highest wages. The employer does the same when he gets all the labor he can for his savings. The tendency of both efforts, taken together, is not to raise or lower all wages, but to create uniformity in wages.

Freedom of competition surely destroys nothing. All that men produce they have as the reward of their labor and waiting, — competition or no competition. All that the saving classes save, the hired classes receive as wages, whether with or without competition. This is all they can in any case receive; freedom of competition affects only the mode of sharing it among them.

4. Temporary Obstructions to Competition. — Under division of labor, the wages and profits of each industry depend on the value of the product. When the market value of the product rises above its natural value, the first effect is to raise the profits of the employers. Under the stimulus of the higher profit, additional savings are attracted into the business, and the increased demand for laborers qualified to produce the commodity causes their wages to rise.

In the same way, when the market value of a commodity falls below its natural value, the first effect is a fall of profits for the employers who produce it. But the fall of profits causes less savings to be invested in producing the commodity. As a result, the wages of the laborers in the industry fall.[1]

Now if laborers could change their occupations quickly, these changes of wages would be slight and of short duration. But here we come on one of the many obstructions to perfect freedom of competition. Changes of employment are not easily made. Every occupation, above the very rudest and most elementary, requires some degree of training and special knowledge. A change means forfeiture of the skill already acquired, and loss of time in learning a new kind of work.[2]

Rather than incur the loss and trouble of changing, men usually persevere in their old calling, even under

[1] To the extent of the difference between producing at high pressure and producing at low pressure, the change of demand for labor in any industry may take place at once. In the industries using a great deal of fixed capital, the change cannot well exceed these limits in any brief space. Even this, however, is enough to make a serious difference for the laborers.

[2] The concentration of single industries in particular towns increases greatly the difficulty of changing employments. Laborers who would change must move to another town in addition to making the sacrifice spoken of in the text.

reduced wages. In the main, the re-adjustment of wages has to be brought about through the choice of occupations made by the new laborers who are constantly coming forward. These can mostly be counted on to choose, among the industries open to them, those that offer best wages. By their action it is that the supply of labor in each industry is eventually adjusted to the demand, and wages are made to have, or tend to have, only such differences as correspond to permanent differences in the quantity of labor involved.

We thus see that competition among the laborers acts somewhat slowly; also that the length of time necessary for bringing the market value of each commodity into agreement with its natural value, is the length of time necessary for bringing the market wages of its producers to the level of other wages.

5. Permanent Obstacles to Free Competition.—Freedom of competition implies that the choice of occupations shall be made without constraint or compulsion. It is not indeed necessary that this shall be so in every case, since all occupations must have some recruits. If, when any industry happened to have a comparative deficiency of laborers, a sufficient number could come into it to restore the equilibrium, that would be enough to keep all wages under the equalizing influence of competition.

We know, however, that even this condition is not fulfilled in practice. The range of free competition is limited and checked by a great variety of circumstances. These may be classified, in the main, under three heads:

First, those that are local in their nature. Here the obstacle to competition is distance, with all that this implies: cost of travelling, the trouble of finding employment among strangers, reluctance to leave home and friends, etc. These local impediments are greatly intensified by the differences of climate, language, and religion which prevail in the world. The contrasts of wages between countries are very striking. In Japan, for example, wages are hardly one-fourth as high as in the United States. Even in Europe, they are not much more than half as high as in our country. If it were a simple and easy matter for laborers to move from one country to another, these wide contrasts in wages could not last.

In the second place, there are obstacles to free competition growing out of the need of much longer training for some employments than for others. This point has already been spoken of in connection with the value of products of skilled labor (Chap. XII., § 3). The principle is, however, of much wider application than could be shown in connection with value. A considerable proportion of the occupations demanding long preparation have no specific products, being connected with transportation, exchange, banking, the learned professions, etc. Further, there is, strictly, no commodity wholly produced by skilled labor, nor is there any wholly produced without it. The so-called products of skilled labor are merely those into the production of which such labor enters most largely. Even if skilled labor entered equally into all production, in which case it would have no effect on values, the scarcity of it would still cause its remuneration to be high. It is scarce only because the cost of long training acts as a permanent barrier to freedom of competition.

Thirdly, many obstacles to free competition arise from the fact that many occupations call for natural gifts of mind or body that the great mass do not possess. Any employment that requires native intelligence, quickness of discernment, artistic instinct, clear judgment, the faculty of organizing and commanding, or any other special faculty, is thereby closed to the great majority of men. Even those employments which simply require muscular strength are thereby closed to more than one-half of the whole community.

Commonly enough, obstacles of this third kind are in addition to the need of long training and education. In the higher employments, or "professions," this is uniformly the case.

6. Permanent Inequalities in Wages. — It would be impossible, in this little book, to go into all the details of differences in wages arising from these impediments to freedom of competition. The general principle governing them is clear. At the bottom of the scale we find the great body of common or "unskilled" laborers: farm-hands, lumbermen, teamsters, miners, firemen, navvies, hodmen, sailors, fishermen, etc. Between these employments, in any given region, there is fairly complete freedom of competition, so that the permanent differences of wages from one to the other depend on the greater or less attractiveness of each employment. Comparing different countries, however, there are considerable contrasts owing to absence of free competition.

At the other end of the scale, we find those whose occupations require special gifts and costly training: superintendents, hired managers, architects, bank cashiers, lawyers, doctors, etc. Wages in these occupations vary greatly from personal causes; but they are ordinarily many times higher than those of the unskilled mass.

Between these extremes there are many gradations of wages, depending in each case on the greater or less potency of the obstacles to freedom of competition. Thus, next above the common laborers come the artisans or mechanics,—the men who have to learn a trade. Next above mechanics, those who, in addition to acquiring a particular kind of skill, must also have a good degree of education and general intelligence: engravers, modellers, engineers, chemists, teachers, proof-readers, etc.

No rigid classification of occupations by earnings is possible. Wages in each trade vary widely on personal grounds. Energy, integrity, diligence, and special aptitude for the work are pretty sure to raise the possessor above the general level of his calling. The opposite qualities are pretty sure to have the reverse effect. A good teamster may earn more than a poor tailor,—a skilled engraver more than an indifferent lawyer, and so on. In general, the higher the occupation the wider this range of difference in earnings.[1]

Of course a certain proportion of each kind of labor is needed in a country: the precise amount depending on the nature of its industries. The source of the chief permanent inequalities of wages for different kinds of labor is the fact that the laborers sag heavily toward those employments that make least call for intelligence, education, and skill. In proportion to the demand there is always a vastly greater supply offering of unskilled labor than of skilled.

7. **Wages of Women.** — The low wages of women afford a good illustration, though a lamentable one, of the principle controlling differences of wages. The number of women who need to work for wages is fortunately much smaller than the number of men. But their lack of physical strength bars them out from all but a few productive employments. The conventional standards of feminine modesty limit still further the range of occupations open to them. The result is that, in the comparatively small number of employments to which they have access, there is a constant oversupply of their labor in comparison with the demand. Consequently, women's wages are much lower than men's; and there is no remedy for the inequality except in either lessening the

---

[1] It is one of the least hopeful features of the labor organizations that they seem to aim at a dead level of wages for all who happen to be doing the same kind of work. Nothing could be more fatal to the industrial success of a community than the adoption of that principle.

number of women who work for wages, or in extending the range of employments open to them. Fortunately, a movement in the latter direction seems to be going on in all civilized countries.

It is easy, in cases of this kind, to mistake the true nature of the difficulty, and to blame the " hard-heartedness of employers" for evils which employers are powerless to prevent. Business men could hardly be expected to employ any class of laborers at a loss. The wages they can afford to pay to women, in productive occupations, are limited by the low exchange value of the product. The low value of the products of female labor is due to the excessive supply of them, in comparison with other commodities; and this, in its turn, is due to the fact that women crowd into a few occupations.

If the community could be induced to pay higher prices for the commodities produced by female labor, and to buy, at the advance, the whole supply offered, wages of women would soon rise. Till the employers can get higher prices it is foolish to reproach them for the low wages.

8. Normal Wages of Individual Laborers. — It follows from the principles stated in this and the preceding chapter, that there is, in any given industrial situation, a normal rate of wages for each kind of labor. This rate holds to the market rate much the same sort of relation that natural value holds to market value. It is the rate that, with a normal volume of savings, would cause the supply of each kind of labor to be equal to the demand. Differences of wages are not normal when they tend to a shifting of laborers from one industry to another.

When anything occurs to raise the market wages of laborers in general, above the normal rate, saving is checked and wages fall. When wages are, for any reason, below the normal level, saving is stimulated by the high rate of profits, and wages rise.

When wages in any occupation are above the normal relation to other wages, an increased proportion of laborers are attracted into it, in preference to other occupations of similar grade, and wages in the employment are brought down. In the reverse case, laborers seek other occupations by preference, and wages in the given employment rise.

In order to save space, I shall assume that the reader can see for himself the truth of the following propositions regarding the normal level of individual wages:

First, that it is high in communities where the spirit of saving is strong, and where the product of industry is large in proportion to the number of laborers. If the spirit of saving be weak, or if the product be relatively small, the normal level of wages will be low. Two communities equal in producing capacity may have unequal wages. Again normal wages may be equal in two communities, notwithstanding a considerable difference in the productiveness of labor.

Secondly, the normal rate of wages for any particular

kind of labor, is above the common level if the general mass of laborers be hindered in any way from performing that kind of labor. The greater the obstacles, the greater the inequality in wages. Conversely, if the rate of wages in any employment be permanently above the common level, it is so only because the general mass of laborers are hindered from entering the employment.

Thirdly, so far as freedom of competition prevails between employments, differences in normal wages depend on differences in the character of the employments, as viewed by the laborers.

Fourthly, the narrower the range of employments open to any class of laborers, the lower their normal wages will be. Conversely, a normal rate of wages below the common level can exist only for laborers whose range of competition is restricted.

Fifthly, a rapid increase of laborers in any country tends to depress the general level of wages. It keeps the number of laborers always larger in proportion to the total volume of savings than it would be if the increase were less rapid.[1]

9. Wages of Non-productive Laborers. — It is necessary, before leaving the subject of wages, to consider briefly the wages of non-productive laborers. The services of these laborers are sought, not with a view to profit, but for the sake of the comfort, improvement, or other benefits they confer on us. Their wages are therefore drawn,

[1] There is another highly important consequence of increasing numbers, which will appear in connection with economic rent.

not from the savings, but from the spendings of the community. This is a highly important fact in relation to the general level of wages. It means that the fund for paying wages is larger than we have hitherto assumed Not, however, larger by the full amount paid for non-productive services; for it is to be observed that these services are in part paid for by the productive laborers. Teachers, ministers of religion, physicians, and public servants in general are in part supported by the contributions of those who live by wages. But the wealthy classes use non-productive services much more freely than the wage-earners. They spend much in the hire of household servants, footmen, coachmen, companions, etc. Whatever amount the laboring class receive in these ways is a clear addition to the wages paid from savings. Or, looking at the case from another point of view, we can easily see that the demand for these non-productive services keeps a considerable number of laborers out of the competition for savings, and thereby enables the productive laborers to get higher wages than they could get if the whole body of laborers were thrown for employment on the savings offered for profitable investment.

Yet it is clear that, in a very important sense, payments for non-productive services are not so beneficial to the laborers as the offer of savings would be. It is only better for them that the wealthy classes, if they are to spend instead of saving, should spend in hiring services rather than in buying luxurious commodities. What is spent in commodities is entirely lost to the laborers. What is spent in hiring services the laborers get, so to say, a single use of, and then it is gone. The kind of labor they give in return leaves no product to be used in paying them for further labors. If the amount were saved and used in hiring them to produce useful commodities, the product of industry would presently be increased, and the wages of laborers would be raised. This on the hypothesis that those who have dispensed with personal services, persevere in the saving they have begun. Of course if they should turn out to be merely changing the form of their spending: if they or other wealthy persons should increase their consumption of good things to the extent of taking up all that the new producers add to the product of industry, wages would not be raised as a result of the change.

Or, putting the same case in a different way, body servants, footmen, etc., live on the products of other men's labor. If, for the wages they are receiving, they were set at work as productive laborers, they would presently add to the product of industry enough commodities for their own support, with a surplus over as profit for their employers. What they now consume, as non-productive members of the community, would in that case, go to swell the wages of other laborers,—provided, of course, that the change denotes a real increase of the saving spirit in the community.

If all non-productive laborers were simply discharged, their present employers spending in increased purchases of commodities what they now pay for non-productive services, there would be a serious fall of wages. The number of laborers thrown on savings for their wages would be increased without a corresponding increase of savings. The case would be similar in its effects to the increase of laborers spoken of in the first section of this chapter.

10. Checks on Competition in Non-productive Occupations. — Wages of non-productive labor tend to conform in a general way to those of productive labor, quantity for quantity, so far as competition prevails between the two.[1] Between the lower forms of the one and the lower forms of the other, there is, so far as the laborers are concerned, a basis for freedom of competition; also between the higher grades of the two. The most important limitation on freedom of competition exists on the side of the employers. In hiring non-productive laborers, the employer is not aiming at profit, and does not therefore feel so strongly the need of proceeding on strictly "business" principles. He is spending, and in spending it is not dignified to higgle over trifles.

Further, the employer of non-productive laborers has them much of the time about him. His personal com-

[1] Remember, once more, that in measuring quantities of labor we must take the judgment of the laborers; and that their judgment has reference to the whole sacrifice. For example, non-productive services are, for the most part, lighter in the mere physical exertion they call for than productive labor is. But the household servant has less personal freedom than the productive laborer; and this difference causes household service to be regarded by the laborers as less dignified than productive labor. It is an element in their judgment as to the quantity of labor involved in either occupation.

fort and convenience require that their service shall be cheerful and willing. This it could hardly be if they felt that their services were poorly paid.

For these reasons, wages of household servants are higher than they would be if fully controlled by competition. It is not open to the general mass of other laborers to come in and do the same service for lower wages. The masters and mistresses do not give them the chance. The difference in wages, however, is not very great.

Again, no man drives a hard bargain with his doctor when he needs medical aid; or with his lawyer when he gets into a lawsuit. The services which professional men render are so important that we feel the necessity of getting the very best help they can give us. The pay of this class of laborers is therefore not wholly under the control of competition.

CHAPTER XX.

FURTHER CONSIDERATIONS REGARDING WAGES.

1. Combinations to Fix Wages. — No discussion of wages can be regarded as complete which fails to notice the strong tendency towards organization that exists among the hired laborers of our time. The tendency is not new, but in recent times the efforts at organization have become more extended than formerly.

The labor unions have more than one object. Largely they are associations for benevolent purposes, for assisting members who are out of employment, for relieving families that are left destitute, etc. Much good has been accomplished by them in these ways.

Commonly, however, the associations have shown a tendency to intervene in questions of wages. The members seem to believe that, by acting as a body, the laborers may force the employers to pay higher wages than they would pay if left to themselves.

The question is one of great practical interest both to laborers and employers. It is at the same time, I think, a much broader and deeper question than the leaders of the labor unions suppose. A full discussion of it would require much space, since it touches, in one way or another, almost every principle of political economy. Only the chief points can be touched on here.

The most general form of the question is whether, by a general combination, able at will to order a universal strike, the hired laborers of the country could succeed in raising the general level of wages. Political economists hold that they could not; the labor agitators seem to hold that they could.

2. Strikes Tend to Discourage Saving. — The general grounds of the answer given by the economists can be stated very briefly. It is easily demonstrable that the wages of productive laborers are drawn from savings, and that the total volume of wages can be increased only by increase of savings. Now, saving is a voluntary act; it is for the most part an act of present self-denial, or sacrifice, submitted to for the sake of the future gain it will bring. Other things being equal, the greater the prospect of gain, the greater the volume of savings will be. We may safely assume, in any given case, that the total volume of savings is already as great as the community is willing to make it for the existing inducement. Normal wages are therefore as high already as the situation will bear.

A general strike might succeed in getting temporary increase of pay for some laborers. The trouble would be to find employment for all at the advance. Wages could be raised at any time, even without a strike, by inducing a portion of the laborers to withdraw from work; but the rise could be maintained only by their staying out. The whole body of laborers would not be benefited by such a rise of wages.

A higher level of wages could be maintained only by an increased flow of savings. But if wages should be raised, profits would be lowered; the inducement to save would be less, not greater, than before; savings would therefore fall off instead of increasing.

The conclusion seems unavoidable that even a universal strike for higher wages must fail of success. It would fail just as an attempt to raise all prices of goods, without an increased supply of money, would fail. There would not be a sufficient supply of savings forthcoming to make the increased wages possible. The doctrine of the labor unions requires us to believe that men would save more for a less inducement than for a greater. It is therefore contrary to the fundamental principle of wages.

The only way by which the laborers can make sure of raising their wages is clearly by adding all they can to the productiveness of their labor. By greater diligence, better care of machinery and materials, more disposition to turn everything to the best account for their employers, they would increase very much the value of their services; the product of industry would become greater; both the means of saving and the inducement to save would be increased. That the speedy result would be an increased demand for labor and a general rise of wages, does not admit of a doubt.

Strikes, with their attendant interruption of industry, with the disorders, violence, and destruction of property that so commonly grow out of them, are poor incentives to induce people to save their income with a view to investing in business enterprises. Till the laborers are willing to save the means of providing capital of their own, it is clearly their interest to do nothing that tends to check the saving spirit in others.

3. Futility of Strikes in Practice. — The common result of strikes against individual employers shows plainly enough the weak point in the theory that strikes may raise the general level of wages. Commonly the strikers fail, because it usually turns out that there are many other laborers who, having either no employment or poorer pay than the strikers, are glad to accept the terms these have rejected. The few cases in which this is not true, in which therefore strikes succeed, are cases in which a rise of wages is on the eve of coming about, without a strike, by the action of supply and demand.

A strike for advance of pay in any industry, if made when business is improving or has improved, may hasten the rise of wages. Strikes against reduction of wages nearly always fail. They come at a time when employers may have little or nothing to gain by going on with production, even at the reduced wages. A stoppage of work for a while may be a welcome relief to the employers at such a time. A strike, in these circumstances, is sure to fail. In no case is it sure to succeed. There can be no doubt, looking at the history of strikes in general, that they have been on the whole a source of great loss to the laborers.

One further reflection as to strikes is, that they are never directed against the most obvious source of low wages. The real wages of laborers depend as much on the prices of the things they buy, as on the amount of money they receive from their employers. The great loss of real wages comes in the difference between the prices the producing employers get from the traders and the prices we all have to pay at retail. Even if the direct employers of the great mass of laborers should raise wages to the point of foregoing all their profit, the difference in wages would be slight. On the other hand, if the cost and risks of making the exchange of products could be reduced one-half, the gain in real wages would be great. The establishment of co-operative stores by the laborers in England was, therefore, a move in the right direction. It has proved a great success. If our American laborers would but devote to a similar plan a part of the energy and money they have wasted and still waste in strikes, there can be no doubt of their opportunity to raise very materially their real wages thereby.

4. High Profits Favorable to High Wages. — It may seem to some that this puts political economy on the side of the capitalists in the struggle about wages. That is not the case. Economists have always sympathized deeply with every feasible plan for improving the lot of those who work for wages. They have always denounced all harsh and unfair treatment of laborers. But they cannot allow their sympathy to blind them to the facts of the case. They see what the labor agitators too often fail to see, namely, that people cannot be coerced into saving. Further, the economist does not look with jealousy on the profits of employers, for he knows that the higher profits are, the better hope there is for the laborers. He knows that high profits to-day are the best ground for expecting high wages to-morrow.

What the laborers fail to get of the product of industry, is not what the employers gain, but what they consume. So far as profits are saved, they become wages. The profits of to-day are not high at the expense of the wages of to-day, they are high at the expense of past wages, which are now beyond the reach of change by strike or other means. Instead, therefore, of fretting over the high profit of capital, laborers ought to rejoice in it. The thing they have some reason to grudge is the lavish expenditure of the capitalist class. Their loss is not what the capitalists gain, but what they spend. This is so important a principle and so contrary to popular theories that we shall do well to consider it fully.

5. Do we Help the Laborers by Buying Goods?— There is a wide-spread belief that whoever buys goods of the merchants helps the laborers. Those who, having the ability to spend freely, choose to live economically are commonly regarded as churlish and unfriendly to those who live by wages. On the other hand, those who are lavish in buying luxuries for themselves are often spoken of as benefactors of the laborers. Their purchases are supposed to create a demand for labor and to promote high wages.

This is one of the many popular ideas which political economy has to reject and refute. It is not true, though it looks true. Anybody who thinks carefully about the matter for a little while ought to be able to expose the fallacy. Observe that the question is, at bottom, whether it is better for the laborers that you should spend your money in getting enjoyable things for yourself, or should turn it over to them to spend. If you save and invest it in any form, it is sure in the end to reach the laborers as wages. Even if you merely put it in a savings' bank, the bank lends it to some business man in whose hands it soon becomes wages. The result will be that your saving adds just so much to the amount the laborers receive for their work.

Perhaps the easiest way of perceiving the error of the popular theory is to consider it in connection with the circulation of money. Looking again at the diagram on page 134, it ought to be easy to see that the greater the amount returning to 1 through a, d, g, j, and q, the less there is left to pass through the channels for wages, b, e, h, l, and o. In other words, the more the wealthy classes spend in buying commodities for their own consumption, the lower the wages of the laborers will be.

The laborers get, not what is spent, but what is saved. Those who hold that the mere purchase of products of labor helps the laborers, forget to ask what would happen if everybody acted on that principle. If, for example, the merchants and the manufacturers, instead of hiring laborers with the money we pay them for their goods, should at once spend it in buying things for their own enjoyment, where would the advantage to the laborers come in? It is only by taking for granted that the business men will do what we have not done,— will save what they receive and hire laborers with it,— that anybody could hold the doctrine for a moment. But if saving on the part of business men be good and even necessary for the laborers, why should it be less beneficial when practised by others?

6. The Argument from the Need of a Market. — To the question just asked, the advocate of the time-worn fallacy usually replies by urging the necessity of a market. Briefly stated, his argument is that "If nobody bought things, there would be no call for labor to make things." This may be freely admitted, but it has no bearing on the case.

The question is not whether there are to be any buyers or no, but Who are to be the buyers? When hired laborers spend their wages, they are buyers quite as truly as any other class. In saving money, we simply transfer buying power to those who live by wages. The question, therefore, is simply Who shall have the privilege of buying? Whoever has that, constitutes the market. The higher wages are, the greater is the market offered by the laborers. Even if all income could be saved and paid for labor, it would only amount to making the laborers a market for the whole product of industry.

As to the call for labor, there would be the same need of labor to make things for working men and their families that there is to make things for the wealthier classes. The precise things to be made would no doubt be different; but that would be merely a question of the sort of production to be carried on, not a question whether any sort of production would be needed.

7. Increase of Saving does not Lessen the Total Demand for Commodities. — The fact that the commodities laborers buy with their money are not the same that the person who saves the money would have bought, makes it easy to fall into a wrong view of the effect of saving. When persons who have been accustomed to spend freely abandon their extravagant habits, we are apt to think of the shopkeepers with their stocks of cigars, wines, silks, and laces. We see that until they sell these, they will not order a fresh supply; and so the manufacturers may not venture to produce further stocks. When the buyers appear, they seem to set the whole productive machinery in operation, and thus to create the occasion for the hiring of laborers.

But to look at the matter in this way is to omit the most important feature of the case. Wines and laces are produced only because there is a demand for them. Had people always saved their money instead of spending it in buying luxurious articles, such articles would not have been on the hands of the merchants awaiting buyers. If people should suddenly give up buying wines and silks, of course the manufacturers and merchants might lose a large part of the savings they have invested in the production and sale of these commodities. But let us suppose the change to be foreseen, or even to be gradual, so that the producers and dealers may have time to withdraw from the business in time. In that case they would still have their savings, and would still wish to use them so as to make profit. They would, therefore, continue to employ as many laborers as before,— merely changing the precise mode of employing them. On their part, then, the payment of wages would not be lessened.[1]

Attending now to those who save the amount previously expended in the purchase of luxuries, there ought to be no difficulty in seeing that all they save and invest is a clear addition to the wages of labor. If anybody doubts the existence of a market under these conditions, for all that the laborers could produce, let him consider the case from the side of the laborers. Why do they labor? Is not the mere fact of their working for wages a proof that they desire products of industry? The only

[1] Some loss of fixed capital would be likely to attend the change; but the opposite change (that is, a decrease of saving and a fall of wages) would involve a similar loss. Such losses attend every change of fashion, and even every improvement in production. This is one of the risks that producers have to run. The danger tends, no doubt, to discourage saving, and so tends to depress wages. The ordinary expectation of profit must, in other words, be high enough, after allowing for these losses, to induce men to save and invest.

possible doubt in the case would be, What particular products do they desire as their increase of wages? Whatever these products, the increase of demand would call forth an increased production of them. Even if they wished only money to lay by for future use, money is a product of labor. Such a demand would simply raise the value of money, and divert an increased amount of labor into the production of gold and silver.

The whole result, then, of increased saving is to raise wages, to diminish the demand for certain articles and to increase, to the same precise extent, the demand for certain other articles.

8. Obscuring Effect of the Use of Money.— We have seen already how much the use of money obscures the true nature of buying and selling. We now see that it has the same effect on the payment of wages. If employers were accustomed to pay their laborers in actual commodities, I think that the error we are considering would never have arisen. Nobody could then fail to see the absurdity of supposing that the rich help the poor by lavish consumption of commodities, and injure them by saving as much as possible for investment. Everybody would perceive that the wages of those who work for hire consist precisely, not of what other men consume, but of what other men do not consume.

The use of money brings the payment of wages into close connection with the exchange of commodities. It separates the receipt of wages into two acts: first, the receipt of the money from the employer, and secondly, the purchase of commodities with the money. The second of these acts has nothing in it, at least on the surface, to distinguish it from other purchases of goods. Yet in a very important sense it is the true payment of wages. The amount of money received for a day's work is a matter of small consequence in itself; the real question of wages is how great a quantity of needful commodities a man can obtain for his labor.

Further, as we have seen in a previous chapter, this connection between payment of wages and the sale of goods, makes it easy to mistake the real nature of the trouble, when, for any reason, there is a falling off in the investment of savings. The obvious thing, at such a time, is the decrease in the sales of goods. The accumulation of uninvested savings in the hands of bankers and others, is either not noticed, or is regarded as a mere consequence of the failing demand for goods. In this way, unthinking persons are confirmed in the erroneous opinion that when we buy commodities for our own use we give employment to laborers. If they reflected at all, they could hardly fail to see that the commodities which do not sell are in fact awaiting use in the payment of real wages; and that, but for the presence of money, these commodities would appear as savings in the hands of the employers, rather than as unsalable goods in the shops.

9. Wages an Advance. — The question we are considering goes to the foundations of political economy. A whole group of important practical questions depend upon the answer we give to this one. It may therefore be well to consider the matter from another point of view.

The fundamental reason why demand for commodities is not a demand for labor, is found in the fact that the production and exchange of finished commodities requires so much time. If every commodity could be produced in a day, or a week, and could be immediately exchanged for such things as the producer happened to desire, there would be no essential difference between paying a man wages and buying his product. There are, in fact, a few cases in which the purchase of the product answers the same purpose as the direct hiring of the laborer would serve.

If, for example, at the proper season, one should offer to buy wild flowers, or berries, or autumn leaves, or shells from the beach, or any other thing that can be obtained without much previous labor, the offer would be as good for the country boy as the offer of wages would be. It would be a demand for his labor.

But very different is the offer to buy a suit of clothes from a journeyman tailor who is looking for employment; or a car-load of potatoes from a farm laborer in the like case; or a house from a carpenter who is out of work; or a roll of cotton cloth from a mill operative; or a ton of coal from a coal miner, etc.

A little careful thinking about these two sets of cases will make clear the reason why, in civilized industry, the offer to buy goods does not give employment to needy laborers. Production takes too long to make the offer of any service to them.

In considering the matter the student must take care to include the whole case. The production of each commodity must be viewed as a whole. All the labor of preparing the natural agents, of raising or procuring the materials, and of making the requisite machinery, must be included in the labor of producing the enjoyable commodity which finally results from them. This point is of great importance in the study of wages. It is the simple fact that labor spent in getting ready to produce good things, has itself no immediate result that is good to eat or to drink or to wear.

Though machinery and materials are bought and sold; and though, on the surface, there is nothing to distinguish such sales from the sale of enjoyable commodities to consumers, yet a little reflection shows us that there is a very wide difference. In sales of the latter kind, the purchaser is taking his reward for labor or waiting. In the purchase of materials or machinery he is investing savings.

If men receive any immediate return for labor spent in providing the capital used in production, it must come from the saved products of other labor. No matter in what form, or under what name the return is obtained, it is in the nature of an advance out of savings.

For example, an agreement to buy of the laborers, at the end of each day or each week, the unfinished results of their work up to that point, would not differ in principle from an agreement to pay them wages. No man could do either without a fund of savings to be used for the purpose. He could not use the very things produced by the laborers themselves, until they had got by the work of creating capital, and had begun to turn out true commodities. All the finished commodities received by the workmen for their labor up to that point are advanced to them out of the saved products of other labor.

10. Extent of the Advance.—Perhaps the simplest way of estimating the extent to which wages are advanced out of savings is to look at the industrial system as a whole. All the contrivances and arrangements for producing and exchanging enjoyable commodities, the three classes of things to which we give the general name of Capital, represent labor which could not have been rewarded by anything of its own producing.

If the whole existing apparatus of production and exchange were swept away, a great deal of labor would be required for restoring it. That labor would have to be applied without immediate return of its own yielding. Anybody getting a weekly allowance of enjoyable commodities, or the means of buying such, in return for this labor, would be getting payment in advance of his own production. The length of time it would take to replace the capital of the country, measures pretty accurately the extent to which wages, in our existing system, are paid in advance of the natural return for labor.

The extent to which wages are advanced is much disguised by the division of labor among employers. Each employer seems as a rule to recover pretty quickly, by the sale of his product, the amounts paid out to his laborers. The manufacturer of cloth, for example, may sell his product from week to week, almost as quickly as it is made; and with the proceeds he pays his laborers. So that his advance of wages seems to be slight.

But this is to look only at the surface of the matter. The manufacture of cloth is but one stage of the work of producing coats. When the manufacturer buys his materials, he in fact advances wages; he pays for all the work already done upon them; he gives free savings for capital, just as if he had himself hired the laborers who produced the materials.

Further, at the very outset of his enterprise he had to make large outlays of savings in the construction of buildings and in the purchase of machinery. These advances consisted mainly of wages paid to the laborers who produced the buildings and machinery. It is quite immaterial whether he himself appeared as the direct employer of these laborers, or simply took over by purchase the work of other employers. In either case, whatever the laborers receive for producing capital can only come from savings. And, as to the extent of the advance, we readily see that years must elapse before the savings paid for clearing land, opening mines, constructing railways, ships, buildings, machinery, etc., can be fully recovered through the commodities which these help to produce.

A Practical Test Suggested. 247

11. Fallacy of Denying the Advance of Wages. — Mr. Henry George and some other writers deny that wages are a real advance, alleging that, before receiving wages, the laborers always add a full equivalent to the possessions of their employers. The question may easily be put to a practical test by anybody who accepts Mr. George's doctrine. It is only necessary that he shall prevail on a body of laborers sharing his view to join him in demonstrating, by actual experiment, that wages can be paid without the advance of savings.

It would only be necessary that he and they should withdraw by themselves, and begin the production of any commodity or commodities they please. The leader must pay his men week by week, just as ordinary employers do; but he is to avoid the use of savings in doing so. He is even to avoid the indirect use of other men's savings. If he resorts to exchange of products with outsiders, he is to offer only finished commodities. Further, he must make no covert use of savings by anticipating the results of the exchange through advances from the dealer. He must wait until his product finds its way to the consumers and their return commodity finds its way to him. On these terms he is to use the results of each week's labor with entire freedom, as resources for the payment of wages to his men.

Anybody who tries this experiment, or even considers how it would be likely to work if tried, will scarcely be disposed to doubt the advance of wages. He must perceive that the addition a laborer makes to his employer's possessions each week, is a very different thing from the assortment of enjoyable commodities the laborer must have as wages. The difference constitutes the whole occasion for the existence of wages.

12. Production by Prison Labor. — The foregoing principles have an obvious bearing on the vexed question of prison labor. There are two chief objections made to the employment of such labor in production; first, that it lessens the demand for free labor, and secondly, that it imposes an unfair competition on free laborers.

The first objection assumes that there is a limit to the total demand for commodities; that, therefore, if any portion of the demand be supplied by prison labor, the opportunities for free laborers to earn wages are, to that extent, abridged. The assumption is plausible; but a little careful thinking shows that it is not true. It is simply one form of the notion that general overproduction is possible. If it were true, it would follow that every invention which increases the productiveness of labor is injurious to the laborers. It would even follow that destruction of commodities by fire, shipwreck, etc., is a good thing for those who live by wages. In fact, one occasionally hears these corollaries of the doctrine gravely advanced as unquestionable truths.

However great the supply of commodities may be, it can never outrun the desire to possess commodities. You will never hear of anybody who has more than he wishes to have, or who is ready to part with his product without an equivalent of other products. There is, in fact, no limit to the desire for wealth.

The owners of the existing supply of goods and money can safely be counted on to use a portion for their own enjoyment. The rest they will wish to use so as to gain more wealth, and this can be done only by hiring productive laborers. The question, then, is whether there is a limit to the amount of commodities the laborers are willing to receive as wages. Those who assert that the demand for commodities is limited, forget that the laborers constitute the great market for the products of labor; and that they stand ready to receive all, and more than all, that others may spare.

If prison labor adds anything to the general supply of good things, the addition can have no tendency to check the desire of the capitalist class to gain increase of wealth. Neither can it diminish their resources for saving; on the contrary, it tends to increase them. Consequently, the most effective use of prison labor can only tend to raise the wages of free laborers.

The second objection rests on the fact that prisoners do not work for wages. Those who employ them are therefore said to have an unfair advantage over employers of free labor, unless the free laborers are willing to accept very low wages. Herein lies the unfair competition of which so much complaint has been made.

This objection is, at bottom, identical with the other. It assumes that there is not field enough for free labor without coming into hurtful competition with the malefactors. But evidently there is no reason why the classes of commodities to which prison labor is applied should not be kept in due proportion to other commodities. Unless there be needless changing of the articles produced by prisoners, this contribution can be reckoned on as a regular portion of the supply; and ordinary industry can as easily adjust itself to the situation as it could if the prisoners were so many free laborers.

Unless the mistake be made of producing too great a relative supply of those particular articles, there is no reason why they should not sell at their natural value; and if they sell at their natural value, the fact that a portion of the supply comes from the prisons can have no ill effect on the wages and profits of those who produce the remainder.

There is, in fact, no necessary competition, fair or unfair, between free laborers working for hire, and prisoners undergoing penal labor. The feature to which objection is made is precisely the point at which, so far as free laborers are concerned, the benefit of prison labor comes in. If the prisoners were free they would be drawing full wages from the savings offering for investment; they would be in real competition with other laborers of their grade. Being in prison, all they receive for their labor is their prison fare, and this they would receive even if they were kept in idleness. All that they produce is therefore a clear gain to the rest of the community. The more they produce, the more there will be for honest men to enjoy. Even if they should steadily furnish the whole supply of some articles, and should do so at prices far below the natural value, the result would be a benefit and not an injury to the rest of the community.

CHAPTER XXI.

PROFITS OF INDIVIDUAL EMPLOYERS.

1. Outlay and Return of the Individual Employer. — The aggregate profits of the whole body of employers are measured, as we have seen, by comparing the product of industry with the cost to them of getting it produced; that is, by comparing their outlay with the return. Further, the whole outlay, in this general case, resolves itself into the real wages paid to the laborers.

The profits of the individual employer must also be measured, of course, by comparing his outlay with his return. But there is a very important difference between the two cases. The outlay of the individual employer does not consist wholly of wages; the larger part of it usually consists of payments made to other business men for materials, machinery, etc.[1] Again, on the other side of the account, his return, in the sense in which his profits depend on it, does not consist of the product he obtains by the outlay. It consists rather of the amount

[1] For an illustration of this see the table on page 103. Of course the proportion of wages to other outlay differs widely in different industries. The whole matter depends on the extent to which division of labor is applied to the work of employing labor. The more minute the subdivision, the greater the ratio of other outlay to wages.

he receives for the product when he sells it; and this depends quite as much on the price he gets as it does on the quantity he has to sell.[1]

2. Two Sources of Individual Profit. — Evidently, then, the profits of the individual employer do not rest on so simple a basis as aggregate profits. There is but one way by which the whole body of employers may make profits, namely, by getting the laborers to produce a greater quantity of wealth than they pay them as wages. But there are two ways by which the individual employer may gain profits: first, by getting laborers to produce more than he pays for their services; secondly, by gaining, through fortunate trading, a part of the profits produced by other men's laborers.

In practical business these two ways of gaining profit are inseparably combined. Under division of labor no man can be an employer without being also a buyer and seller. His profits depend on his success in both capacities. Both the cost to him of his product, and the return for his outlay, depend in large part on the results of his dealings with other business men. Though the necessary

[1] This point did not arise to trouble us in the case of aggregate profits. In the general case we can compare real wages with product by physical measurement, because all the commodities included in wages are reproduced in the product,—with a surplus over, which constitutes the general profit. Aggregate profits are not affected by changes of value, since, when one commodity falls in value, others rise. In fact, value can hardly be said to belong to commodities in the mass, or to the sum of wealth. It belongs rather to one commodity as compared with another, when the question is of exchanging one man's wealth for another man's.

buying and selling between employers create no profits, they do determine very effectively who is to own and enjoy the profits that are created by the general industry of the community.

3. Money a Common Measure of Outlay and Return. — In computing individual profits we need to have the outlay and the return expressed in terms of the same denomination. Otherwise, we cannot compare them and say how great the difference is. We cannot, for example, in the case of any one employer, compare the general assortment of commodities constituting the real wages of his laborers with the case of shoes or the bale of cloth they help to produce. Both wages and product must be expressed in terms of a common measure.

For this purpose it is most convenient to use money. In point of strict fact the individual employer does not pay the real wages of his laborers; his agreement is to pay them certain sums of money. In spending their money the laborers may buy shrewdly and get higher real wages; or they may buy badly and get less for their labor. But this does not affect the profits of their employer. His outlay is, in strictness, the money he pays. The real wages of his laborers are drawn from the general capital of the community: from that portion of the general capital that consists of commodities in the hands of the retail dealers.

Expressing both outlay and return in money, we have a basis for reckoning profits. This mode is, of course, open to the danger of error through changes in the value of money. But it has the advantage of being simple, and the further recommendation of being the one in practical use. Of course, real profits consist in increased command over commodities in general. In order that profits reckoned in money shall represent the real result of an employer's outlay, it is necessary to apply a correction for any rise or fall occuring in the value of money between the outlay and the return. This is particularly necessary where, as happens in the case of fixed capital and many other forms of productive expenditure, considerable periods of time intervene between the outlay and the completed return.

4. Factors on which Individual Profits Depend. — Understanding this correction to be made wherever necessary, we may say that each employer's share in the aggregate profits of industry depends on three factors:

(1) The cost to him of his product (meaning thereby the amount of money each yard, pound, bushel, or other unit costs him).

(2) The price he obtains for it.

(3) The quantity he produces (or acquires in other ways).[1]

---

[1] The word "employer" is to be understood as including all persons who operate with savings, whether they actually hire laborers or not. Similarly the word "produce" is used in this discussion, to include all ways of acquiring products with a view to profit. It would cumber the treatment of profits too much to speak separately, in every case, of merchants, bankers, carriers, speculators, etc. Further, it is to be remembered that the word "laborer" includes salesmen, book-keepers, hired managers, etc.

Each of these factors is variable. Each of them may differ in the case of different employers. It remains for us to note the principal causes of variation and the ways in which individual profits are affected thereby.

5. Cost of Capital Differs to Different Employers. — The cost of a product to the employer may be divided, as we have seen, into two general classes of payments: first, the amounts paid for machinery and materials to other employers; secondly, the amounts paid as wages to his own laborers. The cost of capital bought from other employers may vary in two distinct ways: it may differ in price at different times and to different buyers; secondly, the quantity or quality of product it yields may differ to different employers.

One employer may have the sagacity and good fortune to buy the most suitable articles, and to buy them at the most favorable time, and on the most favorable terms. Another, through incapacity or inadvertence, may buy less shrewdly, buying less suitable articles, or buying them at the wrong time and place, or in wrong quantity. Prices, it must be remembered, are never long stationary and are never quite uniform. It is usually possible to get a good bargain, if one knows how to go about it. There is always danger of getting a bad bargain, unless one has the requisite knowledge and takes the requisite care to avoid it.

Now, in paying for materials or machinery, the purchaser does not merely replace to the seller the savings spent in getting them produced. The price includes also whatever of profit the seller is to have for his share in producing the commodities which ultimately result from the machinery or materials. How much the eventual profit is to be cannot be known yet. The buyer takes over the chances, paying the seller a sum which may later prove to have been indefinitely greater or less than his fair proportion. The effect on the profits of each is obvious.

Of course prices of machinery and materials, like the prices of other things, tend to conform, on the average, to the cost of production. But the price in any particular case may vary widely from this standard. Also, the cost of production itself is subject to changes. The employer who buys when the market price is lowest makes higher profits, other things being equal, than the one who buys when the market price is high. The employer who buys his machinery just after an important improvement has been introduced in the production of it, has a great advantage over the one who had the misfortune to buy just before the new inventions were made. One has the ill fortune to have laid in a large stock of some necessary material just before a great cheapening of it through the discovery of new sources of supply, or just before the discovery of a cheaper and better substitute makes the material no longer necessary. Another has the good fortune to escape loss by the change. And so on. Employers take individually the risks of industry. It makes a great difference to each whether his risks in the purchase of capital turn out well or ill.

Secondly, the cost of machinery and materials may vary according to the employer's success in getting the best results out of them in actual use. One employer may have great skill in arranging the internal economy of his establishment, in keeping down the wear and tear of machinery and buildings, in preventing waste of materials, and in turning everything to the best account. Another may fail in one or all of these respects, through lack of superior judgment, or want of energy, or through over-confidence in the faithfulness of subordinates. Besides these and similar elements of difference, which good management may be supposed to control, there are not a few others which no human sagacity can foresee or wholly prevent, — such as ill-health, accidental injuries to machinery, destruction by fire or flood, and (in such industries as farming) ravages of insects, local drouths, etc. These are matters as to which scarcely two employers fare wholly alike. The result is considerable divergences in the proportion of product to outlay for machinery and materials.

6. Cost of Labor Differs to Different Employers. — As to wages as an element in the cost of products to the employer, it is evident that here again two things are to be taken into the account: first, the rate of wages paid, and secondly, the efficiency of the laborers. Each of these may differ in the case of different laborers. Both must be taken into account in order to determine the cost of each man's labor to the employer.

Wages for any given grade of labor may differ considerably, as we have seen, in different parts of the country, owing to the expense and other difficulties that laborers meet in changing their abode. The employer who has his business in a region where wages are low, has, in this respect, an advantage in cost of labor over producers of the same commodity in other parts of the country.

Again, on the side of efficiency, it is certain that some employers have the faculty of disposing and directing their laborers in such a way as to turn their labor to better account than other employers in the same business. With no greater outlay in wages they succeed in obtaining a greater product. It makes a great difference whether the parts of the productive process are or are not apportioned in the best way; whether labor is economized in every possible way or is wasted; whether the workmen perform their work with energy or with slackness: and so on. These are points that depend chiefly on the ability of the manager. Other things being equal, the employer who is most successful in these respects gets his product at the lowest cost.

7. Cost of Natural and Other Advantages. — There is, finally, a whole group of circumstances connected with the natural advantages for production, as to which scarcely two employers in the same industry stand on a footing of entire equality. Possession of the best kinds of the requisite natural wealth, nearness to the best sources of materials, nearness to the best markets for the product, cheap transportation, and other similar advantages, are of great importance to employers. It is true, as we shall see later, that those who have the use of special advantages such as these, may have to give a full equivalent for them. But the amount of the payment in any particular case is a matter of agreement between men. Here, as in the purchase of machinery and other capital, one employer may obtain special advantages for less than they are worth. Another may make a bad bargain, may find that he has overrated the extent of the advantage, and, by paying too much for it, has increased considerably the money cost of his product.

8. Interest on Borrowed Savings. — Most employers make more or less use of borrowed savings. The interest they pay for these loans may be regarded as an item in the cost to them of their product. The loan, it is true, is presumably a source of gain to the borrower. It enables him to do a larger business than he could have done without it; and from this additional business he expects to make more than he pays for the loan. But, it remains true that the interest is an item in the cost to him of the additional product he obtains by means of the loan. The lower the interest he pays, the greater his gain, in any given circumstances, from the additional business done by borrowing. Here, as in so many other things, the employer of large means and established credit has an advantage over employers of small resources and inferior credit. The great companies and strong business houses can get loans at considerably lower rates of interest than ordinary employers can, with corresponding advantage in making profits.

It must not be supposed, however, that a low customary rate of interest is on the whole a thing to be desired by employers. On the contrary it is a sign of low profits. It shows that the prospects of making gain by the use of savings, whether one's own or borrowed, are not very encouraging. In other words, it shows that wages are high in comparison with the productiveness of labor.

9. **Advantageous Sales as a Source of Profit.**—Assuming the value of money to be constant, or that a correction is made for variations of its value, it is easy to see that the profits of the business man in respect of any given quantity of product, are measured by the difference between the money cost of it to him and the price he obtains for it.

When the price of a product is above that of other things produced by the same amount of labor and waiting, either the employers engaged in producing it, or the laborers, or both, have higher rewards than the producers of other things. The sharing of the extra returns between employers and laborers depends on the greater or less readiness with which the laborers in other industries can be drawn in at need, to take part in the production. In cases where this can be done freely, the benefit of the high market value accrues to the employers. If, however, there be any serious barrier to free competition on the part of outside laborers, the laborers who are in the industry may obtain a part of the advantage. If the barrier, and consequently the high market value, be permanent, they are certain to get all of it.

Apart from the special profits due in particular industries to high market value of their products, it is often possible for the individual employer to get a higher price for his product than others are getting for the same article, or one equally good. In the many fluctuations of price, it often makes a considerable difference whether one sells his product to-day or holds it back till to-morrow. The man who can best foresee the course of the market has a decided advantage. This is especially true in those industries in which contracts are made to deliver goods in the future at a fixed price. Much extra profit is often made by contracts entered into at the right moment.

Again, the great body of consumers are either too busy or too careless to take the trouble of investigating and comparing the qualities of different makes of an article. They are apt to buy the kind they have found satisfactory in the past, just as they are apt to buy of the same dealer year after year. This gives an enormous advantage to producers who have an established reputation. They can charge more for their goods than those can whose reputation is yet to be made; and even at the higher price they can find a steadier market and a more ready sale. Many a fortune is made simply by the possession of an established brand, or a well-known name. The immense extension of "advertising" in our day, and the many devices adopted to bring new wares into notice are sufficient to show how great is the commercial value of having one's particular "make" of an article, or one's particular shop, favorably kept in mind by as many persons as possible.

10. Losses in the Sale of the Product. — Passing now to the cases in which commodities have to be sold at a low price, it is clear that the losses resulting from this cause must usually fall on the employer. The laborers may suffer reduction of wages, but the employer may suffer total loss of profits. Hard as it is for laborers to change occupations, it is still harder, in fact practically impossible, for the employer to change. It often happens that the employers in an industry are obliged to go on for a considerable period without any profits, — perhaps even at a loss, though at a smaller loss than total cessation would imply. This is one of the risks every employer must run. Whatever he produces, it may happen that other men shall unduly extend the production of the article, thus involving him in difficulties and losses, which no skill or forethought on his part could avert.

There is, connected with the sale of the product, a further danger of loss growing out of the fact that products are so largely sold on credit. Every producer is practically compelled to follow the custom of his trade in this respect. Those who are fortunate enough to receive payment, when due, for all they sell, probably make higher profits because of the risk they have run in selling on credit. Those, however, who are unfortunate in this regard, not only fail to make a profit, but even lose the original savings invested in the venture.

A few serious losses of this kind may undo the profits of years, or may even involve in bankruptcy the employer who incurs them. Of course here, as in other matters, the risk may be greatly reduced by careful management; but it is never wholly absent from sales on credit.

11. Scale of the Employer's Transactions. — A comparison of the money cost with the selling price of the product, shows the ratio of the employer's outlay to his return, or the rate of his profit. To determine the total amount of his profits a third factor is necessary, namely, the amount of business he does on these terms. The greater his capital, the greater, at any given rate, will his share of the general profits be.

The importance of the scale of his transactions in this respect is too obvious to need discussion. There is, however, another less obvious way in which an employer's profits are influenced by the volume of business he carries on. Some of the items in the money cost of a product are less in proportion to the quantity produced, where business is done on a large scale than where it is done on a small scale. This is especially true of what may be called the general expenses. It is about as easy to conduct a business of a million a year as one of half a million. The purchase of supplies, the book-keeping, the correspondence, the general oversight and planning of the work, are not much more onerous or costly in the one case than the other. There is, therefore, a comparative saving of cost, in these respects, in the larger scale of business.

Again, the large buyer can usually buy things more cheaply than the small buyer. The employer who produces on an extensive scale can get his materials and machinery at lower prices than the employer who uses but small quantities in comparison.

Thirdly, in a large establishment more effective division of labor is often possible; also more complete application of labor-saving devices. In a large business it often happens that machinery can be economically used to do things which, in a small business, have to be performed by hand; because there is not enough of it to be done to keep a machine busy.

In these and some other ways, various economies in the cost of the product can be introduced as the scale of operations is enlarged. On the other hand, a very large business is under some disadvantages. The larger the scale of operations, the more difficult it becomes for the employer to exercise a minute supervision over all the details. He has to leave more to the care of hired assistants, whose interest in the business can never be as keen and stimulating as his own. In a very large establishment there is apt to be a good deal of waste, through neglect of opportunities for small economies of various kinds. The little odds and ends, which, in the yearly aggregate amount to a considerable sum, are not sufficiently cared for. Then, there is a limit beyond which no ordinary business can be extended without the danger of losing, even in its greater features, that unity of management which is essential to success. There is,

I suppose, a most advantageous scale of production, or of trade, in each case; and the employer who hits this happy mean has the benefit of his sagacity in enhanced profits.

The most economical and effective scale of operations would seem to depend in part on the nature of the business, and in part on the capacity of the employer himself. The tendency of our time is undoubtedly towards large industrial establishments. Large mills, factories, and stores seem to be gradually superseding the smaller ones. Business that used to be carried on by single individuals and "firms" is now passing into the hands of incorporated companies, with large capital stock and highly extended operations. This is practical evidence that, in spite of some drawbacks, the cost to the employer of each unit of product is less where production is on a large scale than where it is on a small one, — provided only the management be in competent hands. Men who have demonstrated their ability to conduct large enterprises successfully are much in demand as managers, and are able to obtain for themselves salaries which, a century ago, would have seemed fabulous.[1]

The new system seems to be especially applicable to

[1] In the case of corporations whose business is conducted by hired managers, with or without a board of directors, the company is the real employer, since it supplies the savings and takes the risks of the enterprise. The hired manager, as such, is simply a skilled laborer in the company's service. The arrangement gives persons of means the chance to get more than mere interest for their savings, while escaping most of the personal labor of management.

industries that need large fixed capital, as is the case in transportation, mining, and most kinds of manufacturing. Perhaps the most notable example is seen in the case of railroads. A generation ago a railroad extending a couple of hundred miles was considered a large one to be under one management. Now a few great companies control the bulk of the railroad business of the country, each of them owning thousands of miles of track; and the process of consolidation is still going on. The great improvement and cheapening of the service that have accompanied the movement, though mainly due to other causes, are no doubt partly to be ascribed to the greater efficiency and economy of the new plan. It seems to be a real industrial improvement.

We may note, in passing, that the recent tendency towards combinations and "trusts" among mining and manufacturing companies, is a very different thing from the movement just spoken of. The enlargement of the scale of business was the result of an effort to lessen cost; the trust is primarily designed to keep the price of an article higher than it would be under free competition. That trusts do sometimes lessen cost, by preventing the waste of savings that attends reckless competition, is no proof that they are an improvement in industry. Free competition has some drawbacks, like every other human institution; but it offers the only sure guarantee that every known device for lessening the cost of commodities shall be faithfully and promptly applied, and that the general mass of men shall have the benefit.

Inequalities of Profits. 267

12. Uncertainty of Individual Profits. — It is clear from what has been said that the profits of the individual employer depend on too many variable elements to be either uniform or certain. The business man has to bear the risks of industry. At every step in the complicated round of transactions he carries on, he is face to face with many chances of loss as well as of gain. The wages of the laborer, the interest of the lender, and the rent of the landlord, may be settled and secured in advance. The employer alone must rely on his own skill and good fortune to win his profits in the results of his venture. While, therefore, wages, interest, rent, and even the aggregate profits of the whole body of employers, are governed by fairly definite principles, the profits of the individual employer must always remain largely a matter of chances. It is impossible that certainty or uniformity should characterize the incomes of men to each of whom every change in modes of production, in the courses of trade, in public taste, in prices, every shock to credit, the accidents of times and seasons, may bring increased gains or heavy losses.

The yearly profits of the individual are not made at a uniform rate on every transaction. They are rather a compound result reached by many strokes of business, some of them highly profitable, others indifferent, and still others a source of loss. Nearly every man who operates with savings has his good periods and his bad periods. At times fortune seems to turn against him; many things go amiss and losses multiply. At other times most things turn out well and his gains are large. Each man's rate of profits depends on the proportion of his ventures that turn out well; and this, as everybody knows, differs widely in the case of different employers.

While, then, we hold that, under free competition, profits tend to equality in the various industries, we must not infer that this implies a tendency to equality in individual profits. It means only that freedom of competition tends to keep all the industries about equally promising, as fields for the employer's enterprise. It remains true that the employer who has energy, skill, foresight, large savings and good fortune, is likely to make much higher profit in any industry than the one who is deficient in any of these respects, even though the two should engage in the same business, at the same time, and in the same town.

NOTE.—It may seem to some that the foregoing treatment makes too little of the connection between the individual employer's profits and the production carried on by his laborers and himself I think, however, that all who consider with care the whole case, will conclude that there is no way of identifying the profits of the individual employer with the contribution made towards the product of industry by his laborers, over and above their real wages. In the first place, as pointed out in the text, their real wages are drawn from the capital of the dealers from whom they buy rather than from their own employer's savings. In the second place, though we have to speak of their product, as if it were something made by them wholly apart from other producers, we know that in fact they do only a part of the work of producing a commodity, since they use, at every turn, the results of other men's labors. Their share in production is consequently merged in the general product of industry, in ways that defy distinction, except through the slippery and changeable medium of value.

It may, however, be urged that their product and their real wages may be compared with each other in terms of the quantity of labor represented by each. That is no doubt true, but the comparison would give us, at best, their contribution to the general mass of profits. It would give no certain measure of their own employer's profit, so long as prices may fail, and in not a few cases do always fail, of conforming to the quantity of labor each article represents. A man's laborers may do as well for him in every respect this year as last year, and for the same rate of wages; yet he may be losing this year, although last year he may have made large profits. If the prices paid and received by each employer always followed cost of production, or even employer's cost, the problem of individual profits would be vastly simpler than it is.

If we include in employers' cost interest on borrowed savings, it may seem that we ought also to include the self-denial (or abstinence), through which employers provide savings of their own. This would be true if our object were to make a complete analysis of the sacrifices employers must make in getting commodities produced. In that case we should have to include the personal labors of employers, as well as their abstinence. But the abstinence and the personal labors of the employer are not elements of cost in the sense in which profits depend on it. They are rather the double sacrifice of which profits are the reward. Cost, in the sense in which it determines profits, consists wholly of payments made to other men. The name "Money Cost" describes its real character.

CHAPTER XXII.

INTEREST ON BORROWED SAVINGS.

1. Nature of Interest. — There are in every community many persons who have savable income, but are themselves either not willing or not qualified to become employers of labor. On the other hand, there are always employers who see ways of profitably extending their business beyond the limits their own savings would impose. Out of these two facts has grown up a very extensive system of commercial loans. Under this system, persons who merely save are enabled to obtain a part of the profits of industry. They loan their savings to employers who agree to repay the loan at a fixed date, with an increase called Interest. It is a part of our task, as students of political economy, to consider how the rate of interest is determined.

On the side of the borrower interest is a payment for the use of other men's savings. On the side of the lender it is chiefly a reward for abstinence. Since there is always a possibility, greater or less, that the borrower may fail to pay back the loan promptly and fully, the rate agreed on includes something for the risk the lender runs, — a sort of premium levied from all borrowers to make good the losses caused by the failure of some among them to repay their loans. In common usage, the name of Interest includes both the reward of abstinence and the compensation for risk. Economists usually restrict the term interest to the first alone. It does not greatly matter which use of the word we follow, so long as we are clear as to the existence of both elements in the payments made by borrowers.

The rate of interest, in the popular sense, differs considerably to different borrowers. This arises mainly from differences in the quality of the security given for the repayment of the loan. It arises in part, however, from differences in the form of the loan, the period for which it is to run, the provisions of law regarding it, etc. The more completely any given investment meets the wishes or the needs of borrowers in these respects, the lower the rate of interest the borrower needs to pay. Thus, as between bonds otherwise equally desirable, borrowers prefer those that have long to run. Again, the law singles out certain bonds for the investment of trust funds. United States bonds are the only ones that can be lawfully deposited as a pledge for the redemption of National Bank notes. Of course bonds are singled out in this way by reason of the superior credit of the issuers. The interest on them would therefore be low in any case. But the special advantages conferred by law on these bonds enable the issuers to borrow at still lower rates than they could otherwise do.

While, then, we must speak of the rate of interest as if it were uniform for all borrowers, we must bear in mind that, in practice, borrowers pay very different rates according to the quality of the assurance given for repayment and all the special features of the loan in each case.

2. Relation of Interest to Profits. — It is to be understood that interest, as here discussed, relates only to payments for the use of savings actually borrowed. As to savings owned by the employers themselves, we have no need to say anything. For his sacrifice in abstaining from the use of this wealth, each employer has no doubt the prospect of a reward; but it is combined when he receives it, with the reward of his personal labor. There is nothing in the nature of profits, nor in the process by which they are gained, to tell us how much is for the abstinence and how much for the labor of management. As well seek in the hewn timber for some sign to tell us how much is due to the axe, and how much to the man who has wielded it. No man can be a true employer without savings of his own as a basis for his operations. If it be assumed that for these savings he has a separate and definite reward, called interest, there is at least no ground for assuming that this reward corresponds with the interest he might obtain by lending his savings to other men, or that any other man would have loaned him the amount on any terms.[1]

[1] Wages and profits (or outlay, return, and difference) are quantities definitely marked out by the very process of carrying on production by means of hired labor. But interest, considered as a reward of all abstinence, has no such basis of determination. It is merely inferred that because employers pay such and such rates for loans,

Interest, so far as actually determinate, is mainly a reward of abstinence separated from the labor and risks of employment. Interest in this sense is not a universal element or share in all profits. It is simply a payment made by employers for the use of savings in addition to their own; the amount of the payment being fixed in advance, and due to the lender in each case, whether the loan has been a source of gain or of loss to the borrower. Of course there is a relation between the rate of interest employers will agree to pay for loans, and the profit they expect to make by means of them. Interest can never be, for long, as high as the general rate of profit. How far it may ordinarily stand below the rate of profit depends very much on the disposition and inclinations of those who, in each country, own the mass of the general savings. If they be much averse to active business, they may forego a large part of the profits of capital, for the sake of the ease and supposed dignity of living without a commercial occupation. If, on the other hand, they be well inclined to the stir and enterprise of business life, the rate of interest may ordinarily stand well up towards the rate of profit. But we may safely assume that it can nowhere be always equal to it.

3. Interest Depends Immediately on the Demand and Supply of Loanable Savings. — Interest being a payment

they get the same, and only the same, returns for their own original savings. Remembering that it is by means of his own savings that the employer lifts himself out of the condition of a wage-earner, and makes the gains of an employer possible for himself, we easily see the fallacy of the inference.

fixed by agreement between borrower and lender, it is largely governed by the same principles as the price of a commodity. There is a current or market rate depending on the supply of savings offering for loan at the moment, as compared with the demand for loans. There is also, for each country and time, something like a natural rate of interest, to which the market rate tends to return after every fluctuation. The market rate tends to be such as to make the demand from day to day equal to the existing supply. The natural rate is that rate which causes people to save for loan as much, and only as much as there is a demand for at that rate. The market rate has reference to some particular condition or case of supply and demand. The natural rate has reference to the strength of the saving spirit among non-employers who have savable income, and to the permanent or average demand for loans.

The amount saved from month to month by non-employers is fairly constant. Many of them save without reference to the interest they can obtain. Most of the saving "for a rainy day," for old age, for children, etc., is probably of this character. Some may even save more strenuously, after what promises to be a lasting decline of interest, than they did before; since the lower the rate the larger the principal necessary in order to yield a given income. Yet it is reasonable to suppose that non-employers, as a body, are stimulated to save more copiously by a high rate of interest than by a low one. To the multitudes of people who have no very definite object to save for, except the general one of increasing their income, the difference between six per cent. and four per cent. may be decisive. The ever-present temptation to spend needs to be met by a strong counteracting influence; and the higher the rate of interest on loans the stronger the motive for denying one's self the immediate enjoyment of one's savable income.

We may therefore assume that when the market rate of interest rises, the supply of savings offering for loan will increase; and that when interest falls, the reverse will happen. Changes in the supply of loanable savings tend, in turn, to react on the rate of interest, in the manner already familiar in the case of market prices.

4. Variable Character of the Demand for Loans. — The objects for which loans may be desired are very numerous; but they may be classed under two general heads: namely, commercial and non-commercial. Commercial loans are those made by business men with a view to profit. Non-commercial loans are those raised by governments, cities, and private individuals for special objects, such as the prosecution of a war, the construction of water-works, the paving of streets, the building of houses, etc. The usual motive in borrowing of the latter kind is to spread the burden of the cost over a number of years, instead of taking it wholly out of the income of any one year.

The call for non-commercial loans is subject to very sudden and extensive changes. The breaking out of a war between two great nations increases it enormously.

The restoration of peace causes an equally sudden and extensive decrease of the demand. At times governments and cities are seized with a feverish activity in the construction of public works; at other times they are overtaken by a spirit of economy, and large expenditures by way of loan are avoided. These changes in the non-commercial demand for loans have striking effects on the rate of interest.

Periods of large borrowing ought to be followed by periods of debt-paying on a large scale. But unfortunately, the payment of public debts is a practice very little in vogue. It calls for a degree of fortitude which governing bodies rarely possess. Obviously the payment of public debts, wherever it does occur, has an effect on the rate of interest exactly the reverse of that produced by the public borrowing. The bond-holders whose bonds are paid off are under the necessity of finding new borrowers. This throws on the loan market a mass of old savings in addition to the amounts coming forward from current saving.

The demand for commercial loans depends on the condition of business; and this as we know is highly variable. When the product of industry contains the right proportion of each article; when the general level of prices accords well with the supply of currency, and when money wages are in such ratio to prices that profits are high, we have the situation known as "good times." At such a time there is a strong demand for commercial loans. Business men are able to see many openings for the profitable use of savings, and accordingly are eager to extend their |operations. Under the strong demand for loans, interest rises, and savings increase. Also, the banks extend their deposit loans and bank currency increases.[1]

How long this situation may last, and why it must come to an end, are questions to which no very simple or satisfactory answer can be given. Probably no two cases work out quite alike, for there are many ways in which the highly complicated arrangements of civilized industry may become deranged. In the various extensions of old enterprises and starting of new ones, there is always a danger that the due proportion of commodity to commodity may not be preserved. There is a danger that wages may be raised to such a level as to leave no sufficient margin for profits. There is a danger that the advance in prices, resulting from the increase of bank-currency, may give rise to excessive bringing in of goods from other places, and that an outward drain of specie to pay for them may bring the banks into difficulties. There is, finally, and above all, a danger that something may occur to shake the general confidence, — especially the confidence of the banks and other lending institutions in the ability of business men to repay their loans at maturity. If any of these things happen, the prosperous course of affairs usually comes to an end.

[1] Were it not for the artificial increase of loanable savings by the expansion of bank deposits, the rate of interest would rise higher at these seasons than it does. (See Chap. XV., § 7.)

We have seen how largely business is conducted on credit. Now the great centres of credit are the banks. When manufacturers or wholesale merchants sell goods on credit, they usually get the notes or bills they take of the buyers discounted at the banks. With the money thus obtained they meet their own business obligations.

If the banks begin to curtail their discounts, two important results follow. The men who fail to get loans must at once cut down their business operations, — they may even have to suspend business altogether. Secondly, the volume of bank currency becomes reduced, and there is no longer enough currency to match the existing scale of prices. The sale of goods begins to slacken. In a word, the season of prosperity is over.

5. Interest in Times of Commercial Crisis.—The extent and violence of the revulsion that follows depends on the circumstances of each case. Where the expansion of credit has been excessive, and there has been much speculative trading based upon it, many failures are sure to occur, and the revulsion may develop into a "panic." Where the over-use of credit has been less extreme, the immediate effects may not pass beyond a few failures, a general check to business activity, and a prevailing distress among business men.

In either case the first effect a business revulsion has on the demand for loans is greatly to increase it. Business men, who have counted on their ordinary "collections." for the means to meet their current obligations, suddenly find this resource failing them. They are compelled to seek in borrowing the means of maintaining their solvency. Some men also, who have money enough to meet their present needs, are apt to become apprehensive at such a time lest they may fail to get the means of meeting future obligations. They therefore try to borrow now enough to make the future secure.

This new and more or less nervous demand for loans is very different from the ordinary commercial demand. The object in view is not to make profit, but to avert business ruin. The demand is accordingly intense. In time of panic it becomes headlong and unreasoning.

While the demand for loans is thus more urgent than usual, the supply is usually much smaller than usual. The great lending institutions, having stretched their lending power to its utmost limit in the "flush" time just preceding the trouble, have little power to aid the business community with fresh loans. There is, therefore, a great dearth of loanable savings.[1]

[1] The law prohibits our National Banks from granting new loans whenever the reserve falls below the lawful ratio to the deposits [25 per cent. for city banks]. This restriction tends to aggravate the situation in time of crisis, because it forbids the banks to do the only thing that can restore confidence and save the business community from wide-spread ruin. In the crisis of 1873, the only one since the National Bank Act was adopted, the banks of New York combined their resources and broke the law, — granting new loans when their joint reserve was less than half of the legal requirement. The Bank of England, which is the centre of the English banking system, has learned by long experience that the best way to quiet a panic is to lend more freely than at ordinary times, — charging, however, high rates of interest. This course it follows freely, not being under any legal restriction as to its reserve, nor as to the rate of interest that

There is no assignable limit to the rise of the rate of interest in such a situation as this. Men have been known to pay two per cent. a day for short loans at such times.

When the crisis is past, the rate of interest suffers a sharp decline; and in the period of depression that always follows a commercial revulsion, interest is low. It is a time when business men find it very difficult to turn savings to profitable account. It is a time of falling prices, owing to the diminished supply of money. (See Chapter XIII.) Sales of goods, especially sales on credit, are fewer than before the crisis; and this means that there are fewer bills and notes offering to the banks for discount. Loanable savings accumulate on the hands of the great lenders. In order to attract borrowers, the rate of interest has to be placed very low, and even this usually fails of complete success.

These periods of depression are in turn succeeded by a time of increased confidence and reviving credit. Prices again come into accord with the supply of money, and money wages with both. A promise of reasonable profits again presents itself to those who have managing skill

may lawfully be charged for loans. The high rate checks merely nervous borrowing. The attempt so commonly made in old times, and still made in some of our States, to keep down the rate of interest by law, has never had the effect of protecting borrowers. The result is always to make the rate higher in time of trouble than it would be if no legal limit existed; for the lender charges more on account of the risk he runs in violating the law. All such laws are foolish and injurious,—as foolish and injurious as the kindred attempt sometimes made in former ages, to regulate prices by law.

and capital. The revival of industry means an increased demand for loans and a rise of the rate of interest. It remains high until a new revulsion overtakes the business world.

We thus see that the rate of interest moves in cycles, following pretty closely the profits of employers. When profits are high, interest is high also. When profits fall off, interest falls too.

6. Significance of the Prevailing Rate of Interest. — The fact that the rate of interest follows so closely the ups and downs of business profits, suggests that there is a connection between the ordinary rate of interest in a country and the general condition of its industry. The ordinary demand for loans is a good index of the ordinary rate of profits. If the demand be strong enough to sustain a high rate, we may safely infer that employers are making high profits. We can also infer that, in comparison with the productiveness of labor, real wages are low in the country.[1]

This does not mean that a high rate of interest is, in itself, a cause of high profits or of low wages. Wages depend on the volume of savings offered for labor, — no matter by whom offered nor at what rates of interest some part may have been borrowed. Profits, in turn, are the excess of product over wages, and this also is uninfluenced by the rate of interest. A high rate of interest is merely a sign and a result of the fact that

[1] It must be remembered that a rise of prices, without a corresponding rise of money wages, means a decline of real wages.

savings are small in proportion to the product of industry. Further, it tells us nothing as to the volume of savings, nor as to the productiveness of labor in the absolute sense. Interest may be high where industry is highly productive, because the spirit of saving is weak among those who have savable income. It may also be high where the productiveness of labor is low, because however strong the inclination to save, the amount of savable income is small. In the one case high interest and high wages prevail side by side; in the other case high interest and low wages, — wages being spoken of in the absolute sense in both cases.

The rate of interest, then, tells us nothing about the actual level of wages. But it does convey an intimation as to one of the factors on which wages depend, — namely, the strength of the saving spirit among the owners of wealth. Other things remaining unchanged, a decline of the ordinary rate of interest in a country implies a rise of wages; for it implies a greater readiness to save on the part of those who have savable income. The rise of wages and the decline of interest are both effects of the same cause; namely, the increase of saving. Other things being equal, then, a low customary rate of interest indicates a condition of things more favorable to the laborers than a high customary rate does. For employers the indication is reversed. Though they pay low rates for what they borrow, the situation implies that they are making low gains on all the savings they invest, — their own as well as what they borrow.

7. The Rate of Interest does not Depend on the Supply of Money. — It is common to suppose that a high rate of interest denotes a scarcity of money, and a low rate an abundance of it. This view is entirely erroneous, as there is no necessary connection between the rate of interest and the quantity of money in the country.

It is true, no doubt, that savings offering for loan are always in the form of money, but it is not true that all money is in the form of savings offering for loan. The money in general circulation does not help anybody to borrow, for the holders have no thought of lending it. It is only the money actually offering for loan that tells on the rate of interest.

If the bankers and other lenders should spend their money, instead of offering it for loan, there would be no less money in the country than there was before; but interest would rise very much all the same. In fact it would be an advantage if we could drop money out of view in this matter, and regard the offer of loans simply as the offer of savings in the form most convenient to borrowers. The newspaper phrase "money market," in the sense of loan market, is a standing misuse of words. The true money market is where money is actually sold, that is, where it is exchanged for goods, — not where loans are made in money to be repaid in the same article. If money did not exist, there would still be loaning of savings, and the rate of interest would depend on the same principles as at present.

The rate of interest, then, is no indication of the

quantity of money in the country. It only indicates whether a large or a small proportion of the existing stock is offering for loan. Accordingly increase of currency does not lower the rate of interest. If the currency were increased a hundred-fold, there would be a hundred times more dollars offering for loan no doubt, but the number of dollars needed by borrowers would be a hundred times greater also. As soon as prices and money-wages became adjusted to the new volume of currency, each borrower would need a hundred dollars to do the work previously done by one dollar. Loanable savings, in the sense of means to carry on business, would be no greater than before the increase of currency.

Looking at the case in another way, both loan and repayment consist of money. If dollars be cheapened for borrowing, they are also cheapened for repaying loans and for paying interest. A man can as easily pay five dollars for the use of a hundred when dollars are dollars, as when each dollar is only worth a cent. Both terms of the ratio are affected alike whenever dollars are cheapened by increase of currency.

A high rate of interest then is no sign of a scarcity of money, nor is a low rate a sign that the currency is large in amount. The high interest that prevails in a commercial crisis is due to the scarcity of loanable savings, not to the lack of money. The low rate that prevails during a depression is due to lack of demand for savings, not to any excess of money. In fact money never seems scarcer to the mass of men than in times of depression, when interest is at the lowest point.

An increase or decrease of the currency may temporarily affect the rate of interest, if it be unequally distributed between the money offering for loan and the money in ordinary circulation. For example, the importation of money from abroad always lowers the rate of interest for the time, but this is because the new money is imported by the bankers and brokers, and consequently presents itself, in the first instance, as an addition to the loanable savings. Every dollar of specie imported adds several dollars to the lending power of the banks. Similarly a drain of coin for exportation raises the rate of interest, because every dollar exported lessens by several dollars the ability of the banks to grant loans. But the effect in each case is only temporary. As soon as the increase or diminution has time to distribute itself equally over the whole volume of the currency, interest returns to its old rate.

If money be brought into a country in the pockets of travellers and emigrants, it has no tendency to lower the rate of interest even temporarily. It adds nothing to the loanable savings of the country. In fact, it would tend to raise the rate of interest until such time as a due proportion of the increase of currency should reach the reserves of the banks; for, by raising prices, it would stimulate borrowing without adding to the volume of loanable savings.

CHAPTER XXIII.

PRODUCTIVENESS OF NATURAL AGENTS.—ECONOMIC RENT.

1. Natural Advantages for Production. — We have already had occasion to note the fact that the natural advantages for the production of any given commodity are not everywhere equally good. In the production of coal, for example, one mine may have its deposits nearer to the surface, or in thicker seams, or of better quality than another. In the production of wheat, one piece of ground may have better qualities of soil, a better situation, or easier access to fertilizers than another; one region may have a more favorable climate than another. In the manufacture of paper, one mill-site may have a more convenient water supply, or easier access to fuel and other materials, than another. In all kinds of production, nearness to the market is an advantage. And so on.

Now these differences in natural agents have an important effect on the productiveness of the labor applied to each. Those who have possession of the better natural facilities in each industry, are obviously in a position to obtain greater results for a given outlay of labor and waiting than those who carry on the industry under less favorable conditions. If those who work under the relative disadvantage are able to earn ordinary wages and profits, the others must be getting something more than this.

2. Economic Rent.—We have here a case of what is called Economic Rent. The term is applied to every excess of product or of return that is due to the possession of superior natural agents, or of facilities that are not open to everybody.

In studying this subject the student must dismiss the idea that the word rent, as used in political economy, necessarily means a sum paid for the use of anything. The rent of which we speak here has no necessary reference to payments between men. It means simply an excess of product or of return that is due to the use of a natural advantage not open to all producers.

It makes no difference whether the person using the superior agent hires it of another or owns it himself. If he hires it of another, the rent may be claimed by that other. If he owns it himself, the rent is his own. In either case, the term denotes simply the extra product or income that is due to the natural advantage.

Again we use the word rent, in common speech, to denote payments for the use of property of any kind. We speak of the rent of a house, or of an office, or of a piano. But payments of this kind are never wholly economic rent. They are largely, and in cases like the rent of a piano, wholly compensation for outlay expended in getting the hired article produced. Real rent, when it takes the form of a payment, must be for the use of a natural agent such as land, mines, water-power, etc. And even in the case of natural agents, the payments called rent are seldom wholly rent in the economic sense. If, for example, a man hires land that has been improved, or a mine that is already in operation, a part of the payment, perhaps the greater part of it, is merely a return for the outlay made in preparing the land or the mine for use. Economic rent is not a compensation for labor and waiting. It has reference to the inherent qualities of the natural agent that yields it, regarded in its original or unimproved condition.

At the same time it is evident that the advantages of a particular spot of ground may depend greatly on the state of its surroundings; and these may be indefinitely improved by human exertions. Where the owner of land or any other natural agent gets the benefit of other men's outlay in this way, the gain to him is as if the whole advantage had been conferred by nature. To him, therefore, though not to the community as a whole, the results of the improvement are in the nature of rent. When, for example, a new railway is built, bringing cheap transportation to a region hitherto cut off from the great markets, the increased letting value of the lands may be regarded as rent for the land-owners, — provided, of course, that the road has been built without corresponding expense to them.

3. No-Rent Stage of Population. — Mere differences in the quality of natural agents of any kind would not of themselves give rise to rent. In fact, we shall presently see that any class of natural agents might yield rent even if they were all equal in point of advantages. The true cause of rent, in any class of these agents, is scarcity of them in comparison with the demand for the product obtained by means of them. This demand depends primarily on population.

Perhaps the easiest way of getting clear ideas regaiding rent is to consider what happens everywhere as population increases. Let us take the production of food as an example. We may assume that the people of a country are interested in obtaining their needful supply of food in the easiest way. While population is still small in proportion to the area of land, there is a wide option as to the portions to be tilled. We may assume that the farmers of the community can discern the lands that are most favorable for their purpose, and that these will be cultivated in preference to poorer lands.

While there are still lands enough and to spare of the best grade, the value of food of any kind will correspond to the cost of producing it on these lands. That is to say, its value will be such as to afford ordinary wages and profits for those who raise it, but nothing over as rent for the land. For if the value were high enough to yield a rent for the cultivated area, those who own other lands just as good would quickly bring theirs into use, and too much food would be raised. We have these two points to start with: first, that while population is small, the value of food is governed by the cost of raising it on the most advantageous lands; and, secondly, no agricultural land affords a rent.

4. Beginnings of Rent. — At a comparatively early stage in the growth of a community, there comes a time when the most advantageous portions of the soil are no longer sufficient to supply the wants of the whole population. When that point is reached and passed, two new facts appear. The first is that the value of food begins to stand at a higher level than before: the old price does not induce farmers to raise enough for all. The value rises until farmers find it profitable to till less advantageous lands than formerly, and it stays permanently higher than before. If it did not, the less advantageous lands would not be cultivated, and the needful addition to the supply of food would not be raised. Higher than is sufficient to afford ordinary wages and profits for raising the needful addition the value will not go, — at least so as to stay. If it did, more than enough of these lands would be cultivated and too much food would be raised. We can therefore say that the natural value of food will now be that which affords ordinary wages and profits for raising it on the less advantageous lands, with nothing over as rent for these lands. This is the first fact.

The second is, that those who till the best lands are now able to sell their crops for more than enough to afford them ordinary wages and profits. It is no harder than before to raise food from these lands; yet each bushel of the crop sells for more than before. The extra gain thus accruing from the higher natural value of the crop is rent. If the owners of these lands do not themselves till them, they may exact from the cultivators an annual payment roughly equal to this extra profit.

5. **Extension of the Rent Area.** — So long as there is enough land of the second grade in point of advantages to supply the whole demand for food, the necessary additions to the crop can be obtained without higher cost, the natural value of food will remain steady, and no lands of the second grade will afford rent, But when population grows to such a point that these lands no longer suffice, the supply of food again begins to be deficient, the value rises, and cultivation is extended to lands of the next inferior grade in point of advantages. In this new situation, the natural value will be that which affords ordinary wages and profits for cultivating the third grade of land, with nothing over for rent. This higher value gives rise to a further extra profit, or rent, from the cultivation of the best lands. It also makes the cultivation of the land of the second grade yield more than ordinary wages and profits: these lands also now afford a rent.

The rent of the better lands may be looked at in two different ways. Comparing the cultivation of rent-yielding land with all other ways of investing savings, we may regard rent simply as extra profit, due to the fact that the value of the product is higher than it needs to be in order to afford ordinary wages and profits to the producers using the better natural agents. This is the simpler view. Secondly, we may regard it as extra product over and above the amount obtainable from the least advantageous lands, by an equal outlay of labor. The two views come to the same result, since the cultivation of the poorest lands must yield ordinary profits. If the labor that produces one hundred bushels from the best lands produces only eighty bushels from the least advantageous lands in use, then twenty bushels in every one hundred produced from the best lands are economic rent. The extra profit coincides with the value of this extra product, or twenty bushels.

Every time that cultivation has to be extended to less productive lands than those already in use, the extra profit from cultivating. the better lands rises in two ways. The excess of product over the least productive land becomes greater than before; and, secondly, the value of each bushel must have become higher, or cultivation would not have been extended. Money rents, therefore, rise more rapidly than rent in kind.

6. General Principles of Rent. — Such is the nature and origin of economic rent. From a consideration of the facts in the case, we are enabled to lay down the following general principles:

(*a*) The poorest lands in cultivation at any time yield no rent, so long as there are other lands of the same quality lying unused. The latent competition of the unused portion keeps rent down to zero on the portions that happen to be in use.

(*b*) The natural value of food corresponds to the cost of procuring the most costly part of the whole needful supply, — that is to say, the portion raised on the poorest lands in cultivation.

(c) All lands superior to the poorest yield a rent proportioned to their superiority. This superiority is measured, in the case of any given land, by the difference between the cost of its crop and the cost of producing an equal quantity from the poorest land in cultivation.

7. Meaning of "best," "poorest," etc., as applied to Lands. — It is necessary to bear in mind that the superiority of one tract of land over another, as a source of supply for a given market, has reference to all the points of difference in the case. It would be a great mistake to think only of differences in fertility of soil, or to suppose that rent is ever a mere question of bushels to the acre. The superiority of the better land over the poorest may consist in easier access to fertilizers, greater nearness to the market, cheaper means of transportation, or in any other circumstance that affects the comparative cost of the product obtained from each, when brought to the place of consumption. The inferior land may be in itself more fertile than the other, but so much farther from the place where the food is needed that its superior fertility is more than counterbalanced by its disadvantageous position. Rent has reference to the whole advantage, and this is nearly always a compound result, or balance of many points of difference. The words "best," "poorest," etc., applied to lands in the discussion of rent, mean best or poorest taking all the circumstances into account.

Again the relative advantages of different lands change with changes in agricultural knowledge, improved implements, better facilities for transportation, etc. The lands that are best at one stage in a people's history may be far from being thought best at another stage. Lands are good or poor, in relation to rent, according as they are good or poor for the people who are to use them.

8. The Law of Diminishing Returns.— Our view of economic rent would be very incomplete if we left out of sight an important principle, not yet touched on, relative to the use of natural agents. The amount of product that may be obtained from any given supply or extent of these agents is not subject to any fixed or definite limit. The modes of using them are such that a greater or a less quantity of labor can be applied to them at will. The product may be increased by additional labor at any time. But here we come on the so-called law of diminishing returns. The increase of product is usually found not to be in proportion to the increase of labor.

The principle may be conveniently illustrated in the case of farming. In any given condition of the agricultural arts, the amount of food that may be raised from a given piece of land, has no fixed or inflexible limit, but depends on the amount of care and skill bestowed on the cultivation of it. It has been well said that no man has ever yet developed the full productive capacity of a single acre of ground. Whatever the crop already obtained, a larger crop may be obtained another year by more assiduous cultivation. The soil may always be more completely pulverized or further enriched; seeds may be more carefully selected or more favorably planted; more care may be given to weeding, watering, and otherwise nursing the growing plants, etc. Every such additional exertion causes the yield to be more copious in quantity or better in quality than before.

All this is quite true, and is most fortunate for the human family. But the fact remains that high cultivation is a costly method of adding to the food supply. The same labor expended in looser cultivation of a larger area would procure a much larger quantity of food.

In the application of labor to any given piece of land, there is a point of maximum return in proportion to labor expended. This point is found in a comparatively rough and hasty cultivation of it. Once the point of greatest proportional yield is reached, any additional expenditure of labor is met by the law of diminishing returns. Further, the higher the pressure already put upon the soil, the smaller the addition to the crop by any new application of labor.

These are principles applicable to all the extractive industries. The point of maximum return is, of course, a matter to be settled by practical experience in each case. It cannot be known by any general or abstract rule. Further, it is likely to vary with every new discovery or improvement in the mode of using natural agents of any kind. But for every natural agent, and for every state of the productive arts, there is such a point; and it is nearly always found to lie on the side of working it at a comparatively low pressure, rather than a high one.

Up to the point of diminishing returns it is obviously a saving of labor to draw needful food and materials from the agents already in use at any time, before extending the area of operations. We may therefore assume that, when new lands or new mines are brought into use, being naturally no better than the old ones, the point of diminishing returns has been reached upon those already in use.

Conversely, while there are still new lands open to cultivation, as good in all respects as the old, we may assume that additional supplies of food will ordinarily be obtained by extending the area of cultivation rather than by applying additional labor, with diminishing returns, to the area already in use.

When this is no longer possible, when all the most advantageous lands are already in use, there are obviously two ways of obtaining needful additions to the food supply, — the one by bringing less advantageous lands into use, the other by higher cultivation of the old lands. In practice, both methods are applied simultaneously. But in order that men shall raise additional supplies in either way, the value of food must rise sufficiently to make the raising of the increase a source of ordinary profit.

But, if the raising of the addition yields ordinary profits, it is clear that, taken as a whole, the crop raised on the old lands must yield more than the ordinary rate of profit. This extra profit is economic rent.

9. Rent not Due Solely to Differences in Lands. — We

now see that the existence of economic rent does not depend on the differences between lands in point of advantage. These differences simply give rise to one form or phase of rent; it may be that, in the long run, they will only cause differences in rent. Even if all lands were equal in point of advantage, rent would arise as soon as needful additions to the supply of food could be obtained only by cultivating some portions of the whole beyond the point of maximum return. The value of food would then have to be permanently higher than it was while increase could still be obtained by extending the area of cultivation,— enough higher to make the raising of the addition profitable in spite of its greater cost. The value of the whole crop would now follow the cost of the addition.

We must suppose that, at the old value, farming yielded ordinary profits. At the new value it does more than this, and the excess is economic rent. This point may be made more clear if we keep the increase distinct in our minds from the old amount of crop. Of course it is optional with individual farmers whether to raise the increase or not. If for any reason some of them should simply go on in the old way, raising only the old quantity from their lands, they would have the benefit of the higher value just the same. The addition to their returns would be economic rent. We may assume, however, that the opportunity to employ additional labor, with the prospect of ordinary profits on the additional outlay, would be generally taken advantage of by farmers.

This opportunity would be as good as those offered by the common run of industries in the country. It would simply yield no excess of profit.

10. Rent and the Price of Food.—If all the farming lands in the United States were cultivated by tenant-farmers, each paying a full rent for his land, would the rents thus paid cause the price of food to be higher than it now is? In countries where the farms are held at a rent, would the price of food be lowered if the landlords should make a present of the farms to the tenants?

These are questions which may seem, at first sight, to require an affirmative answer. But anybody who considers carefully the nature of economic rent ought to have no difficulty in seeing that both questions must be answered in the negative.

Where the food supply is drawn from lands differing in point of advantages, we have seen that the cost of procuring it from the least advantageous lands fixes the natural value of the whole supply. We have also seen that the least advantageous land yields no rent. It follows that rents have nothing to do with settling the value or the price of food. If all rents were remitted to the tillers of the better lands, this would not alter in the least the cost of procuring food from the poorest lands. If the value should fall, this portion of the supply could no longer be raised with a profit, and consequently would cease to be raised at all. So that if the price should fall, it would have to rise again. The tenants of the better lands, whose rents are remitted, would find no greater difficulty than before in disposing of their whole crop at the old price. To offer it for less because now they "could afford" to do so, would simply be to hand over to sharper men gains that were fairly their own. We may safely hold that they would make no such mistake, and that even if they did, the lowered price would not last many days.

Rent as a payment to the owner of a natural agent by the employer using it, may well enough be regarded as a part of the cost to the latter of the product he obtains from it: the more he pays in any given case the less his profit. But this is only half of the case. The reason why the employer pays rent is the fact that he gets the use of a corresponding advantage. For the special item of rent in his outlay, he expects to have an equivalent special item in his return, — namely, the economic rent yielded by the natural agent of which he has the use.

Of the true cost of production that fixes the value of the commodity, it ought to be clear that rent is no part. The cost to which the value must conform is that of the last needful addition to the supply. The last needful addition, whether obtained by extending cultivation to poorer lands or by higher cultivation of the lands already in use, is obtained free of rent. We conclude, then, that even if all rents, in the sense of payments, were remitted, economic rent would still continue to accrue, and would simply remain, as extra profit, in the pockets of the employers having the use of the superior natural agents.

We see then that, instead of rent causing the product

to have a high value, it is rather the high value that makes the rent possible. The high value and the rent that goes with it are both due to the scarcity of the natural agent (or of the superior portions of it) in comparison with the demand for its product. The strong demand keeps the value of the product above the point that would correspond to the cost of producing it under the most favorable conditions: that is to say, the cost of obtaining it from the most productive sources within reach, by applying labor to them up to, but not beyond, the point of highest proportional return. As soon as value is such that production from any natural agent can be pushed beyond this point, with ordinary profit, that natural agent has begun to yield rent. So that rent follows value, not value rent.[1]

[1] There is, however, one form of rent of which this is hardly true, at least to the full extent. I refer to the rent of land used for manufacturing purposes in and about cities. To a considerable extent these rents are due, not to any peculiar advantage possessed by the land, in and of itself, for the purposes to which it is applied, but to the fact that it could be let at the same rent for other purposes. Many kinds of manufacture can hardly be carried on, at least on the modern scale, at a distance from the great centres of population and commerce. The advantage lies as much in the mere aggregation of men as in the natural fitness of the place. But the aggregation of men causes the land occupied by the necessary buildings and the dwellings of the workmen, to be at a scarcity value and to command a considerable rent. For this rent, so far as it is unavoidable, the employer and his laborers must be compensated in the value of their product. Of course any rent of manufacturing sites that is due to special natural advantage for the purpose, follows the ordinary rule, — being offset by the extra return which the advantage brings.

11. Improvements in Farming Lessen Rents.— Rent, as we have seen, depends immediately on the value of farm produce. Every rise of natural value implies a rise of rents. Railways lessen rents in the crowded portions of the world, by supplying the inhabitants with cheaper food. Any other agency that tends to lower the value of farm produce has the same tendency to reduce rent.

Of course, therefore, all agricultural improvements have this tendency. They lessen the cost of food, just as inventions in manufacturing lessen the cost of manufactured goods. But their action, especially in its bearing on rent, is less simple than that of improvements in manufacturing. They are peculiar, in that they affect the value of food, and thereby the rents of the better lands, not in proportion to their effect on agriculture as a whole, but in proportion to their effect on the cost of that part of the necessary food supply, which is most difficult to procure.

Agricultural improvements are of two general classes. Those of one class save labor in farming, but add nothing to the crop; for example, the gang-plough or the reaping-machine. Those of the other class add to the productiveness of the land, but without lessening the labor required for cultivating a given area; for example, the introduction of rotation of crops or the discovery of new fertilizers. Labor-saving machines tend to lower the value of food simply in the ratio in which they lessen the cost of raising it on the least advantageous lands in use. Improvements of the second kind have this effect also;

but they may go farther and make the cultivation of the poorest lands needless. By increasing the crop from a given area, they may make a smaller area sufficient. Any improvement which should do this would lower the value of food, and consequently rent, in two distinct ways: first, by making a naturally better land the regulator of cost; secondly, by increasing the productiveness of this land.

By way of illustration, let us suppose the supply of food for a community is drawn from three grades of land; and that the quantity of labor which produces ten bushels from the poorest grade, produces twelve and fifteen bushels from the other two grades respectively. Of course, the value must be such as to make ten bushels sufficient to afford ordinary wages and profits for this labor. That being so, the price of two bushels in every twelve, or one-sixth of the crop, raised on the second grade of land is rent; and the same of every third bushel raised on the best grade. If the price be one dollar a bushel, there is a rent of two dollars for every twelve bushels raised on the second grade, and five dollars for every fifteen bushels raised on the best grade.

If now a labor-saving improvement lessens by one-fifth the outlay required for raising these quantities, it will lower the price to eighty cents a bushel; the money rent of the second grade will fall to a dollar and sixty cents for every twelve bushels produced from it; and that of the best grade to four dollars for every fifteen bushels produced from it. The saving in outlay is the same for all three grades (say two dollars); but the fall of price affects the better lands more heavily than the poorest, because their crop is greater.

If, instead of a labor-saving improvement, a new fertilizer be discovered that increases by say one-third the productiveness of labor applied to agriculture, the result may be to make the cultivation of the poorest grade no longer necessary. In that case the value will fall to correspond with the cost of producing food, with the aid of the new fertilizer, from the second grade of land.[1] The labor that previously raised twelve bushels on this land will now raise sixteen; but the sixteen bushels will have the same price that ten had previously; namely $10, or 62½ cents a bushel. This leaves nothing over as rent. The same quantity of labor will now raise twenty bushels on the best land; but the price of sixteen bushels will be required to pay ordinary wages and profits, leaving only the new reduced price of four bushels for rent. The rent of the second grade disappears entirely, and that of the best lands is reduced to one-half of the old amount, namely $2.50, for the given outlay of labor.

It is well to note that the fall of rent in this case is not due to the fact that the poorest land ceases to be cultivated. The fall of rent and the abandonment of the poorest lands are both effects of the same cause, namely, the decreased value of food. The same effects would follow from an equal fall in value caused by cheapened

[1] Strictly this result requires that not all even of the second grade shall be needed for cultivation.

importation of food from other regions. In fact, it must be said of all strictly agricultural improvements that they have seldom had in practice the effect of actually lowering the value of farm products. The art of tillage has undoubtedly made progress; but in comparison with manufacturing and transportation the progress has been very slow. The improvements in farming would not, of themselves, have done more than to retard the rise of rents. The great and striking effects on the value of farm products, and consequently on rents, have been brought about by the wonderful cheapening of transportation.

12. Railways and Rent. — The application of steam to transportation has kept down the value of food in two ways: first, by enabling people to move away easily and cheaply from the crowded parts of the world to regions where population is sparse; secondly, by enabling those who remain in the thickly peopled parts, to draw their food and materials from distant places at slight cost. The first of these effects has been spoken of already. The second is equally important.

The great abundance of fertile land in America would not keep the value of farm products down in all parts even of our country, if it were not possible to carry the product with little labor from the western farms to the crowded districts of the centre and East. Farm products are bulky and heavy. Without powerful means of transportation they could not be moved far except at great cost.

This was the ordinary case in old times. Before the

introduction of canals and railways, it was costly and difficult to carry things from one place to another, except where transportation by sea or river was possible. To transport wheat even a hundred miles, by means of draught animals, added enormously to its cost. Consequently, in a region of dense population, farming lands might yield a considerable rent, even though abundant land could be obtained rent free in regions comparatively near.

But the improvements in transportation made in the last fifty years have changed all this. It is now possible to carry food and other products of labor long distances at slight cost. A barrel of flour is now carried one thousand miles by land for the sum of one dollar. The application of steam to transportation, both by land and by water, has in effect brought the most distant places very close together for purposes of exchange.[1]

The effect on agricultural rents, especially in the Old World, has been very marked. Wheat may now be carried from Dakota to London for less than it cost formerly to carry it from the centre of England. Agricultural rents have therefore declined very much in the British Islands, and are likely to decline still farther. Even in the United States the cheapening of transportation has produced effects hardly less striking on the value of lands in the older States. Many lands that

[1] Mr. Edward Atkinson computes that the labor of one man is now sufficient to transport the wheat supply for a thousand persons from Dakota to New York, a distance of 1700 miles.— *Distribution of Products*, page 286.

formerly yielded a good, if not a bountiful, return to savings expended upon them, have now quite fallen out of cultivation. The opening up of the great West has so lowered the value of farm produce that there is little profit to be made now in ordinary farming in the East.

The present condition of things will last until the virgin soils of the West and North-west have been so far exhausted, that the manuring and other burdensome processes necessary in the older countries have to be resorted to. When that time comes rents will begin to rise again.

It remains only to add the obvious remark that a decline in the value of farm products caused by cheapened importation, is much more disastrous to agricultural rent than a decline caused by home improvements in agriculture. In the latter case, the better lands have at least the benefit of the improvement as a partial offset to the fall in value; but in the former case the fall in value is wholly at the expense of the landlords. Thus, if the fall to eighty cents, spoken of on page 302, were caused by cheapened importation, the rent of the best land would fall to two dollars instead of four.

13. Rent of Building Lands.—City rents are more conspicuous in this country than agricultural rents. The modern tendency of population is toward the towns, and the growth of building rents is correspondingly rapid. The sum paid for the use of a building in a city consists of two parts. One part is simply a payment for the use of the building itself, which is a product of labor.

The other part is for the use of the land on which the building stands. The first is mainly replacement of savings with interest thereon; the second is true rent.

The rent of city lots is determined by the same general principles as the rent of agricultural lands. The chief difference is that here we start usually from a condition in which the land is already yielding rent for agricultural purposes. Of course, land will not be turned into building lots until there is a prospect of its yielding somewhat better returns than it yields as farming land.

The new building lots in the outskirts of a city may be regarded as having their rent determined roughly by the agricultural rent of the land. As quickly as there is a gain to be made by converting farming land into building lots, we may assume that the conversion will ordinarily be made. At the meeting line of the two kinds the difference of rents must always be slight.

Building lots nearer to the centre of the town have of course many advantages for business purposes over these newly-made lots. The economic rent of each more central lot is equal to the rent of an equal area in the outskirts, plus the equivalent of its special advantages over the latter. Since the rent of newly-converted lots must usually be small, we may say for brevity that the rent of central lots is a sum equivalent to their superiority, for the uses to which they are put, over equal areas in the outskirts.

This is a question of business advantage mainly. Other things being equal, the merchant who has his store in the crowded thoroughfare can sell much more than the one who has his store in a remote corner of the town. Without charging higher prices, he can make much larger profits.

If he does not own the ground he occupies, the owner may exact as rent the full equivalent, in the view of business men, of this special advantage. The competition of business men for the possession of the best sites may safely be counted on to enable him to do this. Thus we have for the rent of business sites in cities the same rule of extra profits that we found to apply in agricultural rents.

14. Rent of City Lots used for Dwellings. — In the case of city lots used as sites for dwellings, we cannot lay down any so definite measure of rent as in the case of business sites. Of course, lots that possess special advantages for business purposes are not likely to be let for residences at a lower rent than could be obtained for them, if applied to the other use. Usually, however, dwellings and business edifices occupy separate quarters of the city; so that the rule of extra profit can hardly be applied universally as the regulator of city rents.

In the case of lands adapted, or held to be adapted, for dwellings only, rent depends on the demand. The question is simply how much extra the people are willing to pay for the privilege of living in the most desirable streets or neighborhoods. Here, as in the case of lots used for business purposes, we take the lands in the outskirts of the city as our starting-point. Those lands may be hired, as sites for dwellings, for about the same rent as they yield in agriculture. The better sites will have their excess of rent above these, set by the general estimate of the social and other advantages of living upon them. If there are a hundred of the best sites, the rent of them will be set at such an amount as a hundred persons, and only a hundred, can be found to pay. If later the number of persons willing to pay this amount of rent should increase, then the rent of these lots will rise to a point at which only one hundred applicants for them can be found.

Cities are becoming rather centres of trade than places of residence. The railways enable men whose work lies in the city, to have their homes miles away in the country. This fact checks the rise of house-rent in the cities.

15. The Price of Land. — Land that yields rent, or is expected to do so, may evidently be bought as a mode of investing savings. The price, through the competition of buyers, tends to be equal to the present worth of the expected rent. That is to say, it tends to be such a sum as puts the purchase on a level, in the opinion of investors, with other modes of getting interest on savings. The price of any piece of ground depends, therefore, on two things: namely, the amount of rent it is expected to yield; and, secondly, the prevailing rate of interest on other investments. The lower the rate of interest the higher the price of land is.

Since the future rent is always uncertain, dealings in land are apt to be speculative. The price changes with every change in the general opinion as to the future course of the rent.

CHAPTER XXIV.

CONSEQUENCES OF DIMINISHING RETURNS.

1. Effect of Diminishing Returns on Wages and Profits. — The law of diminishing returns has an obvious bearing on the course of wages and profits in a country as its population increases in numbers. When once the population has reached the stage at which the best sources of food and materials, worked at their point of maximum return, are no longer sufficient to supply the whole demand, individual wages or profits, or both, must tend to decline. Further additions to the number of producers are not followed by corresponding additions to the general product of industry, unless the natural tendency to diminishing returns in the extractive industries, be offset by increased productiveness of labor in other ways.

Of course the falling off in proportional return does not begin simultaneously in all the extractive industries. The different kinds of natural wealth are nowhere in equal ratio to the human need of them. The resources of some kinds may be practically unlimited; but there are others that are never so. Among the latter must be placed the most productive sources of the better varieties of food, fuel, and clothing, — the articles of prime necessity for everybody. In the production of these the point of diminishing returns is reached at a comparatively early stage in the growth of population.

Now, in regions where this stage has been passed, the opportunities for making profit at any given rate of wages are governed, not by the general or average productiveness of labor, but by its productiveness under the conditions which have to be faced in obtaining the last additions to the product of industry. This is a point of great importance in relation to wages and profits in a country where increase of population is attended by diminishing returns. The amount a given number of additional laborers can add to the product of industry constitutes the inducement open to employers for engaging their services. No matter how much other men are producing, the new-comers must stand on the basis of the addition their own exertions can make to the general product.

Compelled by the nature of the case to apply their labor to inferior natural agents, or under less favorable conditions than the previous laborers have done, they cannot produce as much as the same number produced previously. It follows that either their wages, or the profits of their employers, must be less than those previously earned by equally capable producers.

But this is only a small part of the case. Under freedom of competition, there cannot be one level of wages and profits for the former inhabitants, and another lower level for the additional producers. The wages of all equally capable laborers, and the opportunities for profit open to all employers, must be roughly equal. Equality, in this case, is brought about by a decline of all wages and profits to the level of those obtainable by the additional laborers and their employers.

What is lost by the general body of producers in this way goes as rent, to the owners of the better natural agents. Competition forces the employers who have the use of the better opportunities for production, to pay over to the owners of them an amount roughly equivalent to the economic rent, or excess of product due to the special advantage in each case.

For example, let us suppose a country has reached the stage of diminishing returns in her chief extractive industries, with a population of twenty millions, and that the population goes on increasing until it reaches twenty-five millions. The effect on wages, profits, and rents will depend on the extent to which say the last million falls short of adding to the product of industry as much as each of the original twenty millions produced. Suppose they add only nine-tenths as much, then it is, for the employers of labor, precisely as if the whole twenty-five millions produced only twenty-five times as much as this last. Whatever they do in fact produce beyond this may be claimed by the owners of the natural agents as rent. While the number of laborers has increased in the ratio of $20 : 25$, the product from which profits must be drawn has risen only in the ratio of $20 : 22\frac{1}{2}$, (*i. e.* $20 : 25 \times \frac{9}{10}$). The balance, whatever its amount, is rent.

2. Diminishing Returns Counteracted by Improvements. — It is obvious that industrial improvements of every kind have an effect precisely the opposite of that just considered. Every invention or discovery that enables us to produce a greater quantity of any commodity by a given amount of labor, makes the industry of the community more productive than it was before, and thus tends to raise the wages and profits of producers.

The same effect is produced, in the crowded portions of the world, by the importation of cheap food and materials from other countries. This lessens the pressure on the home sources of supply, and thus prevents the rise of rents and the decline of wages and profits as the population increases. Herein lies, for the crowded parts of all countries, the great importance of improvements that cheapen transportation.

We see, then, that the actual course of industrial returns in a country, as its population grows, depends on the question whether the falling off in the proportional yield of labor used in its extractive industries is, or is not, fully counterbalanced by improvements in its industries as a whole.

The rapid and wonderful improvements of the past hundred years have apparently more than counterbalanced the diminishing returns from the chief natural agents, — giving us for the time an increased return for labor and waiting. Whether this can continue much longer, in the face of the enormous increase of population that is going on in the world, is at least open to serious doubt. Discoveries and inventions are striking in their effects; but they are somewhat fitful and uncertain in their coming, and each of them is limited in application. The action of diminishing returns, on the other hand, though silent and gradual, is certain, universal, and always progressive. That it must in the end prevail over human ingenuity hardly admits of a doubt.[1]

3. Checks on Increase of Population. — Reason tells us that there is a limit to the number of inhabitants the world, with its limited resources, can sustain. That we cannot now say definitely what the limit is, is no ground for denying its existence. It is hardly credible that a thousand persons can ever find sustenance in the average space now occupied by one. It is quite incredible that a million should ever do so.

Now the limit to increase of population will be reached, not by a sudden shock, but by the cumulative action of diminishing returns. The precise mode in which the arrest of increase will come about, will depend, in each country, on the behavior of the inhabitants. There are two alternatives, — the number of births may diminish, or the number of deaths may increase.

[1] Those who argue the contrary forget how largely the improved returns of recent times are due to mere redistribution of population by emigration to new countries, and to cheapening of transportation. These are devices that must exhaust their benefits comparatively soon. There are no more New Worlds to be opened up. When America and Australia become as thickly peopled as England and Belgium, cheap transportation will be of comparatively little avail as a means of counteracting the effects of diminishing returns in the older countries.

The first of these is called the "prudential check on population." It is a check that is already operative in every civilized community. It is merely that feeling of common prudence and regard for the future, which prevents intelligent young people from assuming the care of families, without having the means to provide an adequate support for them. As earnings fall off through the action of diminishing returns, this motive may be counted on to restrict more and more the number of births in every community where the mass of the people are governed by prudence and forethought.

This check evidently rests on the standard of living which people are accustomed to, or which prevails in the social group to which they belong. Few persons will lightly adopt a course that is sure to entail loss of accustomed comforts or of social standing. The higher the standard of living among the mass of a country's inhabitants, the slower will be the increase of its numbers and the smaller its eventual population.

This principle has an obvious connection with the law of wages. It means that the general level of wages in each country depends, in the long run, on the degree of self-control practiced by the bulk of its people. Low wages are the inevitable result of reckless increase of numbers; high wages are inseparable from restraints on increase. Nothing can prevent wages from eventually reaching that level, be it high or low, which the mass of the laborers themselves look upon as adequate for the support of a family.

The second or "positive" check on increase of population comes into play wherever the first does not exist, or has proved too weak. The prudential check acts through fear of want; this one acts through want itself. Whereever more people are born than can find proper nourishment and shelter, the death-rate rises. A decreasing proportion of those that are born reach maturity. Diseases of all kinds multiply, finding ready lodgement and easy victims among the badly housed, ill-clad, and meanly nourished masses of poor. Famines occur from time to time, with pestilence following, to carry off the redundant population that other destroying agencies have spared.

These positive checks on increase overtake men, in common with the lower animals, wherever they multiply with brutish disregard of consequences. It is these checks that, in the last resort, keep down all forms of animal life on the earth. Were it not for the attacks of enemies, and the lack of suitable nourishment, there is no animal that could not long since have filled with its increase every inch of the habitable globe. Men have two points of great superiority over the lower animals: they have no living enemies to fear except one another, and they can do much to improve their surroundings. But without due restraint on increase, they eventually expose themselves to limiting forces no less terrible and effective than those that restrict lower forms of life.

These doctrines, as to the ultimate limits of population, are known as Malthusianism, from the name of

Mr. Malthus, the economist who first expounded them. They have been frequently controverted, especially by persons who did not clearly understand them; but they seem to rest on very solid foundations.[1]

4. Sharing of the Loss from Diminishing Returns.—The division, between laborers and employers, of the loss from diminishing returns, follows the principles stated in Chapter XVIII. The question is how the increase of savings, in the sense of real savings, compares with the increase of laborers seeking employment. If savings, measured in the things that laborers need, increase as fast as the number of laborers, the whole loss falls on profits. So far, however, as savings fall short of keeping

[1] It is important to remember that, at any given rate of increase, the absolute growth of numbers in a country becomes more and more rapid as time goes on. If, for example, the United States, starting with a population of sixty millions, were to go on doubling its numbers every thirty-three years, the absolute increase in each successive period would be as follows:—

	Increase.	Population at end of period.
First period	60,000,000	120,000,000
Second period	120,000,000	240,000,000
Third period	240,000,000	480,000,000
Fourth period	480,000,000	960,000,000

In the ninth period (end of three hundred years), the increase would be 15,360,000,000, bringing the total population up to 30,720,000,000. In the thirtieth period (end of one thousand years), the increase would be 32,212,254,720,000,000, bringing the total population up to 64,424,509,440,000,000. It is easy to see that a uniform rate of increase must in the end make the mere question of standing-room a matter of difficulty,—to say nothing as to the means of supporting life. Checks on the rate of increase, and eventual arrest of all increase, would thus seem to be a physical necessity.

pace with the increase of laborers, the loss is thrown on wages.

In order that savings shall increase as fast as laborers, it is obviously necessary that, as time goes on, an increasing proportion of all that is produced shall be saved for investment, — and this in spite of the declining returns. This would imply that profits were high at the outset, and that the spirit of saving is steadily growing. Where these conditions are fulfilled, the loss from diminishing returns may fall for generation's mainly, or even wholly, on the employing class. But of course there is a limit, beyond which the decline of profits could not go without arresting increase of savings. There is a necessary rate below which even the previous volume of savings would not be maintained. As this point is approached, the loss from increased pressure on natural agents must fall more and more on the laborers.

It is well to note the precise mode in which diminishing returns take effect on wages. The two principal items in the expenses of a laborer's family namely, tenement and table, are precisely the things that are most affected by increase of population. At any given scale of money-wages, a rise in house-rents and in the price of food leaves a smaller amount for spending in other ways. Unless, therefore, other things are greatly cheapened, or money-wages rise, it becomes impossible for a laborer to maintain a family in the former degree of comfort. Where this occurs, the decline of real wages may call into greater activity the prudential check on increase of numbers. If it does, the ratio of money-savings to the number of laborers will gradually change in favor of the laborers, and real wages will rise again. If it does not, the result will be a permanent and progressive lowering of the condition of laborers and their families.[1]

The whole matter depends, then, on the working of the principles that govern savings on the one hand, and growth of population on the other. Every circumstance that favors increase of savings, or repression of the numbers seeking employment, tends to preserve the mass of mankind from loss of earnings by reason of diminishing returns from natural agents.

5. Results Modified by use of Rents in Paying Wages. — On the side of savings there is one further circumstance to be considered. There is one kind of income that increases as the proportional return for labor diminishes. The rise of economic rent makes the behavior of the rent-receiving class an element of considerable and ever-growing importance, in determining the course of wages. Though rent must be deducted from the product of industry when the question is to find the profits on past outlay, it remains a part of the product of industry when the question is of present resources for paying wages. Income from rent may be saved and used in

[1] Possible rise in the cost of gold is intentionally omitted. It would doubtless be more accurate, though less clear, to state the principle thus: When, taken as a whole, the things constituting real wages become more costly, real wages must decline, unless an increased proportion of the currency, in its circuit, be turned into money-wages. See p. 200, top.

hiring laborers as readily as income of any other kind. Just as in the case of profits, what is lost to the laborers through rent, is not the amount the landlords receive, but the amount they consume.

Here, then, is a source from which increase of savings may be looked for as population increases. It is probable that rent-receivers spend more freely on themselves than other classes; but they are not exempt from the common eagerness for increase of wealth. Even in countries where they form a separate class, mostly abstaining from active business, their savings have a great influence in sustaining the rate of wages in the face of diminished returns. Further, as a class, landlords usually employ many servants and personal attendants, — so that a part even of their spendings are in aid of wages. It would therefore be a great mistake to suppose that whatever accrues as rent, out of the current product of industry, is thereby withdrawn from the support of laborers. It may be paid to them for their help in the production of commodities that are still in the future, or for any of those non-productive services that rent-receivers so commonly demand.

This, however, does not invalidate the principle stated in § 1. It does not alter the law of diminishing returns. It merely tempers, at any given time, the action of the law in the case of wages. It means simply that, as population increases, the source of wages does not contract, relatively to the number of laborers, as rapidly as the returns for additional labor fall off. Where economic rent exists, the industrial product from which wages may be drawn, exceeds, by the amount of the rent, the product on which employers must rely for their profits.

The situation is, therefore, more favorable for the laborers than it would be if all the natural agents were as poor as the poorest in use. But it is correspondingly less favorable for the employers. So far as rents are turned into wages, thus keeping wages up in spite of diminishing returns, the result is to throw the brunt of the loss on profits. The consequent decline of profits must eventually check the aggregate flow of savings from all sources. The conversion of rent into wages cannot, therefore, in the long run, protect the laborers from the consequences of undue increase. It may postpone, but it cannot prevent, the ultimate fall of wages. Its eventual effect may only be to afford the reduced scale of wages to a larger population than could find employment, even at that rate, if the owners of the better natural agents consumed the whole rent themselves in the form of luxurious commodities.

QUESTIONS AND EXERCISES.

1. What circumstances determine the normal level of wages in a community?

2. Why are wages higher in some countries than in others?

3. Show that real wages depend on the relative height of money-wages and prices (including house-rents).

4. If, for the coming year, all persons who have money to spare should spend it in buying goods for their own use, what would the effect be on wages?

5. What are the grounds for holding that the general level of wages cannot be raised by strikes?

6. Mention circumstances that would be likely to depress market wages below the normal level, and describe the process of recovery in such a case.

7. In what sense do the wages of the present time depend on past savings?

8. How do labor-saving inventions affect wages?

9. Why is it difficult to ascertain the precise rate of profits at any time?

10. What do the aggregate profits of the whole body of employers depend on?

11. Show that aggregate profits may rise without a fall of real wages, and that real wages may rise without a fall of profits.

12. Name the three principal factors on which the profits of the individual employer depend. Show how a change in any one of these affects his profits.

13. How do you account for the notable differences in the profits of individual employers?

14. Distinguish between economic rent and rent in the popular sense. Is the rent of a city house economic?

15. How do railroads affect rents?

16. Explain carefully the connection between rent of land and the price of food?

17. What is meant by the law of diminishing returns?

18. What is the error in assuming that wages may be discovered at any time by deducting profits and rent from the product of industry? What would the remainder be?

19. On what does the normal rate of interest depend? Is it affected by changes in the supply of money? Mention circumstances that cause the market rate of interest to be high.

20. What does the price of land depend on? Why is it more variable than other prices?

CHAPTER XXV.

EXCHANGE OF PRODUCTS BETWEEN SEPARATE COMMUNITIES, OR INTERNATIONAL TRADE.

We must now enter upon a subject involving very considerable difficulties in itself, and made doubly difficult by the apparently endless controversies that are connected with it. It is needless to associate this little book with one side or the other in the issue between Free Trade and Protection. But the exchange of products between whole communities of men is too interesting and important to be passed over without discussion in any general study of economics. I propose, therefore, to set down in this chapter certain general truths and elementary facts in connection with foreign trade, as to which I suppose all intelligent men would agree in substance, however much they might differ in their ways of interpreting them. In the next chapter I shall try to state, as briefly and impartially as I can, the two opposing views as to the benefits, or the injurious effects, of unrestricted foreign trade.

1. **International Trade an Exchanging of Products.** — The first thing to note is, that trade between communities, like all other trade, is always at bottom an exchanging of products. The exchange is disguised, but less so

than in the case of exchanges within each community. It is not involved with the payment of wages. But money is employed with the same complicating effect. The importation of goods is carried on by a different set of men from those who carry on the exportation of goods. Again, the goods exported are not always sent to the place from which the imports come. Yet it is easy to demonstrate that every country pays for its imports by means of exports; and this not in any loose or half figurative sense, but in strict and literal fact.

In the trade between communities a special form of paper currency is used, which has not yet been spoken of, — namely, Bills of Exchange or Drafts. The nature and use of bills of exchange may best be seen from an example. Suppose A. B. of New York sends a cargo of wheat to C. D. in Liverpool, he does not ordinarily wait for C. D. to send him money in return. Instead of this he draws a bill on C. D. for the amount, and sells it to an exchange broker,[1] getting in this way the means

[1] Exchange brokers are a class of bankers who buy and sell bills of exchange. In this country the ordinary banks act as exchange brokers. Bills of exchange vary in form. They differ from checks in two important particulars: they may be drawn on any person who owes money to another; and the time for making the payment (that is to say, whether "at sight" or in a certain number of days "after sight") is always mentioned in the bill. The following specimen will serve to show how A. B. draws on C. D. in favor of Smith, Jones & Co., the purchasing brokers:

Exchange for £1000.   NEW YORK, January 2, 1889.

Sixty days after sight pay to the order of Smith, Jones & Co. one thousand pounds sterling, for value received, and charge the same to account of

  To C. D., Liverpool, England.   A. B.

to buy a fresh cargo. The broker forwards the bill to his London "correspondent," who attends to the collection and places the amount to the broker's credit.

Similarly, when E. F. of New York imports a cargo of steel rails from G. H. in Birmingham, he does not forward cash in return, but goes to the broker for a bill. The broker sells him a bill on his London "correspondent." This is sent to G. H., who readily obtains the money for his steel rails by means of it.

Thus the bill-brokers manage the collections for goods exported and make the payments for goods imported. They are able to do this very cheaply, because they can ordinarily use the proceeds of the bills they buy from exporters, to meet the bills they sell to importers. For example, in the case given above, the money collected from C. D. is simply turned over to G. H. In this way the wheat sent out by A. B. is made to pay for the steel rails imported by E. F. The bill-brokers contrive very easily to balance off all our obligations to the various countries of Europe against their indebtedness to us. In this way hundreds of millions' worth of goods may be paid for without the actual sending of a single dollar. There could be no clearer proof needed to show that international trade is strictly an exchange of products.

2. The Rate of Exchange. — The exchange-brokers make their profit by charging a little more for the bills they sell than they pay for the bills they buy. Both their buying price and their selling price may rise or fall together. Exchange on foreign countries may be at a premium or at a discount, depending on the relative demand and supply of bills.

When exports of merchandise exceed imports, the bills brought to the brokers by the exporters exceed in amount those called for by the importers, — the supply exceeds the demand. In this situation the price falls. In the reverse case, — that is, when imports exceed exports, — importers demand more bills of the brokers than exporters are bringing to them for sale, and the price of bills rises.

Whatever the relative demand and supply of commercial bills, the brokers stand ready to buy all that are offered to them, and to sell as many as are called for. But when they sell faster than they buy, they do so at the risk of having to bear the expense of sending over gold to cover the balance; for, just as in the case of a private person drawing on a bank, they must not overdraw their account with the foreign banker on whom they sell bills. In the reverse case, they buy bills with the certain prospect of having to bring the proceeds home. They cannot go on indefinitely paying out money at home for the right to collect money abroad, without some way of replenishing their home supply. But if customers are lacking for the money they have to their credit abroad, they can at least bring it home for use in buying more bills. The cost of thus sending money in the one case, and of bringing it in the other, gives the limit of the rise and fall of the price of exchange.

In the case of bills on England, par of exchange is

$4.86⅔ = £1. Now brokers can profitably send gold to England and sell bills against it at the rate of about $4.89½ for the pound. This is therefore the upper limit of the premium they can charge for "sight" bills. Exchange is then said to be at the "shipping point." In this situation, the exporter is able to get a premium (about $4.88 for £1) when he sells his bill to the brokers. (Of course bills that are not payable at sight are always lower than "sight" bills.)

There is a corresponding lower limit of the rate for "sight" bills, which depends on the cost of bringing over actual money. Brokers can make a fair profit by buying bills at $4.83 for £1, even if the only use they can find for the proceeds is to have the money brought to America. This, therefore, is the gold-importing point, or lower limit of the rate of exchange on England.

It is to be remembered that gold passes from country to country simply by weight, even although it be in the form of coins. When we say that $4.86⅔ equals the English pound, the meaning is that this is the relative weight of pure gold in the dollar and the sovereign. Incidentally, it is worth noting that bankers do not always send to the mint the foreign coins they import. It may be an advantage presently to have gold in the form of foreign coin for sending back, when the balance of exchange turns the other way.

To be accurate, the balance of imports and exports is only the chief and usual occasion for the movement of money between countries. Every other business relation of each country to other countries must come into the account and help to determine the rate of exchange. For example, if foreign capitalists invest in our railroads or buy our government bonds, we may have a balance of imports over exports equal to the sum they invest, without causing gold to be sent abroad. On the other hand, if we have to pay ten millions annually as interest to foreign holders of our bonds, and ten millions more for the expenses of Americans travelling in Europe, our exports may exceed our imports by twenty millions without causing gold to come to us.

3. How Exports and Imports are kept roughly equal. — A country cannot go on permanently getting from other countries more than she gives them in return. When her debts to foreign nations exceed her claims against them, gold has to be sent to settle the balance. The effect of a continued export of gold is to lessen gradually her home-supply of money, and thus cause a decline in the prices of her products. Not only so, but the increased supply of money in the countries to which the gold is sent causes a rise in the prices of the things she buys of those countries. This double change of prices tends in two ways to bring about an equality of exports and imports, and thus put an end to the outflow of gold. First, it becomes easier than it was before to make a profit by sending things abroad to be sold. Secondly, it becomes harder than it was before to find a profitable sale for imports. In this way exports are stimulated and imports are checked, until equilibrium is reached.

It is thus made certain that a drain of money from one country to another cannot go on permanently; that a country must in the long run give commodities for commodities. A case may easily be imagined in which one country should have all her prices above those of another, to such an extent that a one-sided trade should set in between them,—the country of high prices sending the other nothing but money in return for imports. But such a trade could not last. The transfer of money would soon cause a fall of prices in the one, and a rise of prices in the other, until the difference became too slight to afford a profit for the movement of goods. Then the trade would cease,—that is, if the change of prices failed to open a chance for sending goods, with a profit, where cash was sent previously. The thing certain to happen is the cessation of the outflow of money.

A country cannot long have imports without exporting an equivalent. So neither can it have exports without importing an equivalent. The money of the world could not always move towards one country without in the end stripping other countries of their necessary share.

The principles here stated must be slightly modified for the case of the gold-producing countries. Most of the world's supply of gold is produced in two or three countries. The new gold must find its way out of these and distribute itself over the commercial world. It can do so only through the ordinary process, by going out in payment of balances accruing against these countries on their general trade with the rest of the world. Though gold is, for the gold-producing countries, a commodity and a part of its product of industry, yet it is an article which cannot have a lower price in one country than in another, for gold has no price. The excess of gold in the countries producing it keeps their general level of prices above the level prevailing in other countries: with the result that their importation of ordinary commodities is steadily greater than their exportation. This causes the demand for bills on other countries to be greater than the supply; exchange is ordinarily at or near the shipping point. The brokers have to send gold, from time to time, to cover the bills they sell in excess of those they buy. In this way the gold makes its way to other countries.

4. Prices of the Goods Exchanged must Differ in the Trading Countries.— It may be taken for granted that no man would ordinarily send an article to another country to be sold, unless he expected to get a higher price for it than he could get at home: enough higher to pay the freight, insurance, and other costs, together with some balance over by way of profit on the transaction. Certainly no man would make a business of buying products in one country and selling them in another, unless the difference of price in the two countries was sufficient to give him ordinary profits on the business.

Also, we may assume that the difference in price in the two countries cannot ordinarily be more than enough to cover all costs and charges, and leave ordinary profits for those who carry on the business. The competition of other capitalists may be relied on to keep the profits of this class of traders on a level with those made in other business.

The smaller the value of an article, in proportion to its weight and bulk, the greater must be the difference in its price in the two countries in order to make a trade in it profitable: for the cost of transporting such articles is great in proportion to their value. Thus, the price of coal in Massachusetts must differ more from the price of coal in Pennsylvania than the price of shoes differs in the two States. The price of lumber in the United States and in France must differ more widely than (apart from Customs' duties) the price of silk differs in the two countries.

5. Trade between Communities Due to Difference in Relative Cost — From the fact that the prices of the articles exchanged differ in this way in the trading countries, we can infer a principle of fundamental importance in relation to trade between separate communities. This principle is, that no exchange of commodities can exist between two countries except there be a difference in the comparative cost to employers of producing the commodities in the two countries. If we construct a scale of prices for each country, and compare the one scale with the other, the point will at once stand forth clearly. Suppose wheat to be ordinarily exported from this country to Sweden, and iron to be regularly imported from Sweden. Suppose farther, that the American price of wheat is ninety cents a bushel, and that fifteen cents additional must be obtained in Sweden in order to give the exporter a profit over expenses. Also, that the price of a hundred-weight of iron in Sweden is $1.00, and that the importer must have twenty cents additional for bringing it to the United States. Putting these facts in the form of a diagram, we readily see that the ratio

```
United States.                      Sweden.
$1.20                               $1.20
 1.15          Iron.                 1.15
 1.10                                1.10
 1.05                                1.05
 1.00                                1.00
  .95         Wheat.                  .95
  .90                                 .90
```

of the price of wheat to the price of iron is different in the two countries. In the United States it is 90 : 120; in Sweden it is 105 : 100, (or 90 : 86). This tells us unmistakably that the comparative cost to employers of producing wheat and iron in the United States is different from the comparative cost of producing them in Sweden. For if it were not, this difference in the ratios of the prices could not last; American employers would produce iron in preference to wheat; Swedish employers would find wheat-raising more profitable than the production of iron So the ratio of prices would be changed and the trade would cease.

It is thus easily demonstrable that where a regular trade exists between two countries there must be, for the time being, a difference in comparative cost at least equal to the cost of transporting the goods exchanged. How the difference arises, whether or not it is necessarily permanent, and whether it is expedient in any case to impose countervailing duties to check the trade, are questions not now under consideration. We are here concerned only with discovering the present facts which an existing trade implies. Whatever views we may hold as to the expediency of protective duties, we are in duty bound, as students, to search out the facts which give rise to the tendency to trade between countries.

6. How the Difference in Comparative Cost might be Ascertained. — How great the whole difference in comparative cost may be, in any case, cannot be inferred from the prices at which the trade goes on. We can only be sure that it is at least somewhat greater than the difference between the ratios of the prices. In order to discover how much greater it is than this, the trade would have to be stopped. For the price of wheat in Sweden is kept down by the cheap supplies from the United States; and the price of iron in the United States is kept down by the cheap importation from Sweden.

If two countries wished to discover the extent of the difference between their ratios of cost to cost in the case of the articles exchanged, they might obviously do so by means of import duties. By imposing duties, and raising them year by year until they reached a height just sufficient to prevent the trade, they could find in the new ratio of prices, in each country, a pretty accurate measure of the difference in comparative cost.[1]

Let us suppose that, in our example, it were found that with a duty of thirty cents a hundred-weight on iron, and fifteen cents a bushel on wheat, some trade would go on permanently, but that at any higher rates the trade must cease. Wheat must then stand at $1.20 a bushel in Sweden, and iron at $1.50 a hundred-weight in the United States; these being the prices necessary to give the traders a profit on the business, after paying the additional charges. The ratio of the price of wheat to that of iron in the United States would then be 90 : 150, and in Sweden it would be 120 : 100 (or 90 : 75).

On the supposition that these prices continued, they might safely be taken to show the comparative cost of production of wheat and iron in each country. For, if American employers found the production of iron at $1.50 a hundred-weight more profitable than the production of wheat at ninety cents a bushel, they would gradually desert the production of wheat altogether. And so of the production of wheat in Sweden; if Swedish employers found it more profitable to raise wheat at $1.20 a bushel, than to produce iron at $1.00 a hundred-weight, they would gradually desert the production of

---

[1] Strictly, it would not matter whether the barrier to the exchange were duties imposed by both countries or a sufficiently high duty imposed by one of the two. The former alternative is suggested because it works out more simply,— the trade being checked equally on each side. If the check came from one side only, there would be a transfer of money and a re-adjustment of prices in each country.

iron. If the production of wheat goes on in the United States, and of iron in Sweden, on these terms, it must be because the ratio of cost to cost in Sweden differs from that in the United States to the same extent as the ratios of the prices differ. That is to say, in Sweden seventy-five bushels of wheat cost employers as much as ninety hundred-weight of iron ($75 \times \$1.20 = 90 \times \$1.00$); whereas, in the United States, one hundred and fifty bushels of wheat are produced at the same cost as ninety hundred-weight of iron ($150 \times \$0.90 = 90 \times \$1.50$). Or, changing the form of statement, Sweden's ratio is 1 bu. $= 1\frac{1}{5}$ cwt., whereas ours is 1 bu. $= \frac{3}{5}$ cwt.

7. Difference in Comparative Cost a Basis for Trade in all Cases. — These figures tell us nothing as to the source of the difference in comparative cost; nor does it matter in the least, as regards the course of the trade, how the difference arises. It may be wholly due to inferiority on Sweden's part as a producer of wheat, or wholly to superiority on her part as a producer of iron, or partly due to each of these causes. Or it may be that both wheat and iron can be produced with less labor in the United States than in Sweden, our advantage being greater in the production of wheat than in the production of iron. As to these points our figures give no information; they merely make it clear that where trade exists, a difference in comparative costs must exist as the basis of it.

It may seem strange, at first blush, that a commodity could ever be regularly exported with a profit to a country in which it can be produced with less labor than in the exporting country. But all that is necessary to bring this about is a difference in the comparative cost to employers of producing any two commodities in the two countries. The explanation of the seeming puzzle is, that the money cost of a commodity may be less in one country than in another, while the true or economic cost is greater. Though it costs employers less money to get a hundred-weight of iron produced in Sweden than it does in the United States, the quantity of labor required may be indefinitely greater in Sweden than here. Money-wages and the prices of materials may be lower there than here, because the value of money may be higher there than here. This result would obviously come about, if Sweden should buy freely of our wheat, without having any product of her own cheap enough in price to be profitably exported to us. Her money supply would be gradually drawn away; her general scale of prices and her money-wages would decline. If her inferiority to the United States be less in iron than in other things, it is clear that iron would be the first thing to be made low enough in price to be sent to us with a profit for the sender.

If any person be disposed to doubt whether trade between countries rests on, and implies, a difference in the ratios of costs, he will find it instructive to consider the case of two countries differing strongly in advantages for production, but differing equally in all commodities. In such a case, the ratio of cost to cost would be the same in both countries, and there would be no basis for a permanent trade. It might happen that, for some cause, prices in one should be enough higher than prices in the other to cause a movement of goods for a time. But gradually the return movement of money would bring prices towards a common level; one after another, according to costliness of transportation, commodities would cease to be exportable, until finally, even those having greatest value in the least bulk, would come to be so nearly equal in price in both countries that no profit could be made by sending them. Then all trade would cease. This would come to pass, even if the one could produce every commodity with half of the labor required to produce it in the other. An equal advantage in all things has no tendency to cause an exchange of products. Its only tendency is to cause men to emigrate from the country of poor resources to the country of rich resources. This is the only way by which people living in a country of poor resources can get any permanent benefit from a country superior to their own in all points, and equally superior in all.

8. International Values. — When a trade exists between two separate communities, what determines how much the product of the one shall be worth as compared with that of the other? What determines the amount of iron we shall get from Sweden in exchange for each bushel of wheat? Of course this depends, at any given time, on the price of each. But prices, as we know, may change. If wheat rises in price, or iron falls, we get more iron than before for every bushel of wheat. What determines the relative prices of the two articles, as a permanent rule?

In the first place, we easily see that there is nothing in this sort of exchanging to make the value of each product correspond to the quantity of labor and waiting required to produce it. Value tends to conform to cost of production only where there is freedom of competition between the producers. It is not open to the young laborers to choose freely between the exchanging industries: to choose, for example, between raising wheat in the United States and producing iron in Sweden. We have nothing, therefore, in this kind of exchanging, to keep the values under the control of cost of production.

The comparative costs of production do, however, set limits within which the values must ordinarily stand. If, in our supposed trade with Sweden, the ratio of cost to cost in each country be as given in § 6, it is obvious that the price of our wheat to Sweden cannot exceed the price she gets for one and one-fifth hundred-weight of iron; nor can we take less than the price to us of three-fifths of a hundred-weight of her iron. At a price outside of these limits either way, one country or the other would give up the trade; for her employers could more profitably produce the desired article at home, than the export to be sold in exchange for it.

Within the limits thus set by the comparative costs, the terms of the exchange are fixed by the relative demand of each country for the other's product. If Sweden has a strong demand for our wheat as compared with our demand for her iron, this will cause the prices to approach her own home ratio of costs; our prices will rise and hers will fall until the price of a bushel of wheat is near to the price of one and one-fifth hundred-weight of iron. If, on the other hand, our demand for her iron be relatively greater than her demand for our wheat, the prices will approach our home ratio of costs; the price of a bushel of our wheat will be near to the price of three-fifths of a hundred-weight of her iron.

9. Values Changed by Movement of Money. — This principle works itself out in practice through the movements of money in payment of international balances. It may therefore take many years to accomplish its result; but the result is, in the end, inevitable. It works slowly because it has to change not merely the prices of the articles traded in, but the whole scale of prices and of money-wages in the trading countries.

•By way of illustration, let us suppose the trade with Sweden to open with the prices assumed in § 5; namely, wheat ninety cents, and iron $1.00. If, at these prices, Sweden buys one hundred bushels of our wheat for every ninety hundred-weight of iron we import from her, then the trade may go on indefinitely on this basis. If, however, her demand for wheat be greater than our demand for iron; if, for example, she buys a million bushels a year in excess of the quantity our import of her iron pays for, then for this excess she must send us money year by year. The effect will be a gradual decline in the prices of her products, — the price of iron with the rest;

and a gradual rise in our prices,—the price of wheat with the rest.

This double movement will go on until the high price of our wheat cuts off a part of her demand for it, and the low price of her iron causes us to buy greater quantities of it. In this way the trade will reach an equilibrium and the movement of money will cease. Suppose that when this point is reached, her iron has fallen to ninety-five cents a hundred-weight, and our wheat has risen to ninety-five cents a bushel. It is very obvious that, in the new situation, Sweden gets less wheat for a hundred-weight of her iron than she did at the start. Her strong demand for our product has altered the terms of the exchange to her disadvantage, bringing the values nearer to her own ratio of costs, namely, 1 bu. = $1\frac{1}{5}$ cwt.

If, at the original prices, our demand had been the stronger, the whole movement would have been reversed; our prices would have fallen and Sweden's prices would have risen until the trade reached equilibrium. In the outcome, a bushel of our wheat would pay for less of Sweden's iron than it did at the outset. The values are brought nearer to our own ratio of costs, namely, 1 bu. = $\frac{3}{5}$ cwt.

10. How these Principles Apply in Actual Trade — We have thus far, for the sake of clearness, confined our view to the simplest possible case of exchange between separate countries. Of course, in practice, the trade between different parts of the world is infinitely complex. Each country trades with many others, exporting and importing a great variety of commodities. But the principle governing all exchanges must be the same. Every country exports those things, and those only, that have in some other country a price enough higher than her own to make the exportation a source of gain to those who carry it on. Each country imports only those things that have in some other country a price so much below her own that the importer can make a profit. And these differences of price can exist permanently only as a result of differences in the comparative cost to employers of producing things in different countries.

To the trade of each country it is as if all other countries were one. Her exports go wherever the price is highest, and her imports in return come from wherever their price is lowest. Our wheat may go to England and we may get the iron in return from Sweden, — simply turning over to the latter country our claim on England. That would of course leave England indebted to Sweden; but with that we should have no concern. Our necessity is confined to giving other countries as a whole as much as we get of them.

Trade goes on, at any given time, on the basis of the existing prices. If these prices cause any country to import more than her exports pay for, her prices will be lowered gradually by an outflow of her money. Conversely, if any country's exports are more than sufficient to discharge her liabilities to all other countries, her general scale of prices will be raised by an inflow of money from other countries. In this way, the foreign trade of each country is brought to an equilibrium after every disturbance of the balance.

A general fall in the prices of things produced in any country may increase its exports in two distinct ways. It may cause other countries to buy more of the articles they bought previously. Secondly, it may make it possible to export, with a profit, articles that were not previously exportable, because there was not difference enough between the home price and the foreign price. There are usually some articles that are on the verge of exportability, and a small decline of prices may thus be sufficient to increase considerably the volume of a country's exports. In the same way a small rise of the general scale of prices in a country may cause increase of imports, by introducing new articles as well as by swelling the importation of old ones. The importance of this principle lies in the fact that it makes the establishment of equilibrium more prompt than it would be if the whole burden came on a single commodity. For example, in the case supposed on page 340, the decline of Sweden's prices may not have to proceed far enough to bring iron down to ninety-five cents a hundred-weight. A less decline may open a way for the exportation of some other commodity not previously exported, and this may arrest the further outflow of money.

The higher a country's general scale of prices and money-wages (that is to say, the lower the value of money in a country), the more favorably does she trade with other countries. Everything she exports goes farther towards paying for imports than it would do if the level of prices were lower. For this reason a country that produces gold for other countries has a standing advantage in foreign trade. It gets all its imports more cheaply because of the steadily high level of its prices.

11. Sources of Difference in Comparative Cost.—The chief sources of difference in the ratio of cost to cost, in different countries, may be grouped under three general heads:

(1) Differences in climate, soil, mineral wealth, and other natural resources. Each of the exchanging countries may have great natural facilities for the production of some commodities which the other could produce only with difficulty, or not at all. The trade between tropical countries and countries of cooler climate is largely due to this class of causes.

(2) Differences in the industrial character of the inhabitants of different countries, in their degree of civilization, etc. The trade between a highly civilized and a semi-barbarous country may be due to this cause. The natural resources of the two countries may be similar; but the possession of machinery, and of skill in using it, gives the civilized country great comparative advantages in the production of things that are made by the use of machinery. This makes a basis for trade,—the civilized country giving machine-made goods in exchange for such things that have to be produced mainly by hand. In the same way, any special aptitude possessed by the people of a country may create an occasion for trade with other countries.

(3) Differences in density of population. This is a common source of trade between new and old countries. Two countries may be quite alike in natural resources, and in the industrial quality of their people; but one may be an older country, with denser population, than the other. Of course the one with the denser population is the first to feel the effects of diminishing returns. When its own home resources of any kind, worked at their point of maximum return, become insufficient for the needs of its people, the products affected rise in price. When the rise becomes sufficient to cover cost of transportation, these products begin to be imported from the other country, where increase of the production is still possible without increase of cost.

At first, there may be no commodity low enough in price in the older country to make a return trade possible. If not, an outward flow of money ensues, and prices fall until a return trade is developed, in commodities not affected by diminishing returns. Since manufacturing is practically free from the law of diminishing returns, it is inevitable that the exports of the older country should consist of manufactured articles.

So long as the increasing demand of the older country can be supplied by the new country, without increase of cost, the trade will proceed on this basis, growing in volume as years go by. When, at length, the effects of diminishing returns begin to be felt in the new country also, in the production of the commodity it supplies to the other, the price will begin to rise in both countries.

The more populous country will continue to import the article from the other, but the increase of supply needed by her from year to year, will now be partly or wholly produced at home.

This principle explains why it is that countries so commonly produce a part of the necessary supply of an article at home, and procure the balance by foreign trade. It also indicates the natural limits of trade between new and old countries.

12. Differences in Wages not a Cause of Trade.— It evidently follows, from the nature of the case, that differences in the general level of wages, comparing country with country, make no basis for exchange of products. A high or a low level of wages in a country affects all products alike. For example, the high level of wages in this country extends to the production of wheat and beef, as well as to the production of cloth and steel rails. If that were the only difference between this country and, say England, it could not make cloth and steel rails dearer here than in England, and at the same time make wheat and beef cheaper here than there. Nor can the lower level of wages prevailing in England be the fundamental cause of the lower price of her cloth and steel rails; because it does not make her wheat and beef low in price also. A circumstance that is common to all the industries of each country, could not bring about that difference in the ratio of price to price in the two countries, which alone, as we have seen, makes exchange of products possible.

Remembering, however, that English cloth is brought over here to be sold only when the price is lower there than here, it may seem that a rise of money-wages in England, might so raise the money cost of her cloth as to stop the exportation of it to us. This may be granted, if the meaning be that an increased supply of money in Great Britain, might raise her prices to such an extent as to check greatly, or even stop entirely, her export trade. But in order to judge of the result we must look at the whole case: we must not forget the effect of the higher prices on her import trade. The outflow of money that would arise to pay for imports, would presently bring about a fall of her money-wages and prices, and her export of cloth would be resumed.

If the rise of her money-wages be meant in the sense of greater purchasing power, her supply of money being no greater, but the laborers getting a larger proportion of it, then the answer is that the rise would have no effect on prices, and consequently would have no effect on the international trade. The only result would be a fall of the profits of English employers, and the fall would extend equally to all English industries. The producers of cloth could get no higher price for it at home than before, and would consequently have the same motive as before for sending it to us.

Similarly a decline of money-wages and prices in the United States, caused by a diminished supply of money in this country, might temporarily stop the importation of goods from abroad; but increase of exports would presently bring us increase of money from abroad, and this would raise our prices and money-wages again. On the other hand, a fall of money wages due simply to diminished saving, would not cause our prices to fall. (See Chapter XIII., § 5.) It would only raise the profits of our employers.

The true view, then, would seem to be that where a basis exists for exchange of products, owing to difference in the ratios of cost to cost, the trade itself will bring the scale of money-wages and prices in both countries into the proper relation for carrying on the exchange. But this adjustment does not affect the level of real wages in either. That is governed in every country, not by the absolute height of its money-wages and prices, but by the relation between the two.

13. Much Domestic Trade is "International." — It must not be supposed that the foregoing principles apply only to trade between separate nations in the political sense. The word "international" is, in fact, not aptly chosen to designate the sort of exchanging to which it applies. All trade is subject to these principles, if it takes place between communities that have not free movement of savings and laborers from the one to the other. Much of the domestic trade of every country, especially of every large country, is "international" in the economic sense. In our own case, for example, the trade between north and south, or between the Pacific slope and the Atlantic slope, depends on the same conditions and follows the same rule of values, as trade between the United

States and the United Kingdom. The same is true of the trade between many sections of the country that are less widely separated.

On the other hand, apart from the effects of Customs' regulations, there is nothing to distinguish the border trade of two neighboring countries from the local domestic trade of one and the same country. On the supposition that the laborers on each side of the boundary line pass freely from the one side to the other in search of employment, the value of commodities in the border trade is governed by cost of production. That is to say, it is not "international" in the economic sense.

CHAPTER XXVI.

FREE TRADE AND PROTECTION.

THUS far we have endeavored only to get at the facts of trade between countries. As to the points brought out there is, I think, no room for doubt or difference of opinion. We must now touch briefly on the grounds of the great controversy as to the benefits of international trade. I shall first endeavor to state briefly the general position or thesis maintained by each side in the controversy; then I shall try to give a summary of the chief arguments and counter-arguments, by which the advocates of each theory commonly sustain their position: —

1. **The Theory of Free Trade.**—The thesis of the Free-traders may be stated as follows: ·

"Free Trade increases the productiveness of industry in all countries. It enables the people of every country to use their best natural advantages. It thus allows things to be produced where they can be produced most easily. The result is to make the product of universal industry greater than it could be, if the people of every country were required to produce all commodities at home.

"For example, if under Free Trade, New England were found exchanging shoes for potatoes with Nova Scotia, the mere fact of the exchange would be proof that each country was getting the imported article for less labor than it would cost her at home. For the price of shoes is higher in Nova Scotia than in New England, and the price of potatoes is higher in New England than in Nova Scotia; otherwise the trade would not go on. The ratio of cost to cost must therefore be different in the two countries: how widely different could be known only by discovering how high duties would have to be imposed in order to stop the trade. Suppose the ratio of cost to cost in each country were found to be: for New England 1 pair of shoes = 2 barrels of potatoes, and for Nova Scotia 1 pair of shoes = 3 barrels of potatoes. Suppose further that there are one thousand men in New England whose labor is to be used in procuring potatoes, and another one thousand in Nova Scotia whose labor is to be used in procuring shoes. The New-England laborers can produce 125,000 pairs of shoes in the same time they would require to produce 250,000 barrels of potatoes. The Nova-Scotia laborers can produce 300,000 barrels of potatoes in the same time they would require to produce 100,000 pairs of shoes. If the New-England men produce potatoes and the Nova-Scotia men produce shoes, the product for the two countries is 250,000 barrels of potatoes and 100,000 pairs of shoes. If, on the other hand, the New-England men produce shoes for Nova Scotia and the Nova Scotians produce potatoes for New England, the result is 125,000 pairs of shoes and 300,000 barrels of potatoes. The difference in favor of Free Trade (subject to some deduction for cost of transportation) is 25,000 pairs of shoes and 50,000 barrels of potatoes.

"This superior productiveness of industry in both countries, under free exchange, goes to swell the rewards of producers. If all countries that have set up barriers against free exchange should throw them down, the effect would be like that of an immense improvement in production. Wages and profits would be higher in all of them than before, because the product of industry would be greatly increased."

2. The Protectionist Position. — The general position taken by the advocates of Protection may be stated as follows:

"Every country ought to develop her resources of all kinds in a healthy and symmetrical proportion. The tendency of unrestricted trade with other countries is to create a lop-sided development. Certain lines of production, once entered upon, are liable to be followed to the exclusion of everything else. By the mere fact that they are established, that the requisite machinery, implements, skill, and business arrangements are at hand for carrying them on, they tend to absorb the whole energy of the people.

"The result is injurious in every way. It condemns a people to lasting poverty, because it leads to the neglect of the national resources. The single product which receives all attention is produced in too great quantity, and commands but a small price in the foreign markets to which it has to be sent. Much of even this small price is eaten up in the costs of transportation and the charges of middlemen, so that the producers receive less and less for their labor. Yet there is no avenue of escape for them. The products of foreign labor, coming in without restriction, are sold at such low prices as to make hopeless any attempt to compete with them in producing like articles at home. The foreign producers have all the advantages of an established industry. They have the machinery, the skilled laborers, and possession of the market. They stand ready to crush any attempt at setting up a rival industry here. Rather than lose control, they would place their goods here at prices which would be simply ruinous to the home producer, struggling with the difficulties of starting a new industry.

"Protection, on the other hand, guarantees to the founder of a new industry a safe and remunerative sale for his product. He is enabled to pass, without ruinous loss, through the early stages while he and his workmen are acquiring the necessary knowledge and skill, and while he is making those commercial connections which are necessary to the success of an enterprise. In this way a country builds up for itself a variety of industries. Its people have the great advantages that come from diversified pursuits. The growth of wealth is rapid, because all the national resources are brought into use, and every producer is encouraged by the prospect of sure and adequate returns for his labor."

GROUNDS OF THE PROTECTION THEORY.

3. Answer to the Free Trade Argument as to Cost. — Turning now to the question of the effect of protective duties on the cost of commodities, the advocates of Protection reply substantially as follows to the Free Trade argument:

"Differences in advantages for different kinds of production in any country are largely artificial. The reason why Nova Scotia can produce only one hundred pairs of shoes with the labor that produces one hundred and fifty barrels of potatoes, is found in the fact that she has not applied herself to the production of shoes. If the importation of shoes from New England were prevented, capital would be largely turned into the shoe industry, the machinery would be improved, the laborers would become more efficient, and presently Nova-Scotian labor would become as productive in the manufacture of shoes as that of New England.

"Protection, it is true, may temporarily increase the cost of commodities, but in the long run its effect is rather to cheapen them. It brings the producer and the consumer side by side, and thus saves much needless labor in transporting things between countries. Though it excludes injurious foreign competition, it preserves the healthy competition of home producers. By the mutual rivalry of these, each of them endeavoring to produce his commodity as cheaply as possible, every known device for saving labor is brought into use. The possession of a sure market enables the employers to invest their savings, with confidence, in machinery and appliances of all kinds for carrying on the production in the most effective way. The result is that, in the long run, the productiveness of labor is greatly increased by Protection. Of this fact many notable examples have occurred in our own history under the present tariff. Nearly all the most important commodities are cheaper now than they were before the tariff was adopted."

4. **Compensations for Temporary Increase of Cost under Protection.** — "It follows that, even if there were no immediate compensations, a protective tariff admits of easy defence on the score of cost of commodities. Looked at merely as a device for eventually diminishing cost, any temporary sacrifice it calls for on the part of any class of consumers, is a wise and useful investment of the public resources. But there are immediate compensa-

tions which, in themselves, more than counterbalance the temporary addition to cost. If, by the exclusion of New-England shoes, Nova Scotia must for a while pay more for her shoes, the immediate effect is an extension of her own home industries. The establishment of shoe factories increases the demand for her labor, and wages rise. Profits also rise, because a new opening is presented for the profitable investment of savings. From being a community wholly given up to raising potatoes, she becomes a community enjoying diversified employments, with all the social advantages resulting therefrom.

"On the side of New England, the exclusion of Nova-Scotia potatoes gives needful encouragement to the farmers. These will get higher prices for their crop when they have the home market to themselves; they will therefore increase the production, — will employ more laborers, and will pay higher wages than they could if embarrassed by the competition of Nova-Scotia farmers. The additional price the consumers of potatoes have to pay is not lost as it would be if paid to foreigners; the money is paid to our own people and remains in the country. The farmers of New England will buy more manufactured goods than they could buy when they got less for their farm products. Thus, the money they receive will come back to those who have paid it. Further, the New-England manufacturers will be protected as well as the farmers; they will have a sure home market for all they can produce, and will not be compelled to sell their wares in competition with foreign products. This will enable them to employ more laborers, and to pay higher wages, than they could if they were exposed to foreign competition.

"In these ways Protection tends to make both wages

and profits high. It also makes a nation independent of foreign countries. Supplying all her own needs, she is able to pursue towards other nations a policy of becoming dignity and strength. In case of war, she is not taken at a disadvantage, but has within herself all the resources for self-support and vigorous action.

"While a protective tariff is thus a good thing in itself, it is at the same time a source of revenue for the national government. It saves the people from the necessity of paying taxes. The revenue it yields comes out of the pockets of the foreign producers; because whatever they send to us has to be sold here, after paying the duty, at the same price as the home product that pays no tax. Not only so but the protective tariff, by raising our prices, compels the people of other countries to pay us more for everything they buy of us than they would otherwise pay." [1]

5. Peculiar Necessity of Protection for the United States. — "But the great argument for a high tariff in the case of the United States, is the necessity of protecting our laborers against the competition of the ill-

[1] I am not sure that this latter point is actually urged by protectionists; but it is obviously true, so far as regards exchange of products with free-trade countries. Suppose two countries have had free trade with each other and one of them imposes a protective tariff; the first result is to check the movement of goods to the protected country, leaving the reverse movement untouched. This leaves a balance to be paid in money by the free-trade country. The trade is gradually restored to equilibrium by the consequent rise of prices in the protected country and a fall of prices in the other, — with the result indicated above. Of course, it may be urged in reply that the amount gained in this way is but a small compensation for the loss through diminished trade: and further, that if all countries adopted protection, the gain would disappear.

paid laborers of European countries. Here it is common to introduce statistics showing that wage-rates in Great Britain are very considerably below the level of wages paid in the United States; and that wage-rates in Germany, France, Belgium, and other continental countries, are in many industries not more than half as high as those paid to our laborers.

"Now, if it were not for the tariff, European employers, getting laborers at such low rates of wages, would be able to flood our markets with commodities of all sorts at very low prices; prices so low in fact, that American employers must either give up hiring laborers altogether, or pay greatly reduced wages. The cost of transportation has now been brought so low, that the natural protection formerly afforded by our distance from Europe has practically disappeared. European products can now be sold in America at so slight an advance over the cost to the European employer, that, without the protection of a tariff, American industry must at once sink to the low level of wages and profits prevailing in Europe. In support of this contention, the advocates of Protection cite freely from the statistics of wages and prices in European countries, showing that in every case the level is below ours, — except, of course, the prices of those commodities that are regularly exported from here to Europe.

"Our own home market is the best and only sure market for American products. Much the greater part of everything that we produce finds its buyers here. If we surrender this market to foreigners, they have nothing to tender us in return that we do not substantially enjoy already. To give up our tariff, then, would be to cut down enormously the field for the employment of labor among us. Our most flourishing industries would be instantly struck down.

"The doctrine of Free Trade is an English invention, adapted only to further the interests of British manufacturers. By means of it these hope to keep all other countries in industrial vassalage to England. Every other country that has accepted the theory of Free Trade has been kept in backwardness and poverty. Those, on the other hand, that have pursued the policy of Protection, have grown and advanced in wealth with rapid strides."

In support of this view, protectionist writers appeal to economic history, giving statistics of decline in Free-trade countries, and of industrial growth wherever Protection has prevailed. In fact, the protectionist argument runs throughout very much in that channel. It is largely an appeal to facts, which, in the view of the writers, go to show that Protection is either an industrial necessity, or has proved itself in practice to be a powerful agency in building up national prosperity. This makes it very difficult to state the case for Protection in brief form. It is an argument that does not easily accommodate itself to abridgement.

The favorite field from which to draw proofs of the beneficent action of Protection, is the record of our own national growth under the system, especially the growth since the adoption of the present tariff.

FREE TRADE REPLY.

To these arguments the advocates of Free Trade reply in substance, as follows:

6. Feebleness of Industries that Live by Protection. — "Differences in advantages for different kinds of production in a country are, no doubt, sometimes artificial, but they are not usually so. The intelligence and enterprise of a country's business men may safely be trusted to discover and utilize its most favorable opportunities for the use of capital and labor. If industry be left without interference, it will spontaneously seek out the most productive channels for itself. The fundamental evil of a protective tariff is, that it makes very little attempt to distinguish the differences that are artificial and temporary, from those that are natural and lasting. It invites men to fly in the face of nature, passing by the better chance and taking the worse one. This is why tariff industries never get beyond the need of protection; never are ready to stand on their own bottom.

"If, as protectionists are apt to assume, the question were of giving temporary public aid in founding new industries, which, once established, could stand and flourish on their own merits, most free-traders would gladly share the burden of giving it,—whether by bounty or by temporary tax on the imported article. But the question is very rarely of that character. Men are apt to make the mistake of supposing that because we have reasonably good resources for the production of a given commodity, the producer of it would need only temporary protection. But it may happen that our resources of other kinds are vastly superior. In that case temporary protection would be of no avail; the moment it was withdrawn, trade would seek the easier way of procuring the commodity,—namely, by giving our more copious product in exchange for it. For what is called protection against foreign competition is always, in reality, protection against our own better resources. Such protection can never be withdrawn without the result of sending our labor and capital back into their most productive channels. Witness the industries which are now still, after seventy years of greater or less (usually greater) protection, as dependent on the tariff as they were at the beginning."

7. The Question of Demand for Labor and for Products. — "As to causing increased demand for labor, stoppage of trade with other countries can never do that. It only changes the direction of the demand. In proportion as you stop imports you stop exports too, in the long run. There is as much demand for labor to make shoes to be sent to Nova Scotia, in exchange for potatoes, as there would be to raise the potatoes at home. Further, the rewards of labor depend on its productiveness : and since interference with free exchange prevents us from getting things in the easiest way, it must lessen wages and profits. Any rise of money-wages due to a tariff is more than offset by the higher prices of most things laborers have to buy.

"As to the market for products of labor, when a protective tariff is first imposed, it does for a little while make the sale of some goods easier, by excluding foreign products. But herein it is simply like an issue of inconvertible currency: the effect lasts only till industry adjusts itself to the situation. Further, whatever a portion of the community gain, even temporarily, is at the expense of the rest. For, in the example of New England and Nova Scotia, the producers of potatoes in Nova Scotia and of shoes in New England find the market for their products narrowed by the tariff: what the others gain these lose, and much more besides.

"Would New England gain by the exclusion of Dakota wheat, or of Texas beef ? Nobody argues that free trade between our States lessens the demand for labor, or for products of labor, in any part of the Union. What strange quality is it, in the national boundaries, that makes free trade with people living beyond them, so injurious to the whole country?"

8. Question of Diversified Employments, etc. — "As to diversified industry, there is no danger that any civilized nation shall lack diversity of employments. The number of commodities is many times too great to have any whole country devoted to producing any one, or even any twenty of them. It is mere absurdity to speak as if the whole population of the United States could in any case be farmers. Foreign countries would have no demand for one-half of the surplus crop that would be raised. Without the tariff, as with it, we should devote labor to agriculture only so far as that promised best returns. For the rest we should produce at home all things that we could not obtain more cheaply by exchange with other countries. Prices would arrange themselves so as to make this certain.

"As to war, unrestricted trade between countries is the best guarantee for peace. It cultivates friendly intercourse. Besides, if it would make us dependent on our neighbors, it would make them equally dependent on us."

9. Protective Duties the most Burdensome Taxes. — "So far from a protective tariff being a way to obtain a revenue without taxes, it is, in fact, the most burdensome form of taxation. The duties actually collected are paid by our own consumers, for no man imports a foreign product unless its price here is enough above the price in the other country to give the importer a profit. Without the duty we should get it at a lower price. But the real burden of the tariff does not lie in the taxes we pay under it. It deprives the people of many times more than it gives to the Treasury. The real loss lies in the diminished productiveness of our labor. The tariff closes to us the easiest ways of obtaining many of the things we need, and forces us upon harder ways. It leaves us for our labor, fewer enjoyable commodities than we might have. The loss it inflicts is therefore not measurable. It is precisely such a loss as we should suffer if we were forbidden to cultivate our most fertile lands, to work our most productive mines, or to use our most effective machinery.

"Suppose we had two areas of land, on one of which a given number of laborers could raise 250,000 barrels of potatoes, and on the other 300,000 barrels. What should we think of a law that should forbid the use of the better area? What should we answer if it were said in justification of the injury, that the poorer land could probably be made more productive than the other by improvements in agriculture? — or that it would, at all events, give more employment to labor than the other?"

10. **The Tariff and Wages.** — "On the great question of wages, and competition with the pauper labor of Europe, the free-trader's answer is that wages in the United States will depend on the general law of wages, whether we have a tariff or not. Without the tariff, as with it, our capitalists would seek to make profits by employing labor. The tariff can only alter the direction in which labor shall be employed, and, as already pointed out, it alters it for the worse.

"It is a fundamental error to suppose that the laborers of two exchanging countries are in competition with each other. The only way in which the pauper laborers of Europe can lower wages in America, is by coming over here to compete in our labor market. While they stay at home, the more cheaply they and their employers produce commodities for us, the better it is for all classes of Americans, — hired laborers as well as others. If they stood ready to sell us their products for one-tenth of the prices they are likely to demand, the only effect would be to increase greatly the returns for capital and labor here. It would simply be for us like a labor-saving improvement, that should enormously cheapen those commodities.

"This suggests the central fallacy of the whole protectionist argument on this head. It takes for granted that Europe would overstock our markets with *all* commodities, — forgetting that she would expect products of ours in return. The freest trade could only result in a simple exchange of certain products of American labor for certain products of European labor; and it is mere absurdity to allege that we should suffer injury by getting large quantities of Europe's products for small quantities of our own. It would be for Europe to complain in that case, not for us."[1]

The facts appealed to in support of Protection have been frequently traversed by free-trade writers. These explain and interpret the facts differently, — maintaining that the advocates of Protection make the mistake of attributing all the good that happens where Protection exists, to Protection, and all the evil where Free Trade exists, to Free Trade. The recent great development of

[1] The complaint of European protectionists is, in fact, the reverse of this, — namely that American products are too cheap. In spite of the high wages prevailing here, France and Germany have imposed protective duties on American products.

the United States, for example, these writers attribute to the splendid natural resources of the country, and to the great improvements in production and transportation that have come into use in the last thirty years. Of those resources and improvements, they hold, we should have had even fuller advantage, had not the tariff hampered us in the most effective ways of using them.

The advocates of Protection characterize the whole argument for Free Trade as a mere setting up of abstract theories in opposition to plain and visible facts. Their own view they assert to be that of practical men, familiar with the actual affairs and business necessities of the country.

The advocates of Free Trade allege that the argument for Protection is based on a defective and fallacious view of the facts; that it persistently overlooks quite half of the case, and by resting too much on superficial and variable matters, such as the value of money in different countries, loses itself in a tangled web of mere sophistry and self-deception.

With this brief outline of the arguments on each side, I leave the reader to sift and examine the contending claims for himself. The problem may seem highly complicated, but it is really not more so than most other questions in practical economics. A little careful thinking, using the light of first principles, can hardly fail to lead to a just judgment upon the merits of these rival plans for promoting the general wealth.

CHAPTER XXVII.

CONCLUDING SUGGESTIONS ON VARIOUS TOPICS.

WE have now touched, in one form or another, on all the leading principles of economic theory. The more extended study of the subject consists mainly in amplifying these principles, in tracing out more fully their relations to each other, and in considering the modifications to which they are subject in different states of society, and under different social and political institutions.

By way of assisting the student in gaining a comprehensive grasp of the whole subject, up to the point we have reached, the following notes, suggestions, and practical applications are appended:—

1. **Particular and General Cases.**—Many of the more common slips in reasoning about economic subjects, arise from failure to observe the difference between things that are universally true and things that are true only in limited cases. By way of help towards guarding against such slips, a careful study of the following truths is recommended:

A. Things possible in limited cases but quite impossible universally,—

1. Any one commodity, or any limited number of commodities, may rise or fall in value at any time; but

it is quite impossible for all commodities to rise or fall in value simultaneously. If some rise, others fall.

2. Any one commodity, or any limited number of commodities, may be produced in excess of the demand at any time; but it is quite impossible that all products should be in excess of the demand at one and the same time. If the supply of some things be excessive, the supply of other things is deficient to the same extent.

These two propositions are intimately connected with each other. The only evidence of overproduction, in any case, is a fall in the value of the product. Since all things cannot fall in value simultaneously, there can be no simultaneous overproduction of all things. There can, however, be a general fall of prices; and the situation that brings it may have all the awkward features that would attend general overproduction. But it is highly important to keep in mind the fact that gold is a product of labor, and that a fall of prices is due to a deficient supply of this particular product. The use of money is so peculiar, and the opportunities for producing it are so limited, that one is apt to leave it out of view as a product of labor. A general fall of prices is in fact a call for more money; just as a rise in the value of iron is a call for more iron. (See pages 137–140.)

Remembering that buying and selling are at bottom exchanging of products, it is easy to see that supply of one thing is demand for other things. Supply and demand are therefore simply opposite views of the things offered for sale. Do not, then, make the mistake of looking at one side only; of looking, for example, at the farmer's supply of wheat, and forgetting his demand for the things he wishes to get in exchange for his wheat.

3. Some men may gain by a general rise of prices; but it is quite impossible for all men to gain in that way. What some gain, others lose.

B. Things always possible in limited cases, but not possible universally unless special conditions be fulfilled,—

There are many of these; and they are the source of most of the economic fallacies that prevail in the world in relation to wages, profits, prices, and the like. In dealing with questions relating to these subjects, we have to be very careful to distinguish the two sets of cases. The following examples illustrate the point:

1. The price of any one commodity or group of commodities may rise or fall at any time, by reason of some circumstance peculiar to the commodity itself or to the group of commodities. But it is impossible for all commodities to rise or fall in price simultaneously, unless there be a change either in the supply of money, or in the quantity of goods to be sold (the productiveness of industry).

2. Money-wages in any one industry, or group of industries, may rise or fall at any time for reasons peculiar to the industry or group of industries affected. But it is impossible for money-wages to rise or fall in all industries simultaneously, unless there be a change either in the volume of money-savings or in the number of laborers to be hired.

3. A tax on any one commodity causes its value and price to rise; but an equal tax on all products, including gold, would not raise the value, or the price, of any. It would simply lessen the rewards of producers. [Every tax on commodities has this latter effect, whether it acts through, or without, change of values. Compare the opposite case of improvements, page 106.]

4. If the laborers should begin to abandon coal-mining, wages in that industry would have to be advanced, and the price of coal would rise; but an equal rise of wages in all industries would not be attended by a general rise of prices. There would be a general fall of profits. Similarly, a fall of wages in any one industry, owing to a greater inclination of the laborers to enter it, would bring a fall in the value and price of the product; but a general fall of wages would not cause a general fall of prices. It would only cause a general rise of profits. [The change of wages, in these cases, is not the cause of the change of value. Both changes are effects of the changed conduct of the laborers. See page 97.]

The reason why the single case is so different from the general case is easily seen. In economics, as in other things, results must have adequate causes: you cannot make something out of nothing. If there be a regiment to feed, and only a certain quantity of bread and meat to do it with each day, everybody sees at once that the average share cannot exceed a certain amount. Any one company may have its allowance enlarged; but in that case we readily see that the allowance to other companies has to be diminished. Yet one is liable to argue about wages, prices, and such subjects, as if there could be a general rise at any time, without any additional means for maintaining the rise.

No doubt there is an elastic quality in the agencies that set the level of wages and prices. There is always a reserve of savings awaiting investment, of goods awaiting sale, of money awaiting expenditure, and of laborers seeking employment. In a loosely organized society, such as goes with individual liberty, these reserves are to a large extent necessary, and where not necessary they are unavoidable. The existence of them, and the possibility of increasing or diminishing them, makes the action of economic principles less sharp and sudden than it would otherwise be. By drawing on, or adding to, these reserves, a temporary effect may be obtained at seeming variance with the general principle. The general level of prices may be raised somewhat for a time, without increase of money, on the simple condition of adding to the unsold stock. Wages may be temporarily raised at any time, without increase of saving, simply by drawing on the ordinary reserve of savings, or by adding to the number of laborers out of employment. There is, in fact, no limit to the prices sellers might ask, nor to the wages laborers might demand. The difficulty comes in selling the whole product at prices too high to match the existing supply of money, and in finding employment for all laborers at wages too high to match the current flow of savings.

2. Slow Working of Economic Principles.

The point just considered is a good illustration of a general truth which the student must always keep in mind,—namely, that economic principles take time to work themselves out. They are only certain to prevail in the long run. They have at any given moment very little of the character of physical laws, which assert themselves irresistibly in every case. They are rather principles of human action, true of men in the average so long as they act intelligently. What we call the law of prices, for example, operates mainly as an argument presented to the minds of those who have things to sell, or wish to buy. The argument is weak at first and may be thrust aside; but the longer it is resisted, the stronger it grows. In the long run men find resistance to be a source of loss, and we assume that for their own advantage they will yield.

Every result that depends on competition must have the requisite time to work itself out; and the less mobile the elements in the case, the longer the time necessary. For example, the values of commodities that require long time for their production are slower to conform to their cost than the values of commodities that are quickly made. Again, prices of things are much slower to fall when the situation requires a fall, than they are to rise when the situation warrants a rise. Everybody who has invested savings, counting on the old prices, is pledged to resist a fall. Undertakings that require extensive machinery or other fixed capital,—railroads, for example, — are slower to have their profits brought to the common level, than undertakings that require but little outlay. This is especially true where, as in the case of railroads between most towns, only one such establishment is needed. If two be built there is not traffic enough to keep both fully employed, and the consequence is a "war of rates," which means total loss of earnings for both roads. Competition acts smoothly and effectively only when there is room for several competitors. As the country grows and business increases, it can hardly be doubted that competition will, in the long run, assert its force in railroad earnings as in other things.

3. Temporary and Permanent Results. — Because economic principles take time to work themselves out, it is essential for the student of economics to distinguish, in many cases, between temporary or immediate effects and the permanent results. We have had occasion to note a good many examples of this. Artificial interference with the natural progress or tendency of industry, is very apt to have an ultimate effect very different from that at the outset.

(1) A tax suddenly imposed on the production or importation of any commodity would give, temporarily, high profits to those having stocks of the article but the high gains would not continue.

(2) A strike, in favoring circumstances, may extort a rise of wages in any industry; but if wages were previously as high as competition tended to make them, the rise cannot be maintained.

(3) An increase of the demand for any commodity raises the value temporarily, and with it the wages and profits of the producers; but the permanent effect is to cause increased production of the commodity, without any excess of gains over those made in other industries. The converse is true in the case of diminished demand for an article.

(4) The temporary effect of increasing the supply of money in a country may be to lower the rate of interest; also to quicken the sales of goods. But the permanent effect is only to lower the value of money,—that is, to cause a rise of prices (and money-wages). The rate of interest and the difficulties of trade return to their normal condition.

(5) The temporary effect of increase in the number of laborers is to lower the rate of wages. The effect in the long run may only be to cause a proportional increase of savings, through increasing the product of industry. A constant addition has, however, the constant result of keeping wages somewhat lower than they would otherwise be.

(6) A tariff on imports may have the temporary effect of causing high profits in the production of things previously obtained by foreign trade, and low profits in the production of exports. In the long run, competition diverts capital and labor from the production of exports to the production of things formerly obtained by exchange with other countries; and profits in the tariff industries are brought to the same level as profits in the other industries.

(7) Similarly when duties are abolished, tariff industries are temporarily depressed, and other industries have their gains increased. But the effect in the long run is to divert capital and labor from the production of things previously excluded by the tariff, to the production of things to be exported in return for the new imports.

4. Relation of Wages to Product, Prices, etc. — No part of economic theory presents so many points of difficulty as that which relates to wages, especially to the source and consequences of changes in wages. The subject is so important that the student ought to spare no pains in order to gain clear views regarding it. A careful study of the following cases can hardly fail to be of service in clearing up the relations of wages to profits, prices, and the productiveness of industry.

Changes in the general level of individual wages present themselves, in practice, in one or other of the following forms:

Case I. A change of money-wages, with a corresponding change of prices.

Case II. A change of money-wages, without a corresponding change of prices.

Case III. A change of prices, without a corresponding change of money-wages.

Now it is evident, from the principles stated in the foregoing chapters, that four different elements come into play at any given time, in fixing the scale of money-wages and the general level of prices, namely:

1. The number of laborers.

2. The total volume of commodities produced.
3. The supply of money.
4. The strength of the spirit of saving.

Each of these elements is liable to change. The fourth, no doubt, changes but slowly, since it depends on the general character and temperament of men,—things which are not subject to violent fluctuations. But, in every growing country, the other three are constantly expanding. Every increase of population, every industrial improvement, every change in the supply of gold or in the use of substitutes for it, may have an effect, temporary or lasting, on the earnings of the individual laborer. Assuming the fourth element to be constant, the course of wages depends on the relative rate of increase of the other three. Of course, if the three expand equally, there is (on the assumption named) no effect on individual wages, money or real. But the three may not, and in fact usually do not, expand equally. There are three representative cases:

A. All three expanding, but the supply of money not increasing at the same rate as the number of laborers and the volume of products (the two latter increasing equally); the general level of prices rises or falls, with a corresponding change of money-wages; no necessary change of real wages, nor of profits. [Case I. above.] There may, however, be temporary effects of no small importance, owing to the difficulty of readjusting the scale of money-wages and of prices, so as to conform to the changed (relative) supply of money. (See Chapter XIII., §§ 9 and 10.)

B. All three increasing, but the number of laborers not increasing at the same rate as the volume of products and the supply of money (the two latter expanding equally); the general level of prices remains unchanged, but wages (both money and real) and profits rise or fall. If the increase of products and money be more rapid than the increase of laborers, the first effect is a rise of profits; each employer has more goods to sell than before (in proportion to the number of laborers he employs), and there is no fall of value to offset the increase of quantity. The general rise of profits may be counted on to cause increase of savings, and thus to carry the greater part, or even the whole, of the increased product to wages. These are the effects of all general improvements in the arts of production, such as the invention of the steam-engine; also, of every increase in the personal efficiency of the laborers in all industries. Both money and commodities become more plentiful, in comparison with the number of laborers: each man has more money and more good things for his labor. If, on the other hand, the increase of products and money be less rapid than the increase of laborers, the first effect is a decline of profits and this is followed by a falling-off in savings, — thus throwing a part, or even all, of the loss on wages. [Case II. above.] If the decrease of product be due to the necessity of pressing some classes of natural agents beyond their point of maximum return, there is a rise of some prices, and a fall of others, the general level remaining the same; and rents rise.

C. All three increasing, but the volume of products not increasing at the same rate as the number of laborers and the supply of money: money-wages remain the same, but prices rise or fall and real wages and profits fall or rise. Though each man, whether laborer or employer, gets the same money-income as before, his income reckoned in things is different. In this case the change of real wages is direct and automatic; that is to say, it is not brought about through an antecedent effect on profits. When any of the things laborers consume are reduced in price, whether by improvements in production or by the opening of trade with other regions, the result is an immediate rise of real wages. Further, the rise is permanent, unless by more rapid increase of numbers, the advantage be in part or wholly transferred to the employers. The opposite result follows a rise of price of any of the things consumed by laborers, — whether the rise be due to increased cost of production, or to the cutting-off of trade with other communities. [Case III. above.] The differences between this case and the second, arise from the fact that here the laborer's earning power, measured in money, does not change, whereas in the other case it does. The second case relates to universal changes in the productiveness of labor; this one to changes in particular industries other than the production of gold. As already pointed out (page 107), the course of affairs, in practice, presents a combination of the two cases.

D. If now the general disposition to save becomes

stronger, each of the foregoing cases becomes modified in favor of wages and against profits. First of all, where population, product, and money increase equally, the more strenuous saving causes a rise of individual wages (both money and real) and a fall of profits,—giving, for the laborer the same effect as the first alternative under *B*. In *A*. money-wages rise more than prices, or do not fall so much: real wages rise and profits decline. In *B*. each man's wages (money and real) rise more than his product increases, or fall less than it decreases. In *C*. money-wages rise, and real wages rise more than proportionally to the increase of individual product, or fall less than the product falls off. In every case the advantage gained by the laborers, through increase of the disposition to save, is gained at the expense of the employers' profits.

5. **The Question of an Eight-hour Law.**—It is of the highest importance in the discussion of practical cases, to distinguish changes of wages that are at the expense of profits from those that are not so. In such a question as that of the proposed eight-hour law, for example, everything turns on the effect a reduction of hours would have on the volume of product. If in eight hours the laborers would produce as much as they now produce in ten hours, the change is in every way desirable; it may be made without loss of wages, or profits. If, however, the reduction of hours means a reduction of product also, it involves a fall of profits, or of wages, or both. The question as to the product is one of fact, which economic

theory cannot decide. But we may safely lay down the principle that a diminution of individual product implies an inevitable reduction of individual rewards.

The reduction of hours, it is true, seems to be contemplated only for certain classes of city laborers; and the expectation may be that the decline of product in the eight-hour industries would be made good to the employers by a rise of the value. This is, of course, conceivable; but it is not therefore practicable. The result would obviously be to favor particular classes of laborers at the expense of the rest of the community. To maintain the favored classes in the enjoyment of higher wages for a day of eight hours, than other equally good laborers are getting for a day of ten or even twelve hours, would require that we should, in some way, give them a strict monopoly of the work. Otherwise competition would, in the long run, bring wages to correspond with the quantity of labor.

QUESTIONS AND EXERCISES.

1. Explain the process by which exports of merchandise are made to pay for imports.

2. When a country exports more than she imports, what is the effect on the rate of exchange, and why?

3. How are exports and imports kept roughly equal in money value (or aggregate price)?

4. Show that money-wages may differ more, in two exchanging countries, then the general level of prices can differ.

5. Explain carefully the statement that international trade arises from differences in the comparative cost of producing the articles exchanged.

6. Can differences in the general level of wages in two countries cause a trade between them?

7. Show that the cost to a country of its imports is the cost of producing its exports.

8. Suppose labor became twice as productive as it is, in all our industries, what would the effect be on the cost to us of our imports? Would the change cause us to export or import any articles not now exported or imported?

9. There are two countries, A and B. Each of them produces at home its whole supply of wheat and cloth, and the prices in each are as follows:

In A wheat is $1.50 a bushel; cloth, $1.00 a yard.
In B wheat is $0.80 a bushel; cloth, $1.00 a yard.

If now trade be opened between them, what course will it probably take? What will determine the international value of wheat and cloth? Does it follow that the production of either wheat or cloth will be wholly abandoned in either country?

10. There are two countries, C and D, which have had no trade with each other. Prices and money-wages differ as follows:

In C wheat is $2.00 a bushel; cloth, $1.50 a yard; coal, $8.00 a ton; shoes, $6.00 a pair; wages, $3.00 a day.

In D wheat is $1.00 a bushel; cloth, $0.75 a yard; coal, $4.00 a ton; shoes, $3.00 a pair; wages, $2.00 a day.

If trade be opened between them, what will be the probable course of affairs? [Cost of transportation: wheat, 10 cents a bushel; cloth, 1 cent a yard; coal, $1.50 a ton; shoes, 2 cents a pair.]

11. If in the preceding example, the price of wheat in C had been $1.00 instead of $2.00, what difference would this make as regards the course of the trade?

12. When a high tariff is adopted in a country, explain carefully the effect on the industries producing exports. Give, step by step, the process by which, in such a case, exports and imports are restored to equality.

13. Do the same for the case of a country in which duties on imports are reduced or abolished.

14. Taking the facts given in question 10, as representative of the general character of the two countries, C and D, which of them is best for a laborer to live in?

15. Why does not cost of production regulate the values of commodities in trade between countries? Why does it do so in any trade?

16. Does the importation of goods lessen the market for the products of home labor in a country?

17. What are the chief sources of difference in the comparative cost of commodities in different countries?

18. England buys of us annually about twice as much as we buy of her. [For 1888 the figures were three hundred and eight millions against one hundred and fifty millions of dollars' worth.] How do you reconcile this fact with the general principle of trade between countries?

19. Show that the abolition of our tariff would probably be followed by a rise in the value of money in this country (*i. e.*, by a fall of prices).

20. Would all prices be likely to fall equally in that case? Would the price of wheat, for example, fall as much as the price of steel-rails, or of cloth?

21. Would money-wages be likely to fall in the same ratio as the general level, or average, of prices?

22. Show that foreign products might be excluded from our markets by means of duties on our exports. Show also how the situation would differ from that in which the exclusion was brought about by prohibitory duties on imports.

23. If you had the power of adding ten per cent. to the wealth of the country, should you make the increase in money, or in other things? If in money, would it be likely to remain with us?

24. Would the addition of a hundred millions to the coin in general circulation in the world, differ in effect from an equal extension of bank currency?

25. Why is demand for commodities not a demand for labor? Is it so in any case?

26. How does the use of Prison Labor in production affect the interests of free laborers?

27. Why are the wages of women lower than the wages of men?

28. What is the fallacy of the doctrine that wages are paid out of the product of the labor they reward?

29. In what forms do changes of real wages present themselves? In what precise form do hired laborers receive benefit from railroads? from increased personal efficiency on their own part in all industries? from lessened cost of producing clothing and fuel?

30. Mention cases in which the permanent result of economic changes differs from the temporary result.

31. Give examples illustrating the statement that "many things are always possible in every case singly, which are never possible universally, unless some special condition be fulfilled."

32. Suppose the present owner of every hired house in New York, should make a present of it to the tenant, would house-rents fall in the city?

33. A man mortgages his farm as security for a loan wherewith to build a mill. Supposing the farm and the mill to be taxed at their full value, ought the mortgage to be taxed also? Is the general wealth greater than it would be if the lender had built the mill himself?

34. Show that a special tax on all farms, or on farm products, must fall on the consumers; but a tax on the economic rent of land, falls on the land-owners alone.

35. If a special tax were suddenly imposed on the rent of land, show that it would be a practical confiscation of a portion of the wealth of the present owners. Would future purchasers be burdened by such a tax? [Remember how the price of land is fixed.]

36. Show that the proposed Single Tax on land, in order to be just, must be confined to the increase of rent after the tax is imposed.

APPENDIX.

THE TARIFF ON IMPORTS.

THERE is much discussion of the Tariff, but most persons have very little knowledge as to the precise rates of duty it imposes. The whole document is much too complicated and too long to be given in full here. The following abstract and statistics may be of service to those who desire to get a general view of the subject. It will be observed that the duties on some articles is specific (*i. e.*, so much a pound, gallon, etc.); on others *ad valorem* (*i. e.*, at a given rate per cent. on the value), and on still others an *ad valorem* rate is levied in addition to a specific duty [see, for example, manufactures of wool]. In not a few cases the duty on some grades of a commodity is specific, and on other grades *ad valorem*.

The following table is compiled from the official report of the Bureau of Statistics of Foreign Commerce, for the year 1888. In the case of articles subject to a simple *ad valorem* duty, the rate is given in the last column. When the duty is specific, or a combination of specific and *ad valorem* rates, the character of the duty is noted in the first column; in such cases the figures in the last column indicate the proportion the duty actually collected bore to the value of the goods. The average rate on all dutiable goods imported during the year was nearly 46 per cent.

It is to be noted that about one-third, by value, of all the articles imported, come in free of duty. The leading article on the free list is coffee. The five next in order are chemicals, hides, raw silk, India-rubber, and tea. These six articles constitute two-thirds of the whole free importation.

ARTICLES.	The amount of duty actually collected.	Rate per cent. on the value of goods.
EDUCATIONAL REQUISITES.		
Books, maps, etc.	$721,255	25
Paper, printing	6,828	20
" writing, blank books and envelopes . .	225,731	25
Type-metal (20 per cent.), type (25 per cent.) .	30,698	20
Ink	30,290	30
Pens, 12 cents a gross	61,240	44
Penholders	9,774	30
Pencils, 50 cents a gross, and 30 per cent. *ad valorem* in addition	58,479	56
Penknives, pocket knives, etc.	773,029	50
Scientific apparatus and instruments . . .	13,478	35
Musical instruments	456,964	25
Works of art	432,406	30
Soap, 15 cents a pound, or 20 per cent. *ad valorem*	130,511	29
MANUFACTURES OF COTTON.		
Thread, 10 cents to 48 cents per pound . .	436,704	46
Spools, 7 cents a dozen	59,820	57
Cloth, unbleached, 2¼ to 4 cents per square yard	45,742	46
" bleached, 3¼ to 5 cents per square yard .	393,586	50
" printed, 4¼ to 6 cents per square yard . .	1,145,279	43
Stockings and other knit goods, 35 and 40 per ct.	2,608,435	39
Ready-made clothing (cotton)	133,559	35

Appendix.

ARTICLES.	The amount of duty actually collected.	Rate per cent. on the value of goods.
WOOL AND ARTICLES PARTLY OR WHOLLY MANUFACTURED OF WOOL.		
Wool for clothing, *value under 30 cents per pound*		
unwashed, 10 cents per pound	$1,612,637	48
" washed, 20 cents per pound	129,509	60
" scoured, 30 cents per pound	40,485	72
Value over 30 cents per pound.	-	-
" unwashed, 12 cents per pound	4,458	37
" washed, 24 cents per pound	1,341	61
" scoured, 36 cents per pound	1,144	85
Combing wools, unscoured, 10 cents per pound	553,513	42
" " scoured, 30 cents per pound	7,396	58
Carpet wools, *value under 12 cents per pound*		
unscoured, 2¼ cents per pound	1,367,600	25
" scoured, 7¼ cents per pound	28,877	43
Value over 12 cents per pound.		
" unscoured, 5 cents per pound	981,028	28
" scoured, 15 cents per pound	519	52
Blankets, 10 to 35 cents per pound, and 35 to 40 per cent. in addition	5,068	70
Flannels, 10 to 35 cents per pound, and 35 or 40 per cent. in addition	460,252	70
Stockings and other knit goods, same rates of duty as flannels	1,072,167	62
Woolen and worsted yarns, (same rates)	1,303,373	68
Woolen shawls, 35 or 40 cents per pound, and 35 or 40 per cent. in addition	632,509	65

ARTICLES.	The amount of duty actually collected.	Rate per cent. on the value of goods.
Ready-made clothing (woolen or partly wool) 40 or 45 cents per pound, and 35 or 40 per cent. ad valorem, in addition	$822,847	59
Cloth, cheaper grades, 35 cents per lb., and 35 per ct.	983,395	92
Cloth, better grades, 35 cents per lb., and 40 per ct.	6,747,138	60
Dress goods, part wool, cheaper grades, 5 cents a square yard, and 35 per cent. . . .	2,893,679	68
Ditto, better grades, 7 cents. a sq. yard, 40 per ct.	2,125,022	59
Dress goods, all wool, cheaper grades, 9 cents a square yard, and 40 per cent. ad valorem. .	6,603,535	84
Dress goods, same, better grades, 35 cents per pound, and 40 per cent. ad valorem . .	2,120,260	70
MISCELLANEOUS.		
Silk goods	16,383,371	50
Coal, 75 cents per ton -	665,786	22
Lumber, boards, shingles, laths, etc., various rates, specific and ad valorem	1,086,658	18
Lime	9,292	10
Nails, 1¼ to 4 cents per pound . . .	9,118	79
Screws, 6 to 12 cents per pound . .	2,017	54
Handsaws	9,184	40
Files, 35 cents to $2.50 a dozen	39,279	60
Window-glass, common, 1⅜ to 2⅞ cents per pound	1,563,512	113
" " plate, 3 to 50 cents per square foot	1,127,147	90
Paints, various rates from 8 to 173 per cent. .	411,964	33
Oil, flaxseed or linseed, 25 cents per gallon . .	1,855	54
Crockery and china, various rates, from 20 to 60 per cent.	3,531,467	58
Carpets, hemp, 6 cents per square yard . .	14,977	25

ARTICLES.	The amount of duty actually collected.	Rate per cent. on the value of goods.
Oil-cloth for floors	$133,309	40
Woolen carpets, or partly woolen, 40 per cent. or 8 to 45 cents per square yard and 30 per cent.	651,579	47½
Cutlery	228,740	35
Sugar, 1¾ to 3¼ cents per pound	50,649,760	80
Molasses, 4 and 8 cents per gallon . . .	1,347,327	26
Salt, 8 and 12 cents per 100 pounds . . .	552,788	54
Starch, 2 and 2½ cents per pound . .	154,076	96
Potatoes, 15 cents per bushel . . .	1,239,309	34
Rice, 2¼ cents per pound . . .	1,109,187	113
Fish, cured, various rates	645,652	21
Iron ores, 75 cents per ton	693,501	38
Pig-iron, $6.72 per ton	2,189,435	43
Scrap iron, $6.72 per ton	1,052,035	49
Steel-rails, $17 per ton	2,630,347	75
Structural iron, 1¼ cents per pound . .	187,827	104
Cotton ties	181,637	35
Machinery (iron and steel), 45 per cent. . .	936,033	45
Jewelry	132,043	25
Precious stones (except diamonds which are on the free list)	1,052,966	10
Tobacco, 35, 40, and 75 cents per pound . .	5,886,289	66
Cigars, $2.50 per pound, and 25 per cent. in addition	3,659,140	108
Ale and beer, 20 cents a gallon, 35 cents bottled	666,666	49
Whiskey, brandy, and other spirits, $2 a gallon	2,987,824	153
Wines, various rates	4,019,717	55

SUMMARY.

The following table shows the amount of duty collected on the leading classes of dutiable imports in the year ending June 30, 1888, and the proportion of the duty to the value of the goods: —

ARTICLES.	Duty collected.	Percentage of value.
Sugar and molasses	$52,007,980	75
Wool, raw	4,729,486	34
Manufactures of wool	32,213,120	68
Iron ore, pig and scrap	2,882,886	42
Manufactures of iron and steel	18,391,246	42
Flax, hemp, jute, etc., raw	2,388,002	14
Manufactures of flax	7,914,003	34
Silk, manufactures of	16,351,685	50
Cotton, manufactures of	11,491,807	40
Fruit and nuts	4,477,535	29
Chemicals, drugs, dyes, etc.	4,622,442	36
Tobacco and cigars, etc.	9,734,987	79
Leather, and manufactures of	3,479,249	30
Wines and liquors	7,663,244	72
Wood, boards, shingles, and other "manufactures" of	1,684,998	18
Glass and glass-ware	4,799,252	62
Fancy articles	3,022,742	42
Breadstuffs	1,115,811	14
Earthen, stone, and china-ware	3,568,277	57
Hats, bonnets, and materials for	1,241,915	22
Animals	932,370	20
All other dutiable articles	13,816,591	19
TOTAL	$213,509,801	46

INTERNAL REVENUE.

The internal revenue of the United States is derived from excise duties on the production and sale of whiskey and other distilled spirits, beer and ale, tobacco, cigars and cigarettes, and oleomargarine. The rates of duty and the amount of revenue derived therefrom, are as follows: —

Whiskey and other spirits, 90 cents a gallon	$69,306,166
Beer and ale, $1 per barrel	23,324,218
Tobacco and snuff, 8 cents per pound	16,749,009
Cigars, 30 cents a hundred	11,534,180
Cigarettes, 5 cents a hundred	931,363
Special tax on manufacturers and dealers	1,447,880
Oleomargarine, 2 cents per pound, and license fee	804,140
Other items (chiefly penalties)	169,519
TOTAL	$124,326,475

NOTE ON THE ANALYSIS OF COST OF PRODUCTION.

The reasons which lead me to name "Waiting," instead of "Abstinence," as an element in the cost of producing things, are briefly as follows: —

1. It is desirable to have a definition that applies to all production, under whatever circumstances. Abstinence is not a universal and necessary sacrifice in production. It is strictly applicable only to industry carried on by hired labor.

2. Production must have preceded abstinence. The first wealth abstained from had a cost of production in which abstinence surely formed no part.

3. It is desirable to disentangle cost of production wholly from questions of wages. Now abstinence is intimately connected with wages. The laborer's wages give the measure of the employer's abstinence. If, other things remaining unchanged, wages rise, the employer must submit to increased abstinence in order to obtain

a given product. If wages fall, the reverse is true. If now we say that abstinence enters into cost of production, we are bound to say that cost of production varies with mere changes of wages.

4. Cost of production, as distinct from what economists have usually called "cost of labor," is a question between men on one side, and the materials and forces of nature on the other. It is a question of the total exertion or sacrifice necessary on men's part in order to obtain the products they need. Nature demands only labor without immediate enjoyable result; or, as I have ventured to express it, labor and waiting. How men shall carry or share these burdens, is a question between men themselves; it belongs, as already suggested, to the region of wages and profits, and not to production as such.

5. The abstinence of the employing class may be regarded as an element in what I have ventured to call the "employer's cost." It is a sacrifice made with a view to profit, rather than with a view to production, pure and simple. Abstinence is an element in the cost of profits, not in the cost of production.

6. The substitution of Waiting for Abstinence brings out more clearly the whole cost of production under division of labor, — since it enables us to take account of the time required for exchanging the finished products. It lays the basis for exhibiting, more clearly than was easily possible under the old definition, the true relation of wages to the economic cost of products. It supplies the economic answer to those who assert that labor is the whole burden of production. In a word, it corresponds with the observable facts of the case.

7. Finally, the proposed change of definition lays the basis for a better treatment of wages. It enables us to connect wages directly with savings, and to avoid the confusion that arises from failing to distinguish between savings (which are necessary only for paying wages) and the working capital which is a necessity of production.

INDEX.

THE NUMBERS REFER TO PAGES.

Abstinence, a part of the cost to employers, but not of the true cost of production, 75, 94, 269, 387.

Bank currency, 150.
Bills of exchange, 324.
Bimetallism, 177.
Buying and selling, the separated halves of economic exchange, 26; buying easier than selling, 28.

Capital, three forms of, 59; is consumed, 63; fixed and circulating, 64; the capital of to-day a legacy, 65; represents improvements, 66, 70; how created, 66, 76; owned by a few, 72; how related to savings, 68, 74; cost of, 255.
Competition, in selling, 89; tends to equality of rewards, 105, 215, 226; erroneous view of, 216; combinations to defeat, 118, 231, 266; obstructed in its action, 113, 217, 229.

Cost, to the employer, 92, 254–266, 269; true or economic cost, 94, 104, and appendix note; cost in both senses, made up of many small parts, 102; difficulty of analyzing, 104; economic cost governs natural value, 105; lessened by improvements, 106; does not include risk, 108; relation of to international value, 332; sources of difference in comparative cost, 343.

Demand and supply, action of in fixing market value, 89; demand for commodities not a demand for labor, 237; demand for commodities not lessened by saving, 239.
Deposits (bank) as currency, 151.
Diminishing returns, law of, 294; consequences of, 310.
Division of labor, advantages of, 18; makes exchange necessary, 22; how men know what to produce under, 105.

Double standard, 167.
Dull times, nature of, 138, 164.

Employers, function of, 73; profits of, see Profits; not responsible for low wages of women, 224; employer's cost, 92, 254, 269, 387.

Exchange of products made necessary by division of labor, 22; obscured by use of money, 26; carried on by traders, 28; complicated with payment of wages, 33, 133, 139, 164, 238, 241; must keep pace with production, 88, 128; exchange between nations, 323.

Exports, pay for imports, 325, and tend to equality with, 328.

Free Trade and Protection, 349.

Gold, nominal and real demand and supply of, 142; uses of, 143; has no price, 145; production of, 145; profits of gold-mining affected by changes of prices, 146, note; how the careful keeping of the precious metals affects their value, 147; questions between gold and silver, 166; gold standard, 170; movements of gold between countries, chap. xxv.

Improvements in production, effect of on values, 106; on wages and profits, 107, 373; agricultural improvements, 301.

Inconvertible notes, 182.
Interest, 196, 259, 270.
International trade, 323.
Inventors, importance of, 71.

Labor, as an element in cost of production, 95; cost of differs to different employers, 257; division of, 18; productive labor, 52; productiveness of, 54; non-productive labor, 53, 226, 320; prison labor, 248.

Laborers, classes of, 214; may raise wages by increased efficiency, 233, 235, 374; not benefited by those who buy goods, 236; constitute a market for all they can produce, 238.

Land, grades of, 44; rent of, 288; city rents, 306; why price of land so variable, 309.

Legal tender notes, 154, 156; inconvertible, 183.

Materials, a form of capital, 60.

Money, the struggle for, 17; uses of, 25; value of, 122; circulation of, 124, 130; two functions of, 133; nominal and real demand and supply of, 127, 142; value of differs in different countries, 94, 329.

Money-wages, 123, 198, 372; scale of important only in relation to prices, 34, 197, 235; differ in different countries, 336.

Index.

Natural wealth, 40; law of value of, 46, 109. See also Rent and Land.
Natural value, 105; of money, 123.
Normal wages and profits, 203, 224.

Overproduction possible in single commodities, 78, 262, but not in all, 138, 248, 365.

Particular and general cases, 364.
Population, effects of growth of, 46, 289; checks on increase of, 314; ultimate limits of, 317.
Price, how distinguished from value, 86; how the general level of prices is fixed, 127, 142; prices in international trade, 94, 328.
Prison labor, production by, not injurious to free laborers, 248.
Production, nature of, 41, 52, 94; requisites for, 58; in progress, 62.
Productiveness of labor, 54; relation of to wages, 199, 225, 310, 374.
Profits, nature of 195; normal, 203; rate of, hard to discover, 208; profits may become wages, 211, 236; profits of individual employers, 251.
Protection and free trade, 349.

Questions and exercises, 35, 83, 120, 192, 321, 377.

Rent, 286–309; rents may become wages, 319.
Risk, an element in employer's cost, 78, 262; but not in economic cost, 108.

Savings, relation of to capital, 75; to wages, 76, 197, 373; to the rate of profits, 201, 225: not increased by strikes, 233; increase of saving does not lessen demand for goods, 239; replacement of savings expended, 209, 211.
Selling, difficulties of, 28; these not due to scarcity of money, 190; profit and loss by sales, 260.
Silver, convenience of, 165; decline of value, 172; silver certificates, 154, 158 note, 176 note; our currency approaching the silver standard, 173; the silver in the Treasury not a reserve, 176. See also gold.
Skilled labor, products of, 113; wages of, 220.
Slow working of economic principles, 369.
Strikes, 232.
Supply and demand, 89; in the case of money, 124; supply of one thing demand for other things, 365.

Tariff, on imports, 381.
Temporary and permanent results, 370.

Trusts, 118, 266.

Value, 86; connection with cost of production, 101, 105; how affected by improvements, 106, 375; value of natural wealth, 109; of products of skill, 112; of things having a joint cost, 115; governed by cost of most costly part, 296; relation of value to rent, 298; international values, 115, 337; general rise or fall of values impossible, 87, 248, 365; value not an attribute of all wealth, 46, 252 note; increase in value of natural wealth not a general gain, 50.

Wages, industrial consequences of, 77; principles governing aggregate wages, 194; individual wages, 212; equalizing tendency of competition, 215; normal and market wages, 203, 224; relation of wages to product, 196; not found by deducting profits from the product, 211; raised by improvements, 106, 374; but not by strikes, 232; not lowered by production in prisons, 248; wages and the circulation of money, 133, 198, 241; real wages depend on the relation of money-wages to prices, 34, 198, 235, 372; high profits favorable to high wages, 235, 374; free spending is not so, 236; wages advanced out of savings, 75, 242; extent of the advance, 245; fallacy of denying the advance, 247; wages of women, 223; of non-productive laborers, 226; wages differ in different countries, 220; these differences not a cause of international trade, 345. See also Money-wages.

Wealth, defined, 36; natural wealth and wealth produced by labor, 39; how natural wealth acquires value, 43, 109; production of wealth, 41, 52; value of, 86.

Waiting, an element in cost of production, 72, 95, 99, 387.

www.ingramcontent.com/pod-product-compliance
Lightning Source LLC
Chambersburg PA
CBHW051249300426
44114CB00011B/960